ROUTLEDGE LIBRARY EDITIONS:
BANKING & FINANCE

FOREIGN EXCHANGE ISSUES, CAPITAL MARKETS, AND INTERNATIONAL BANKING IN THE 1990s

FOREIGN EXCHANGE ISSUES, CAPITAL MARKETS, AND INTERNATIONAL BANKING IN THE 1990s

Edited by
KHOSROW FATEMI AND DOMINICK SALVATORE

Volume 13

Routledge
Taylor & Francis Group
LONDON AND NEW YORK

First published in 1993

This edition first published in 2012
by Routledge
2 Park Square, Milton Park, Abingdon, Oxon, OX14 4RN

Simultaneously published in the USA and Canada
by Routledge
711 Third Avenue, New York, NY 10017

Routledge is an imprint of the Taylor & Francis Group, an informa business

British Library Cataloguing in Publication Data
A catalogue record for this book is available from the British Library

ISBN: 978-0-415-52086-7 (Set)
eISBN: 978-0-203-10819-2 (Set)
ISBN: 978-0-415-53880-0 (Volume 13)
eISBN: 978-0-203-10881-9 (Volume 13)

Publisher's Note
The publisher has gone to great lengths to ensure the quality of this reprint but points out that some imperfections in the original copies may be apparent.

Disclaimer
The publisher has made every effort to trace copyright holders and would welcome correspondence from those they have been unable to trace.

Foreign Exchange Issues, Capital Markets, and International Banking in the 1990s

Edited by
Khosrow Fatemi

Dominick Salvatore

Taylor & Francis

USA	Publishing Office:	Taylor & Francis 1101 Vermont Avenue, NW, Suite 200 Washington, DC 20005-3521 Tel: (202) 289-2174 Fax: (202) 289-3665
	Distribution Center:	Taylor & Francis 1900 Frost Road, Suite 101 Bristol, PA 19007-1598 Tel: (215) 785-5800 Fax: (215) 785-5515
UK		Taylor & Francis Ltd. 4 John St. London WC1N 2ET Tel: 071 405 2237 Fax: 071 831 2035

FOREIGN EXCHANGE ISSUES, CAPITAL MARKETS, AND INTERNATIONAL BANKING IN THE 1990s

1 2 3 4 5 6 7 8 9 0 B R B R 9 8 7 6 5 4 3

This book was set in Times Roman by Taylor & Francis. The editors were Virginia E. Dunn and Susan Connell; the production supervisor was Peggy M. Rote; and the typesetters were Phoebe Carter and Wayne Hutchins. Cover design by Michelle Fleitz.
Printing and binding by Braun-Brumfield, Inc.

A CIP catalog record for this book is available from the British Library.

♾ The paper in this publication meets the requirements of the ANSI Standard Z39.48-1984(Permanence of Paper)

Library of Congress Cataloging-in-Publication Data

Foreign exchange issues, capital markets, and international banking in the 1990s / edited by Khosrow Fatemi, Dominick Salvatore.
p. cm. — (Series on international business and trade)

1. Foreign exchange. 2. Capital market. 3. Banks and banking, International. I. Fatemi, Khosrow. II. Salvatore, Dominick. III. Series.
HG3853.F67 1993
332′.042—dc20 92-35613
CIP

ISBN 0-8448-1737-6
ISSN 1052-9160

Contents

Part Three
International Financial Management

Preface

The international economic order that was established at the end of World War II was based on certain premises and conditions. The financial and monetary side of this *new* international economic order had its own postulations, such as the overwhelming dominance of the American economy [48% of the global gross national product (GNP)] and the stability of the American dollar.

During the two ensuing decades, the validity of some of these premises diminished, thus reducing the effectiveness of the system itself. A variety of conflicting forces finally caused the de facto demise of the old Bretton Woods system in the early 1970s, without a parallel creation to replace it.

The rapidly changing environment of international economic areas and the dynamic nature of international financial activities have precluded the development of a generalized system to replace the old one.

The need for continued analysis and evaluation of the international financial system never has been greater. Considering the enormity of the task, it is necessary to concentrate on specialized studies. The current volume follows this line of reasoning by providing an in-depth analysis of certain aspects of the international financial system. Specifically, it addresses four of the most important financial and monetary issues of the present time—namely, exchange rate, capital markets, international banking and external debt, and international financial management.

The studies included in this volume have undergone the normal process of evaluation. In addition, the authors have benefited from the feedback of participants of the First International Conference of the International Trade and Finance Association, held in Marseille, France, May 31–June 2, 1991. The objective of this volume, in short, is to contribute to the studies needed as a prelude for the creation of a new international financial system.

Khosrow Fatemi
Dominick Salvatore

Chapter 1

Introduction

Dominick Salvatore and Khosrow Fatemi

The worldwide deregulation movement of the 1980s and the resultant globalization of financial markets have led to increased efficiency in the utilization of financial capital and direct investments around the world, but also to greater interdependence of financial markets and to the development of many new financial instruments to meet changed needs and conditions. Furthermore, they pointed to the crucial need to fully understand the implications of recent changes for the functioning of the present international financial and economic systems. This volume addresses some of these important issues. Specifically, as the title indicates, it deals with the effect of recent changes in the international economy on the operation of foreign exchange markets, capital markets, and international banking in the 1990s. The volume includes the most important papers on international finance presented at the first international meeting of the International Trade and Finance Association held in cooperation with the Ecole International des Affaires in Marseilles, France, from 31 May to 2 June 1991.

RECENT CHANGES IN INTERNATIONAL FINANCE ADDRESSED IN THIS VOLUME

One of the most striking aspects of the present international financial system is the great volatility of exchange rates and the inability of empirical models of exchange rate determination to explain and forecast exchange rate movements. While exchange rate risks can generally be hedged at a cost, persistent exchange rate misalignments can and have greatly disrupted the pattern of international specialization and created serious disruptions in the international economy. An example of this was the sharp overvaluation of the U.S. dollar during most of the 1980s and the loss of competitiveness of otherwise internationally efficient U.S. manufacturing firms. Indeed, the problem does not seem to end with the elimination of the exchange rate misalignments. Economists have borrowed from physicists the term *hysteresis* to describe a situation in which trade does not return to equilibrium even after the exchange rate misalignment has been eliminated. Thus, is is important to know what the equilibrium exchange rates are and to avoid large and persistent exchange rate misalignments and excessive fluctuations. The fact is that no model has been able to correctly and consistently forecast exchange rates. There are three main reasons for this. First, most models of exchange rate determination emphasize a particular aspect of the economy to the exclusion of other important aspects. Second, exchange rate expectations in exchange rate models are generally based on unrealistic assumptions. Third, new information alters exchange rate expectations instantly and may dominate exchange rate movements. Thus, a more general and eclectic model that incorporates the best of existing models and that can be shown to better predict exchange rates is certainly a welcome development. Such seems to be the model developed by Vincent Dropsy in Chapter 2.

Exchange rate movements also reflect the changed international financial environment, and often, as during the current period of rapid changes, theoretical developments that consider the effect of such changes lag behind actual market developments. A good example of this is in the pricing of currency options in the face of foreign exchange agreements, as for example, the European Monetary System (EMS). It is important to see how arrangements that constrain exchange rate movements affect the pricing of currency options, especially as they become more inclusive and widespread in the international economy. This important aspect is examined in Chapter 3 of this volume. Chapter 4 examines the way in which the large dollar overvaluation during most of the 1980s permanently harmed the international competitiveness of U.S. firms and also interfered with international specialization and trade, because the dollar is still the most important vehicle currency of international trade and finance in the world today. Exchange rate problems, however, do not arise only as a result of misalignment. As pointed out in Chapter 5, if a country such as Japan does not allow the appreciation of the yen toward its equilibrium level from being reflected in lower import prices and higher export prices for Japan, the equilibrating effect of the yen appreciation is not allowed to take place. The same occurs if Japan takes other measures, such as a contractionary fiscal policy that neutralizes the effect of the appreciation of the yen. It is then important to understand that the problem does not lie in the fact that the international economy and international financial markets do not respond to exchange rate changes, but to these other forces that prevent exchange rates from accomplishing their equilibrating function. To examine clearly and isolate the effect of exchange rate changes from other forces simultaneously at work requires the use of counterfactual simulations. If this is not recognized and the problem is attributed instead to economic and financial markets not responding to exchange rate changes, then the wrong policies are likely to be employed.

Another important topic that has traditionally received a great deal of attention is the efficiency of the forward market for foreign exchange. While there is some evidence in support of forward market efficiency, a large body of empirical evidence has rejected the forward rate as an unbiased or efficient predictor of future spot rates. In short, no model seems to outperform a *random walk* of exchange rates in an out-of-sample period. Many conflicting explanations have been advanced for this, for example, the many risk-averse agents of foreign markets, irrational behavior of agents, financial markets that do not clear, fundamentals that exhibit strong short-term volatility, speculative bubbles, and central bank intervention. A great deal of research has taken place, but no firm conclusion has been reached as to which of these explanations is most important. Chapter 6 of this volume examines the notion that the presence of risk premium in the foreign exchange market allows the forward rate to be an unbiased predictor of the future spot rate without sacrificing the notion of market efficiency.

Another important topic of research into exchange rates deals with the theoretical arguments for and against monetary integration. While this is not, of course, a new topic of research, it has acquired great importance and immediacy today as the result of the formation of the EMS and its movement toward full monetary union. It is important, therefore, to revive the old theoretical arguments and examine them in the light of the experience of the EMS today and in terms of projections for its future. These topics are investigated in Chapter 7 by an observer who is very close to the debate.

A second major area of interest in the present international financial system that is very much in the news these days is the operation of capital markets in a global-economy context. One aspect of the topic addressed in this volume (Chapter 8), especially after the merger frenzy of the 1980s, is the optimal level of leverage or debt–equity ratio for a firm. Another important topic (discussed in Chapter 9) is whether diversification in international capital markets is beneficial. The importance of this topic in international finance in general and international capital markets in particular can hardly be exaggerated if one remembers that two decades ago U.S. pension funds had never been invested outside the United States, and investment of pension funds in many other countries was prohibited.

Today many U.S. pension funds have 10 to 15% of their assets invested internationally and the value of foreign assets that they hold has reached nearly $100 billion. A similar trend toward international investments has occurred in Europe and Japan. This has been the result of the deregulation movement of the 1980s and the increasing recognition of the benefits of international diversification in terms of risks and returns. Since 1986 foreign banks and organizations were allowed to become members of the most important stock exchanges around the world, global around-the-clock trading has become a reality, and Europe is moving toward complete financial integration. Besides examining the optimal level of leverage or debt–equity ratio for a firm and the benefits of diversification in international capital markets, the other papers in Part Two of this volume examine defeased debt in international capital markets, evidence of the co-movement of two Scandinavian stock markets, the American experience with the deregulation of savings and loans associations, "round-tripping" effects of debt–equity swaps, and emerging capital markets and economic development.

A third major area of interest is international financial management. While the basic principles of domestic and international financial management are basically the same, international financial management is more challenging and dynamic because it must consider a wider range of possibilities, opportunities, and challenges than purely domestic financial management. International financial management requires the firm to consider the impact of fluctuating exchange rates and international taxation on the management strategy of the firm. The flow of funds within the units of an international firm, the management of international accounts receivable and payable, and the management of long-term assets are much more complicated and difficult than the flow of funds within a purely domestic corporation or the management of domestic accounts. All of this has led to an explosion of interest in the facets of international financial management, some of which are explored in Part Three of this volume.

One aspect of international financial management examined in this study is the investigation of the presence of nonlinear dependence in daily stock returns on several stock exchanges of different countries. While there is no unanimity regarding the best stochastic generating model, the most commonly accepted position is that U.S. stock returns are approximately uncorrelated, but not independent, and described by distributions with fatter tails. It is not known, however, whether this is true for other capital markets around the world, which are generally much smaller and thinner than American markets. Chapter 15 examines this topic for nine countries around the world. Other international financial management topics examined in this volume are the statistical properties of nondeflated and deflated constant dollar accounting signals, the survival analysis theory to business failures, and the desirability of joint ventures in Eastern Europe.

A fourth major area of interest in international finance is international banking as it relates to the external debt of Central and Eastern European and developing countries. There is today a real danger of complete economic collapse in the countries of Eastern Europe and in the former Soviet Union after the fall of communism in the late 1980s and early 1990s. These economies urgently need massive help from the West in the form of capital and technology to restructure their economies along market lines and to integrate them into the world economy. A continuing challenge to the international banking system is also provided by the huge international debt facing many developing countries, which these countries are finding difficult to repay or even service. Large-scale defaults have been avoided so far only by coordinated efforts of debtors and creditors. The problem, however, lingers on. Defaults on such debt could make some of the largest commercial banks in the United States insolvent and possibly lead to a world financial collapse reminiscent of the 1930s. While the danger of default had somewhat diminished by the early 1990s, the persistence of the debt problem was seriously interfering with the process of economic development in many developing countries.

These topics and their suggested solutions are taken up in Part Four of this volume. It is generally agreed today that to avoid complete economic collapse in the countries of Eastern Europe and the former Soviet Union and for the debt problem to be overcome and sustained growth to resume in developing countries, a large increase in the flow of equity capital in the form of direct investments from developed countries and the opening of developed-country markets more widely to the exports of Eastern European and developing countries are required.

OVERVIEW OF THE CONTENT OF THE VOLUME

In Chapter 2, "Diversified Expectations and Speculation in the Foreign Exchange Market," Vincent Dropsy develops an eclectic model of spot and forward exchange rate determination that incorporates both economic fundamentals and expectations. He shows that this model predicts exchange rate dynamics better than purchasing power parity or the monetary approach model. Dropsy also shows the potentially destabilizing role of technical expectations and examines the possible reasons that traders consistently make forecasting errors.

In Chapter 3, "Pricing Options on a Constrained Currency Index: Some Simulation Results," Tom Berglund, Staffan Ringbom, and Laura Vajanne point out that the assumption in the classical pricing of options that the exchange rate has a lognormal distribution is not justified in the presence of an exchange rate agreement, such as the EMS. Using a simulation model, they show that allowing exchange rate movements and the probability of a jump to be mutually dependent has significant effects on the valuation of currency options. In Chapter 4, "Exchange Rate Variations and U.S. Multinational Corporations' Profits: The Case of the 1980s," Luc Moens shows with the use of an econometric model that the appreciation of the U.S. dollar during the first half of the 1980s led to permanent negative effects on the profitability of U.S. firms in tradable goods industries. This resulted because the appreciation of the dollar sharply reduced the profits U.S. firms and the internal funds needed for sustained investments in crucial areas.

Chapter 5, "Real Exchange Rates and the Sectoral Composition of Output: Some Evidence from Japan," by Sadequl Islam, examines the relationship between movements in the real exchange rate and output in the industrial sector of the Japanese economy. Empirical results suggest that the real exchange rate, the relative price of imports, and output are not cointegrated, implying no statistically significant relationship among these variables. The author points out that this may be due to the small "pass-through" between exchange rate appreciations and the price of tradable goods or to expansionary fiscal policies and technological changes that have counterbalanced the effect of the exchange rate appreciation. Chapter 6, "Time-Varying Risk Premia and the Efficiency of the New Zealand Foreign Exchange Market," by Dimitri Margaritis and Phay Hoon Teo, begins by pointing out that a risk premium in the foreign exchange market provides an alternative way of examining the proposition that the forward rate is an unbiased predictor of the future spot rate, without having to give up the notion of market efficiency. The authors tested this proposition empirically by distinguishing between an inefficient market and a time-varying premium, and they found that while time-varying premia do exist in the foreign exchange market, the attempt to model risk premia in the context of the asset price theory was not supported by the data. Chapter 7, "European Monetary Integration: Theoretical Issues and Practical Implications," by André Fourçans, examines the theoretical arguments for and against monetary integration in general and for the European Monetary Union in particular. The study supports the formation of the European Monetary Union with a common currency. This, however, requires increased monetary coordination among its members. The author recommends two basic strategies of accomplishing this. The first is for each country to set up growth objectives for its internal money supply in line with internal price stability and real growth. The second strategy consists of fixing a money supply growth for the European Community as a whole. Both strategies would be facilitated by the establishment of a central bank.

In Chapter 8, "Optimal Leverage of a Dynamically Competitive Firm," Dilip Ghosh determines the optimum leverage of a firm in terms of two alternative hypotheses—payout maximization and utility maximization—by using the income-generating process in a dynamic environment with debt and equity accumulation. The author shows that under perfectly competitive conditions, the optimum equity debt ratio of a firm can be uniquely determined in intertemporal maximization models of investor behavior and that the results are basically the same even under different behavioral hypotheses. Chapter 9, "Is Diversification in International Capital Markets Beneficial?," by Krishnan Dandapani and Jerry Haar examines the benefits of diversifying in international equity markets in terms of different performance measures for the years 1987 to 1990. The authors show that a U.S. investor could have gained substantially by investing in the international equity market during the period examined, even after adjusting for transactions and commission costs. In Chapter 10, "International Co-Movements of Capital Markets: Evidence from Two Scandinavian Stock Markets," Teppo Martikainen, Ilkka Virtanen, and Paavo Yli-Olli examine evidence on the co-movement of two Scandinavian stock markets. This is done by using an internationally extended market model for Finnish stocks, where the return of a given Finnish asset is assumed to be dependent on the return of Finnish and Swedish stock markets. This multimarket model of Finnish securities reveals that several Finnish stocks have significant Swedish risk components. These international risk components, however, do not seem to contain incremental information in explaining the cross-sectional variation of expected stock returns with respect to the systematic risk components produced by the Arbitrage Pricing Model (APM).

Chapter 11, "Defeased Debt in International Capital Markets: Benefits and Problems," by Emiel Owens and Ronald Singer, discusses the potential financial consequences of an in-substance defeasance transaction by evaluating potential levels of wealth transfer among bond and stockholders of a defeased corporation. The authors' empirical results show that the Financial Accounting Standard Board's (FASB) Statement 76 issued in the United States in 1983 resulted in no significant pattern of daily residuals around the announcement date but that the cumulative average residuals became negative throughout the postannouncement period. Because in-substance defeasance can be interpreted as a reduction in the level of debt, the negative abnormal return around the announcement date can be explained by the signaling effect associated with the general reduction in debt. Chapter 12, "Deregulation of Financial Institutions: Lessons from the North American Experience with Savings and Loan Associations," by William Dowling and George Philippatos, examines the question of whether scale economies existed in the U.S. savings and loan industry. The authors employ two distinctly different methodologies to determine (1) whether scale economies existed in the industry, (2) the ranges of asset sizes in which they were significant, and (3) whether there was a change in the cost structure of the economy. They find that cost reduction through asset expansion existed, the minimum efficient scale for savings and loan associations increased, and that substantial change in the cost structure of the industry took place.

Chapter 13, "Capital Flight and the Round-Tripping Effect of Debt–Equity Swaps," by M. T. Vaziri and Hossein Shalchi, tests empirically the relationship between round-trip capital flight and its several possible determinants using pooled data on annual observations for Brazil, Chile, Mexico, Venezuela, and Argentina for the 1980–1989 time period. Round-trip capital flight is shown to be positively related to the domestic rate of inflation and domestic currency depreciation. Growing financial constraints and government deficits, however, have tended to limit the magnitude of round-trip capital flight. Chapter 14, "Emerging Capital Markets and Economic Development," by Edgar Ortiz, presents a synthetic model that highlights the importance of the equity and bond markets on economic activity. Risk is also included as a key variable of savings and investments. The implications of the model on the mobilization of resources and economic development are examined first by assuming perfect markets and leaving government out. The model is then extended to incorporate the relationship between government and capital markets and stresses the role of the state in economic development.

Chapter 15, "Conditional Heteroskedasticity in Stock Returns: International Evidence," by Albert Corhay and Alireza Rad, investigates the presence of nonlinear dependence in daily stock returns on several stock exchanges of different countries. Although daily returns seem to be uncorrelated, the rejection of linear models suggests that the return cannot be seen as an independent increment process. Return-generating models that empirically fit the data best are processes with conditional heteroskedastic innovations. The authors show that the generalized autoregressive conditional heteroskedastic process is best in most cases. Chapter 16, "The Effects of Monetary Gains and Losses on the Univariate Time-Series Characteristics of CDA Earnings," by Hossein Shalchi and M. T. Vaziri, examines empirically the statistical properties of nondeflated and deflated constant dollar accounting earnings signals. Univariate time-series models were identified and estimated utilizing the Box–Jenkins ARIMA methodology, and the results of predictive accuracy of the ARIMA models were compared with those of the random walk with and without a trend model using different loss functions associated with forecast inaccuracy. In Chapter 17, "Survival Analysis of Business Failures," Rafael Solis presents a simplified version of the survival analysis theory (used by insurance companies throughout the world) and its application to the analysis of business mortality (failure). Specifically, the author examines the question of why the rate of failures in most businesses is highest in the early years, why the probability of failure of a business becomes smaller the longer the business survives (other things equal), and why mortality rates differ among business types. In Chapter 18, "Stakeholder Objectives and Government Incentives in Eastern European Joint Ventures," David Bangert examines the desirability of joint ventures in Eastern European countries from the perspective of the major stakeholders and the potential incentives that host governments may use to encourage joint ventures while securing minimum aspiration levels for the various stakeholders.

Chapter 19, "Export Earnings Indexed Debt: Risk Reduction and Linking External Debt to Exports," by Per Mokkelbost, utilizes financial innovation techniques associated with contingent financial claims to model the financing project needs of Central Europe. The author shows that the form of financing best suited to the high risks involved is the export-earnings-indexed-debt facility. In Chapter 20, "The International Finance Corporation and Banks: IFC Syndications of Its LDC Investments," James Baker explores the syndication of a significant portion of its loans to developing countries by the International Finance Corporation (IFC) to encourage international commercial banks and other financial institutions to participate in the development process of developing countries. Syndication is shown to be an important method for the IFC to recycle its investment funds by turning them over into new investments.

In Chapter 21, "Some Issues in External Debt, Domestic Policies, and Economic Development," M. Zaman contends that the debt servicing burden of the major debtor nations is due not only to the domestic economic policies of the borrowing nations, but also to the actions of the lending institutions and countries that provide economic aid. He goes on to say that until indebted nations drastically reform their economic policies, debt-restructuring packages will achieve only debt restructuring and not a meaningful reduction in debt burdens.

Finally, in Chapter 22, "MIGA: A New Kid on the Block," James Baker points out that to develop adequately, developing countries need more private investments. Domestic financial markets are not sufficiently developed, however, to generate the necessary private investments, and political and economic conditions in most developing countries discourage increased flows of foreign direct investments (FDI) from industrial countries. The paper examines the operation of the Multilateral Investment Guarantee Agency (MIGA), the new affiliate of the World Bank, in encouraging the flow of FDI to developing countries by providing investment guarantees to foreign investors.

Part One
Foreign Exchange Issues

Chapters 2–7 deal with foreign exchange issues. They examine diversified expectations and speculation in the foreign exchange market, pricing options on a constrained currency index, exchange variations and U.S. multinational corporations' profits, real exchange rates and the sectoral composition of output in Japan, time-varying risk premia and the efficiency of the New Zealand foreign exchange market, and the effect of European economic integration on exchange rates.

In Chapter 2, Vincent Dropsy develops an eclectic model of spot and forward exchange rate determination that incorporates both economic fundamentals and expectations and that seems to predict exchange rate dynamics better than alternative models. In Chapter 3, Tom Berglund, Staffan Ringbom, and Laura Vajanne show that allowing for dependence between exchange rate movements and the probability of a jump under an exchange rate agreement has significant effects on the valuation of a currency option. In Chapter 4, Luc Moens shows that the appreciation of the U.S. dollar during the first half of the 1980s led to permanent negative effects on the profitability of U.S. firms. Chapter 5 by Sadequl Islam shows that the real exchange rate, the relative price of imports, and output are not cointegrated, implying no statistically significant relationship among these variables in Japan. In Chapter 6, Dimitri Margaritis and Phay Hoon Teo find that while time-varying premia do exist in the foreign exchange market, the attempt to model risk premia in the context of the asset price theory was not supported by the data. Chapter 7 by André Fourçans examines the theoretical arguments for and against monetary integration in general and for the European Monetary Union in particular and supports the formation of the European Monetary Union with a common currency.

Chapter 2

Diversified Expectations and Speculation in the Foreign Exchange Market

Vincent Dropsy

Empirical models of exchange rate determination have individually failed to explain the wide currency movements observed for more than a decade. Three main reasons account for their poor performance: (1) Each model emphasizes a particular aspect of the economy with severe restrictions on the choice of explanatory variables and model specification; (2) exchange rate expectations, certainly a crucial element in the behavior of the foreign exchange market participants, are made endogenous on the basis of unrealistically strong assumptions; and (3) new information instantaneously alters expectations and thus causes unexpected changes in the exchange rate that may dominate its movements.

By concentrating efforts on these first two issues, an eclectic model was developed that takes into account the various alternative channels by which exchange rates may be influenced, namely economic fundamentals and expectations. Allen and Taylor (1989) and Frankel and Froot (1990) infer from their studies that the interaction between fundamentalists and chartists plays an important role in exchange rate dynamics.

In addition, the heterogeneity of beliefs about the right model causes foreign exchange traders and forecasters to have various expected values of current equilibrium rates and future rates. Takagi (1991) examines surveys of exchange rate expectations and finds heterogeneity and absence of rationality in these expectations in almost all studies. Various exchange rate expectations are incorporated into the eclectic model and it is assumed that they are based on two fundamental models (purchasing power parity and the monetary approach) and on technical analysis (for example, time-series methods), to approximate the role of chartists.

Moreover, the roles and expectations of the market participants may change over time, which can be embodied in the time-varying specification of the parameters in the eclectic model. The estimated path of the values of these coefficients can be interpreted in terms of learning processes of the right model by foreign exchange traders over time.

AN ECLECTIC VIEW OF THE MARKET

Exchange rates are affected by the decisions of several types of agents. The Federal Reserve Bank of New York (1989) finds that interbank trading accounts for 95% of the volume of trade in the U.S. foreign exchange markets. The worldwide daily turnover in the foreign exchange markets is estimated to exceed $500 billion and the volume of speculative and arbitrage activities of banks is about 100 times greater than the volume of trade. The traditional trichotomy of the market participants to brokers, hedgers, arbitrageurs, and speculators is extended to model this heterogeneity of agents and the diversity of their expectations in a realistic framework. The aim is to determine the possible channels of demand and supply of currencies in both spot and forward markets. All variables are expressed in logarithms, and exchange rates are given in foreign currency units per US$.

First, brokers are viewed as the intermediaries of export- and import-oriented companies. Their transactions are directly related to purchasing power parity. For example, a decrease in the real exchange rate (that is, a real depreciation of the dollar) induces an amelioration of the U.S. trade balance, and thus some demand for additional dollars. It is assumed that this excess flow demand is a linear function of the logarithmic changes in the deviations of the exchange rate from its relative purchasing power parity value (PPP). The responsiveness coefficient $\Theta_{B,t}$, thus positive, is specified as a time-varying parameter, which embodies several characteristics related to trade, such as export and import price elasticities, trade barriers, and the number of brokers at time t. Hence, the brokers' excess flow demand for \$ (in the spot market) is

$$\mathrm{ED\$}^{\mathrm{spot}}_{B,t} = \Theta_{B,t}(dP^{\mathrm{F}}_t - dP^{\mathrm{US}}_t - dS_t) = \Theta_{B,t}(\mathrm{ECS}^{\mathrm{PPP}}_t - dS_t) \qquad (1)$$

where P_t is the wholesale price index, S_t is the spot rate, $\Theta_{B,t} \geq 0$, d denotes the logarithmic change in the related variable, the superscript F signals a foreign variable, and $\mathrm{ECS}^{\mathrm{PPP}}_t$ is the change in the spot rate implied by PPP between $t - 1$ and t.

Similarly, changes in the deviation from the rate implied by the monetary approach constitute the determinant for the flow demand for dollars by a second type of brokers, who are responsible for long-term capital flows. The monetary excess flow demand for \$ (in the spot market) is

$$\begin{aligned}\mathrm{ED\$}^{\mathrm{spot}}_{M,t} &= \Theta_{M,t}[\beta m_M(dM_t^{\mathrm{F}} - dM_t^{\mathrm{US}}) + \beta y_M(dY_t^{\mathrm{F}} - dY_t^{\mathrm{US}}) \\ &\quad + \beta if_M(d\mathrm{IF}^{e,\mathrm{F}}_{t+1} - d\mathrm{IF}^{e,\mathrm{US}}_{t+1}) + \beta r_M(dR_t^{\mathrm{F}} - dR_t^{\mathrm{US}}) + \mu_M - dS_t] \\ &= \Theta_{M,t}(\mathrm{ECS}_t^{\mathrm{MON}} - dS_t)\end{aligned} \tag{2}$$

where M_t is the money supply, Y_t is industrial production, $\mathrm{IF}^e_{t,+1}$ is expected future inflation, $R_t = (1 + \text{interest rate})$, $\Theta_{M,t} \geq 0$, and $\mathrm{ECS}_t^{\mathrm{MON}}$ denotes the changes in the spot rate implied by the monetary approach between $t - 1$ and t.

Second, the hedgers' objective is to protect their positions against some unexpected currency movements. The flow demand for insurance against currency exposure depends on the change of its relative cost over time, that is, the change in the forward discount. It is again assumed that the demand for additional forward dollars is a log-linear function of the forward discount. The hedgers' excess flow demand for dollars (in the forward market) is

$$\mathrm{ED\$}^{\mathrm{forw}}_{H,t} = -\Theta_{H,t}[(F_t - S_t) - (F_{t-1} - S_{t-1})] \tag{3}$$

where F_t is the forward rate, and $\Theta_{H,t} \geq 0$.

Third, arbitrageurs refer to the traders who take advantage of certain assured opportunities that arise from deviations from covered interest rate parity. However, the liquidity of Eurodollar markets has decreased this spread and numerous studies have confirmed that covered interest rate parity held particularly well for offshore interest rates. Hence,

$$F_t - S_t = R_t^{\mathrm{F}} + R_t^{\mathrm{US}} \tag{4}$$

Fourth, speculators tend to play an important role in the spot and forward markets. They constantly take risks at the pursuit of financial profits, and their demand for currency is based on expectations of exchange rates. For clarity, it is assumed that their position is closed at the end of period, although they can reenter the market immediately. Thus, the possible changes in financial position of different agents at a certain date t, which corresponds to the end of a period and the beginning of a new one, are examined. Speculators can switch their respective profit-searching strategies, expectations, attitudes toward risk, and other behavioral components at that specific time t. Three types of speculators exist:

(1) **Simple spot (SS) speculators,** whose strategy consists of simply buying currency that is believed to appreciate, to make a profit when selling it later. The consequent flow demand for dollars at a certain time t is determined by two terms, which represent the current speculative motive and the closing of the past speculative transaction. The SS speculators' excess flow demand for \$ (in the spot market) is

$$ED\$^{spot}_{SS,t} = \sum_i \Theta_{SSi,t}(S^e_{SSi,t+1} - S_t) - \sum_i \Theta_{SSi,t-1}(S^e_{SSi,t} - S_{t-1}) \quad (5)$$

where $\Theta_{SSi,t} \geq 0$, $\Theta_{SSi,t-1} \geq 0$.

(2) **Uncovered interest rate parity (UIRP) spot speculators,** whose purpose involves the holding of interest-bearing assets instead of cash in different currencies, based on the same strategy as covered interest rate parity, but with some speculative risks involved. Their speculative demand is given by the UIRP speculators' excess flow demand for \$ (in the spot market)

$$ED\$^{spot}_{UI,t} = \sum_i \Theta_{UIi,t}(S^e_{UIi,t+1} - S_t - R^F_t + R^{US}_t) - \sum_i \Theta_{UIi,t-1}(S^e_{UIi,t} - S_{t-1} - R^F_{t-1} + R^{US}_{t-1}) \quad (6)$$

where $\Theta_{UIi,t} \geq 0$, and $\Theta_{UIi,t-1} \geq 0$.

(3) **Forward speculators,** who, for example, can gain from a larger expected depreciation of the franc than implied by the forward rate by buying dollars in the forward market and selling the equivalent amount in the spot market in the future. Their excess demand in both markets can thus be modeled by the forward speculators' excess flow demand for \$ (in the forward market at *t*)

$$ED\$^{forw}_{FS,t} = \sum_i \Theta_{FS,t}(S^e_{FSi,t+1} - F_t) \quad (7)$$

The forward speculators' excess demand for \$ (in the future spot market at $t + 1$) is

$$ED\$^{spot}_{FS,t+1} = -\sum_i \Theta_{FSi,t}(S^e_{FSi,t+1} - F_t) \quad (8)$$

where $\Theta_{FSi,t} \geq 0$.

SPOT AND FORWARD MARKETS EQUILIBRIUM

Equilibrium in the spot market is obtained when the sum of excess flow demands for dollars by all traders (that is, brokers, arbitrageurs, and speculators) is equal to zero. By substituting these terms with their respective expressions, as well as the interest rate differential by the forward premium, it is deduced that the equilibrium value for the change in the spot rate can be represented by a time-varying weighted average of the following factors:

(1) Expected current equilibrium values estimated from *fundamental* models (relative purchasing power parity, monetary approach). If speculation and the forward market did not exist, the spot rate would automatically fall in between the two fundamental equilibrium rates.
(2) Deviations of the future expected spot rate from the random walk model,

from uncovered interest rate parity (equivalently the forward rate), which is the essence of speculation in the spot market.

(3) Deviations of past expectations of the current spot rate from the actual current spot rate and from the past forward rate. Speculators are thus differentiated not only by their strategy, but also by their expectations. According to the previous description of the underlying motivations of traders, relative purchasing power parity and the monetary approach are the two fundamental models used to form expectations.

The assumption is also made that exogenous variables are perfectly anticipated, so as to concentrate on the effects of diversified exchange rate expectations. However, an important class of forecasters use technical analysis (for example, charts) to form their expectations. The potentially destabilizing influence of chartists is studied by specifying their expectations as

$$\mathrm{ECS}_{t+1}^{\mathrm{TEC}} = \Pi_t(S_t - S_{t-1}) \tag{9}$$

The sign of Π_t immediately indicates whether these expectations are stabilizing (Π_t negative) or destabilizing (Π_t positive). The latter are also called bandwagon expectations, whereas the former embody first-order distributed lag expectations. With that in mind,[1]

$$\begin{aligned} S_t - S_{t-1} = {} & \Gamma_{\mathrm{ppp},t}\mathrm{ECS}_{t+1}^{\mathrm{PPP}} + \Gamma_{\mathrm{mon},t}\mathrm{ECS}_{t+1}^{\mathrm{MON}} + \Gamma_{\mathrm{fd},t}[-(F_t - S_t)] \\ & + \sigma_{\mathrm{ppp},t}\mathrm{ECS}_{t}^{\mathrm{PPP}} + \sigma_{\mathrm{mon},t}\mathrm{ECS}_{t}^{\mathrm{MON}} + \sigma_{s,t-1}(S_{t-1} - S_{t-2}) \\ & + \sigma_{\mathrm{fd},t-1}(F_{t-1} - S_{t-1}) + \sigma_c \end{aligned} \tag{10}$$

Identically, the forward market equilibrium condition is that the sum of excess flow demands for dollars by all traders be equal to zero. By substituting these terms with their respective expressions, the forward discount is determined as a time-varying (positively) weighted average of three different expected changes in the spot rate (to which is added a lagged endogenous term to take autocollinearity into account):

$$F_t - S_t = \alpha_{s,t}(S_t - S_{t-1}) + \alpha_{\mathrm{ppp},t}\mathrm{ECS}_{t+1}^{\mathrm{PPP}} + \alpha_{\mathrm{mon},t}\mathrm{ECS}_{t+1}^{\mathrm{MON}} \tag{11}$$

Equations corresponding to the equilibria in the spot (10) and forward (11) markets, and covered interest rate parity (4), therefore, reveal the influences of economic fundamentals and expectations, based on these fundamentals and

[1]Detailed expressions of the coefficients of the reduced-form equations are given in the appendix.

technical analysis, on the spot and forward rates. When expectations become increasingly destabilizing (for example, Π_t positive), a large predominance of technical analysts engaged in speculation can cause an overshooting of the spot rate. Reciprocally, if a large number of technical analysts form expectations "against the wind" (i.e., Π_t negative), then they can actually reverse the trend of the spot rate.

EMPIRICAL RESULTS

An empirical analysis of the previous eclectic model, based on the exchange rates of three countries (West Germany, Japan, and the United Kingdom) for the period January 1976 to December 1987 is provided in Tables 1 and 2. Coefficients are allowed to vary over time (as polynomials of degree four, which maximized the average R^2 of both equations) in order to capture the learning process of structural and expectational changes in the foreign exchange markets. Econometric tests and t statistics in this study are based on heteroscedasticity-consistent matrices of covariance estimates (White, 1980) of a two-stage, least-squares regression. Durbin's H test cannot be used (due to time-varying coefficients), and we report only Durbin–Watson statistics, all close to two. The hypothesis that all the coefficients are stable over time can be clearly rejected at 0.01% for all three countries (the hypothesis is specified as the nullity of all estimated parameters whose degree is greater or equal to one). A closer look at the values of the adjusted R^2 of the eclectic model reveals some substantial improvement in goodness of fit over the two individual fundamental models estimated in this study. The time-varying framework of diversified ex-

Table 1
Spot Market Equation (10)

Parameter	West Germany	Japan	United Kingdom
Adjusted R^2	22.54%	26.08%	16.36%
Durbin–Watson stat	2.065	2.102	2.176
Significance tests			
$\Gamma_{ppp,t}(ECS_{t+1}^{PPP})$	2.67%	1.58%	0.37%
$\Gamma_{mon,t}(ECS_{t+1}^{MON})$	11.14%	1.63%	8.57%
$\Gamma_{fd,t}[-(F_t - S_t)]$	8.13%	7.17%	12.04%
$\delta_{ppp,t}(ECS_t^{PPP})$	5.19%	0.01%	49.77%
$\delta_{mon,t}(ECS_t^{MON})$	1.62%	1.22%	0.13%
$\delta_{s,t-1}(dS_{t-1})$	4.54%	6.63%	10.44%
$\delta_{fd,t-1}(F_{t-1} - S_{t-1})$	0.03%	21.79%	22.49%
δ_c	60.09%	31.60%	9.00%
$\Gamma_{ppp,t} + \delta_{ppp,t}$	0.93%	0.01%	4.88%
$\Gamma_{mon,t} + \delta_{mon,t}$	1.88%	94.25%	8.50%
$\Gamma_{fd,t} + \delta_{fd,t-1}$	57.91%	29.72%	14.37%

Table 2
Forward Market Equation (11)

Parameter	West Germany	Japan	United Kingdom
Adjusted R^2	83.93%	76.90%	67.65%
Durbin–Watson stat	2.282	2.075	2.207
Significance tests			
$\alpha_{s,t}(S_t - S_{t-1})$	0.71%	0.27%	0.13%
$\alpha_{\mathrm{ppp},t}(\mathrm{ECS}_{t+1}^{\mathrm{PPP}})$	88.99%	1.33%	0.01%
$\alpha_{\mathrm{mon},t}(\mathrm{ECS}_{t+1}^{\mathrm{MON}})$	13.33%	6.97%	17.31%
$\beta_{\mathrm{fd},t}(F_{t-1} - S_{t-1})$	0.01%	0.01%	0.01%
β_c	0.16%	0.01%	16.07%

pectations thus appears to be appropriate to study the determinants of exchange rates. Also presented are some tests of the hypothesis that each coefficient has all its components (of different time degrees) equal to zero. The hypothesis is rejected for most coefficients, which indicates that, at least for some subperiods, the various fundamental and expectation terms affect the spot rate or the forward discount.

The values and signs of these coefficients clearly change, as indicated in Figures 1–12. In particular, a striking symmetry is observed between the two coefficients related to the current and lagged interest differentials, which implies that these two variables could be aggregated as one explanatory variable, the change in interest rate differentials. This conclusion is statistically confirmed by a test of the hypothesis of nullity of the sum of the two coefficients ($\Gamma_{\mathrm{fd},t} + \sigma_{\mathrm{fd},t-1}$). Hence, this result can be interpreted as evidence that changes in spot rates are very sensitive to changes in interest rate differentials, instead of the common practice among academic economists of using levels of interest rate differentials as speculative benchmarks to calculate expected profits.

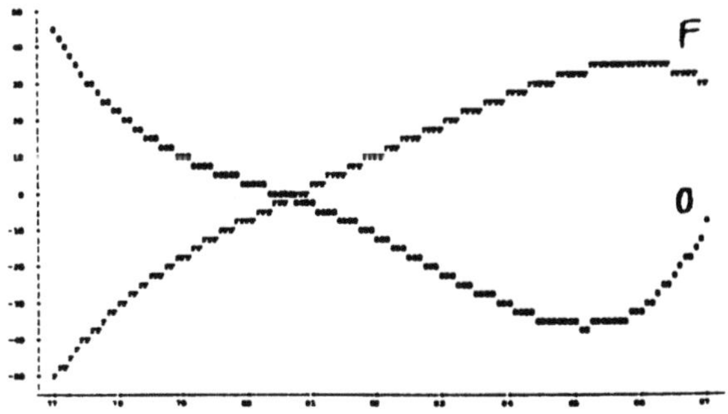

Figure 1 West Germany: Effects of interest rates on the forward discount. $F = -\Gamma'_{\mathrm{fd},t}$; $O = \delta'_{\mathrm{fd},t-1}$.

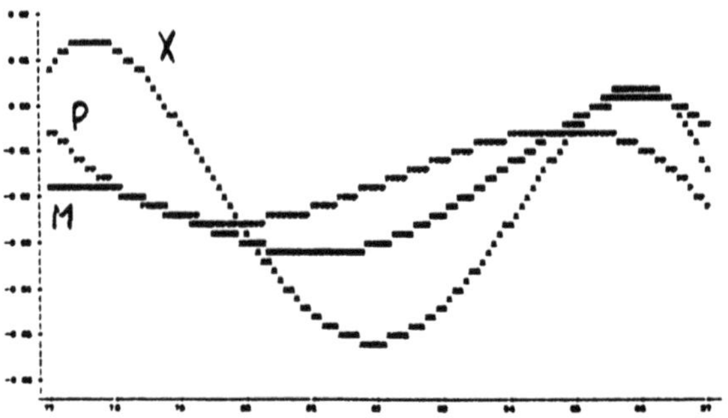

Figure 2 West Germany: Effects of expectations on the forward discount. $X = \alpha_{s,t}$; $P = \alpha_{\mathrm{ppp},t}$; $M = \alpha_{\mathrm{mon},t}$.

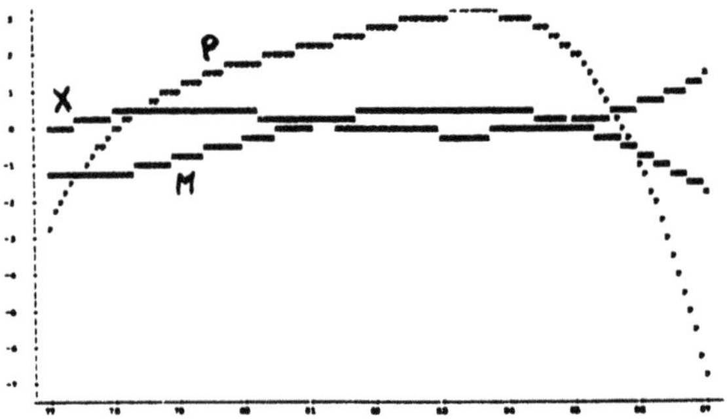

Figure 3 West Germany: Effects of expectations on the change in the spot rate. $P = \Gamma'_{\mathrm{ppp},t}$; $M = \Gamma'_{\mathrm{mon},t}$; $X = -\delta'_{s,t-1}$.

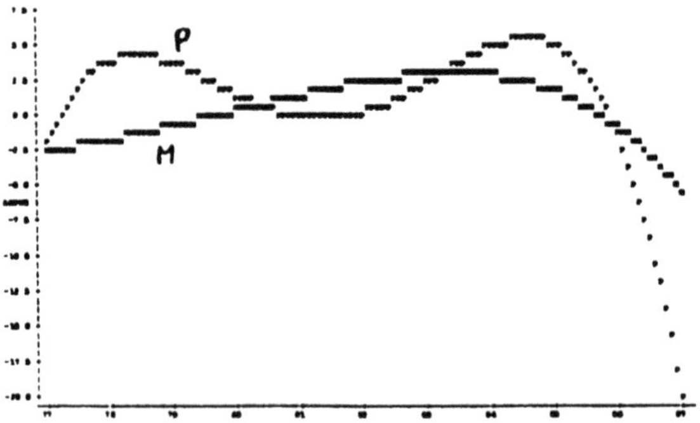

Figure 4 West Germany: Effects of fundamentals on the change in the spot rate. $P = \delta'_{\mathrm{ppp},t}$; $M = \delta'_{\mathrm{mon},t}$.

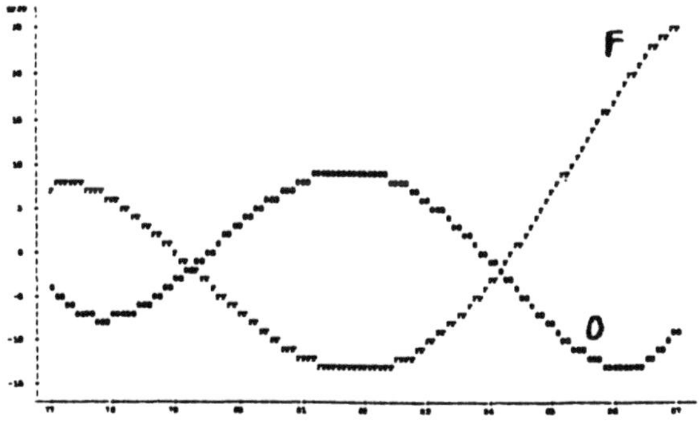

Figure 5 Japan: Effects of interest rates on the forward discount. $F = -\Gamma'_{\mathrm{fd},t}$; $O = \delta'_{\mathrm{fd},t-1}$.

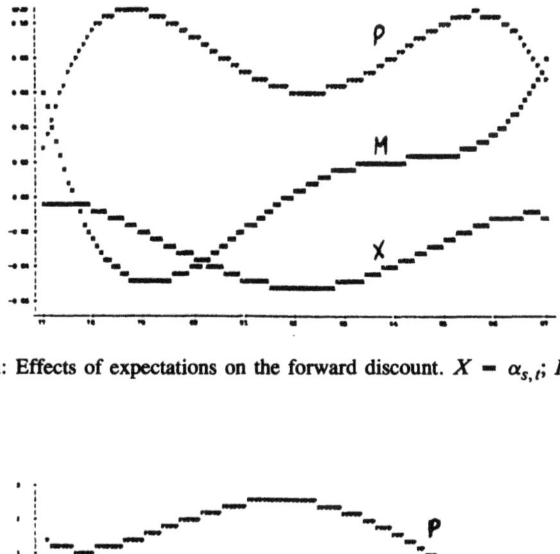

Figure 6 Japan: Effects of expectations on the forward discount. $X = \alpha_{s,t}$; $P = \alpha_{\mathrm{ppp},t}$; $M = \alpha_{\mathrm{mon},t}$.

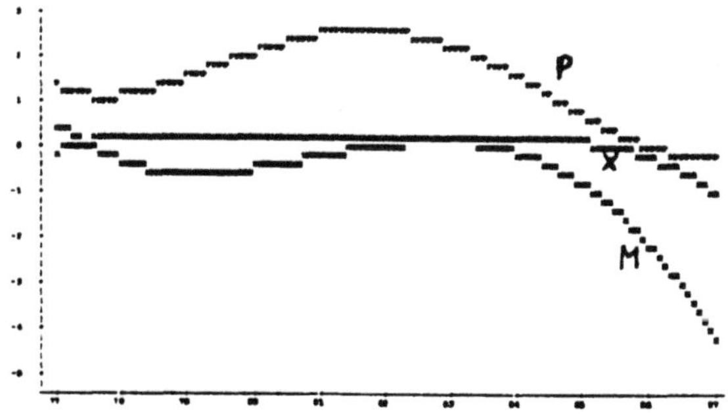

Figure 7 Japan: Effects of expectations on the change in the spot rate. $P = \Gamma'_{\mathrm{ppp},t}$; $M = \Gamma'_{\mathrm{mon},t}$; $X = -\delta'_{s,t-1}$.

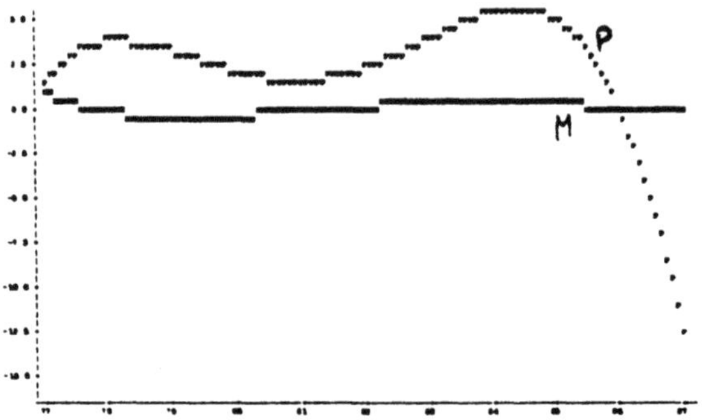

Figure 8 Japan: Effects of fundamentals on the change in the spot rate. $P = \delta'_{\text{ppp},t}$; $M = \delta'_{\text{mon},t}$.

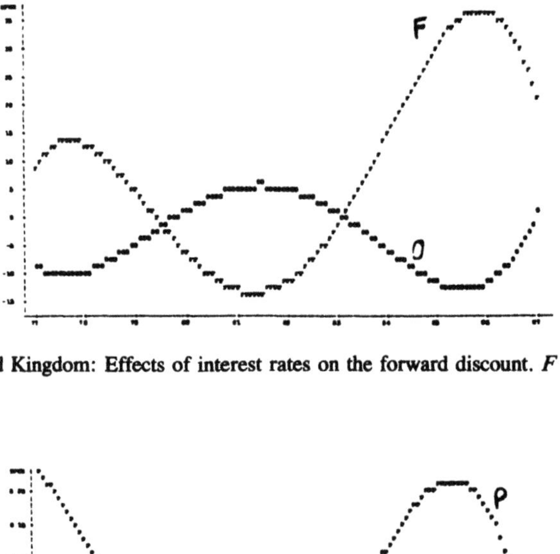

Figure 9 United Kingdom: Effects of interest rates on the forward discount. $F = -\Gamma'_{\text{fd},t}$; $O = \delta'_{\text{fd},t-1}$.

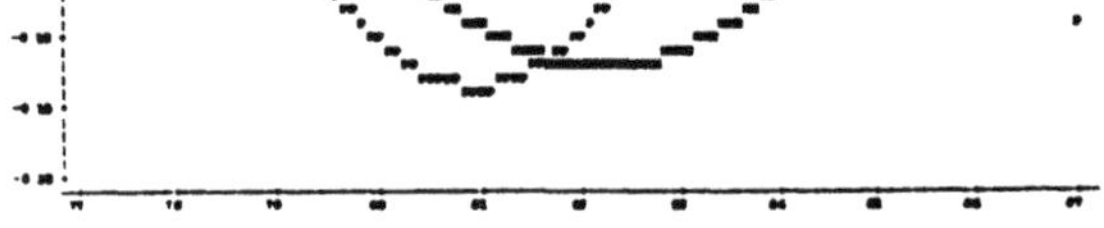

Figure 10 United Kingdom: Effects of expectations on the forward discount. $X = \alpha_{s,t}$; $P = \alpha_{\text{ppp},t}$; $M = \alpha_{\text{mon},t}$.

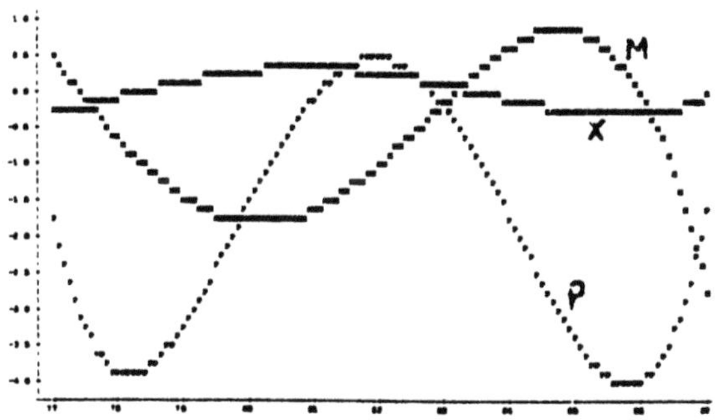

Figure 11 United Kingdom: Effects of expectations on the change in the spot rate. $P = \Gamma'_{ppp,t}$; $M = \Gamma'_{mon,t}$; $X = -\delta'_{s,t-1}$.

Technical analysts also influence the foreign exchange markets. The corresponding coefficients' paths reveal that these technical expectations were most stabilizing in the forward market between 1981 and 1982, but became quickly destabilizing thereafter (that is, Π rose). The role of technical analysts in the spot market ($\sigma_{s,t-1}$) is also highly significant for Germany, in contrast to the belief that the spot rate follows a random-walk process, in which case the lagged change in the spot rate would not significantly affect the current change in the spot rate. It also appears that expectations based on purchasing power parity and the monetary approach can significantly affect the spot rate and the forward discount. However, according to most figures, the values and signs of the corresponding coefficients are subject to large changes over the 12-year period, which may explain the failure of empirical models of exchange rate determination that do not incorporate time-varying coefficients or a learning process about fundamentals. The fact that expectations seem to adapt to changes in the influence of fundamentals does not imply in itself that agents learn the

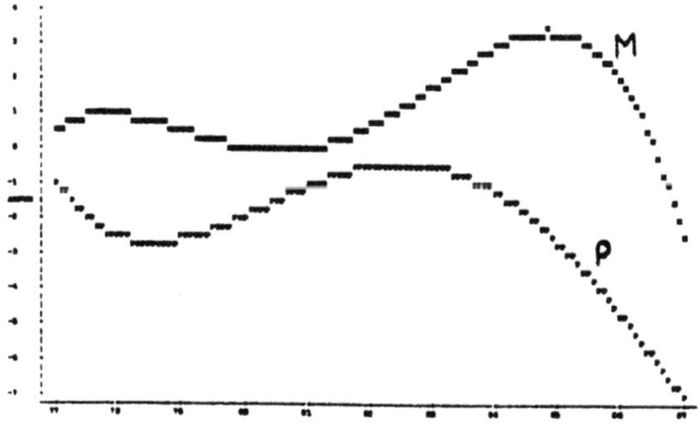

Figure 12 United Kingdom: Effects of fundamentals on the change in the spot rate. $P = \delta'_{ppp,t}$; $M = \delta'_{mon,t}$.

correct structure of the model, which encompasses speculative influences from technical analysts. This fact confirms the yearly ex ante forecasting surveys done by the magazine *Euromoney*, where technical analysts clearly outperformed fundamental models. If the rational expectations hypothesis holds, then agents should switch their expectations toward technical analysis. We then become engaged in a vicious circle of an ever-increasing role of destabilizing speculation.

CONCLUSIONS

The eclectic model and its empirical estimation have provided a wealth of information about the behavior of foreign exchange traders, and especially about the role of their diversified expectations. First, the eclectic model provides a statistically superior framework, as suggested by its goodness of fit (R^2 adjusted for degrees of freedom), compared to the individual models of exchange rate determination, such as relative purchasing power parity and the monetary approach. It is argued that the time-varying structure of the model, which explicitly embodies endogenous diversified expectations, is the main reason for this improvement in predicting changes in exchange rates.

Second, the theoretical assumption that some speculators base their trading decisions on anticipated profits derived from deviations from uncovered interest rate parity has been refuted by the empirical analysis in this study. Instead, the significant influence of changes in interest rate differentials on the change in the spot rate has been detected.

Third, this model indicates that technical analysis tended to increase the volatility of the spot and forward markets in the late 1970s and the mid 1980s. Therefore, the rationality of foreign exchange traders should be addressed in the future in a time-varying framework of diversified expectations that explicitly incorporates the roles of speculators believing in technical analysis and fundamentals, so as to better understand the dynamics of exchange rates.

APPENDIX I

$$\Gamma_{\text{ppp},t} = \sum_{p=1}^{Np(t)} \frac{\Theta_{\text{SS}p,t} + \Theta_{\text{UI}p,t}}{\Phi_t}$$

$$\Gamma_{\text{mon},t} = \Phi_t \sum_{m=1}^{Nm(t)} \frac{\Theta_{\text{SS}m,t} + \Theta_{\text{UI}m,t}}{\Phi_t}$$

$$\Gamma_{r,t} = \Phi_t \sum_{i=1}^{N(t)} \frac{\Theta_{\text{UI}i,t}}{\Phi_t}$$

$$\delta_{\text{ppp},t} = \frac{\Theta_{B,t} - \sum_{p=1}^{Np(t-1)} \Theta_{\text{SS}p,t-1} + \Theta_{\text{UI}p,t-1} + \Theta_{\text{FS}p,t-1}}{\Phi_t}$$

$$\delta_{\text{mon},t} = \frac{\Theta_{M,t} - \sum_{m=1}^{Nm(t-1)} \Theta_{\text{SS}m,t-1} + \Theta_{\text{UI}m,t-1} + \Theta_{\text{FS}m,t-1}}{\Phi_t}$$

$$\delta_{r,t-1} = \sum_{i=1}^{N(t-1)} \frac{\Theta_{\text{UI}i,t-1}}{\Phi_t}$$

$$\delta_{\text{fd},t-1} = \sum_{i=1}^{N(t-1)} \frac{\Theta_{\text{FS}i,t-1}}{\Phi_t}$$

$$\delta_{s,t-1} = -\pi_{t-1} \sum_{c=1}^{Nc(t-1)} \frac{\Theta_{\text{SS}c,t-1} + \Theta_{\text{UI}c,t-1}}{\Phi_t}$$

where

$$\Phi_t = \Theta_{B,t} + \Theta_{M,t} - \pi_t \sum_{c=1}^{Nc(t)} (\Theta_{\text{SS}c,t} + \Theta_{\text{UI}c,t})$$

$$\alpha_{s,t} = \pi_t \sum_{c=1}^{Nc(t)} \frac{\Theta_{\text{FS}c,t}}{\Omega}$$

$$\alpha_{\text{ppp},t} = \sum_{p=1}^{Np(t)} \frac{\Theta_{\text{FS}p,t}}{\Omega}$$

$$\alpha_{\text{mon},t} = \sum_{m=1}^{Nm(t)} \frac{\Theta_{\text{FS}m,t}}{\Omega}$$

where

$$\Omega = \Theta_{H,t} + \sum_{i} \Theta_{\text{FS}i,t} \quad \text{and} \quad N(t) = Np(t) + Nm(t) + Nc(t)$$

REFERENCES

Allen, H., and M. Taylor. 1989. *Charts, Fundamentals in the Foreign Exchange Market.* Bank of England Discussion Paper No. 40, London, England.

Federal Reserve Bank of New York. 1989. *Foreign Exchange Markets in the United States,* New York: FRBNY.

Frankel, J., and K. Froot. 1990. Chartists, fundamentalists, and trading in the foreign exchange market, *American Economic Review, Proceedings* 80(2):181–185.

Takagi, S. 1991. Exchange rate expectations: A survey of survey studies, *IMF Staff Papers* 38(1), Washington, DC.

White, H. 1980. A heteroscedasticity-consistent covariance matrix estimator and a direct test for heteroscedasticity, *Econometrica* 48:817–837.

Chapter 3

Pricing Options on a Constrained Currency Index: Some Simulation Results

Tom Berglund, Staffan Ringbom, and Laura Vajanne

In classical arbitrage pricing of options the specification of a statistical distribution that models the price changes of the underlying security plays a fundamental role. The basic currency option valuation formulas, such as those of Garman and Kohlhagen (1983) and Grabbe (1983), assume that the exchange rate, like the stock price in the Black and Scholes (1973) article, follows an Ito process. The stochastic part of the exchange rate is assumed to follow a geometric Brownian motion, which implies a lognormal distribution of exchange rate changes.

In the case of exchange rates for which there exists a currency agreement, such as the European Monetary System and the currency index system used in Nordic countries, the assumption that underlying exchange rate movements follow a geometric Brownian motion is not justified. In these cases the constraints imposed by the currency agreement and possibility of realignments must be included in a model of the exchange rate process.

In general, option pricing models that allow jumps in the price of the underlying instrument have been studied by Cox and Ross (1976), Cox, Ross, and Rubinstein (1979), and Merton (1976). A generalized valuation formula for the case where the security price is a combination of an Ito process and a random point process is presented by Aase (1988).

The focus of this chapter is to study the effects of allowing the exchange rate movements and the probability of a jump to be mutually dependent as compared to the assumption of the independence of these two stochastic processes. It is shown that this dependence has significant effects on the valuation of a currency option.

THE PRINCIPLE OF RISK-NEUTRAL VALUATION IN THE PRESENT CONTEXT

At the heart of the derivation of the Black–Scholes type of currency option pricing formula is the arbitrage technique by which investors can follow a dynamic portfolio strategy using the underlying currency and riskless borrowing to exactly reproduce the return structure of an option. By following this strategy in combination with a short position in an option, the investor can eliminate all risk from the total position; hence, to avoid arbitrage opportunities, the option must be priced such that the return on the total position equals the risk-free rate of interest.

In the presence of jumps the hedging argument breaks down. Proper pricing requires the market's aversion to jump risk to be taken into account. However, there are plausible reasons why the premium attached to jump risk may be negligible in the case of exchange rates. The most important is that the jump, be it re- or devaluation, is likely to be uncorrelated with the changes in aggregate wealth in the world economy. This should be the case especially if the world market beta for the domestic aggregate wealth against global wealth is close to one, that is, if the systematic risk of the domestic economy equals the global average. In the following discussion it is assumed that no risk premium is required by the market for the jump risk in exchange rates.

The assumption that the domestic and the foreign economy are expected to react alike to exogenous stochastic shocks allows us to derive the domestic risk-free interest rate from the foreign rate by assuming that the instantaneous expected return is the same for default-free holdings irrespective of the currency in which it is denoted.[1] The risk premium is zero, and interest rates are linked by the uncovered interest rate parity condition, which relates the interest differential to expected changes in exchange rates.[2]

EXPERIMENTAL DESIGN

Exchange Rate Movements Within the Index Band When Jumps Are Excluded

The assumption here is that the movements of the currency index within the index band can be described as a discrete time Markov process on a continuous

[1] In practice this is not necessarily true. Due to the extensive dependence on the highly cyclical forest industry, Finland may be more exposed to world market risk. Thus, if the foreign output is considered less "risky" than the home output, there is an expected return on buying foreign exchange forward, and a risk premium should be added to the relation.

[2] Even in a case of risk neutrality, the uncovered interest rate parity may seem to be violated due to Jensen's inequality. This is known as Siegel's (1972) paradox, and since it affects the computation of the domestic interest rate it will be discussed later in this chapter.

state space.[3] In the absence of jumps, the process of the currency index is characterized by[4]

$$J_t^* = \max(0, \min\{2c, [c + b(J_{t-1}^* - c) + \sigma\Phi^{-1}(X_t^{(1)})]\}) \tag{1}$$

where $2c$ is the width of the band, b is the strength of the assumed mean reverting tendency within the index band, and $X_t^{(1)}$ is a standardized uniformly distributed random variable, which through the inverse of the cumulative standard normal distribution function Φ^{-1} produces a normally distributed random shock. The dispersion of the shock is scaled by σ. The boundaries of the index are imposed through the min and max functions, which will keep the index value within the band.

The mean reverting property means that when the system is in a state far removed from the midpoint, it is more likely to move toward the midpoint than in the opposite direction. If $b = 1$, the corresponding unbounded process, the second argument in the min function in (1), is a random walk. If $|b| < 1$, the corresponding process is a stationary autoregressive process of order one. The values for the coefficient b and for the standard deviation σ can be estimated from historical data.

Jump Characteristics

A jump means that the whole index band is moved up or down. Furthermore, the index number jumps to a new location within the new band. Since the range of the band is given, it is sufficient to model the process for the lower bound ($J_t^{(1)}$). The change of the lower bound of the index, that is, a revaluation (A) or a devaluation (D), is defined by

$$\Delta J_t^{(1)} = -1_{A_t}(X_t^{(2)})a_1(X_t^{(3)}) + 1_{D_t}(X_t^{(2)})d_1(X_t^{(3)}) \tag{2}$$

Normally, $\Delta J_t^{(1)}$ is zero. If the indicator function 1_A takes the value one, a revaluation occurs and the size of the jump is given by $a_1 X_t^{(3)}$, and if the indicator function 1_D takes the value one, a devaluation occurs and the size of the jump is given by $d_1 X_t^{(3)}$. $X_t^{(3)}$ is a standard uniformly distributed independent

[3]For convenience the authors talk about movements of the index, although movements of the specific currency (markka) with respect to the index would be more natural.

[4]In the background there is a stochastic base (Ω, $\mathcal{F}$, $(\mathcal{F}_t)_{t\in N}$, P) on which every process is measurable and adapted:

$$\Omega = \times_{i=0}^{\infty} \mathbf{R}^3, \quad \mathcal{F} = \bigotimes_{i=0}^{\infty} \mathfrak{R}^3, \quad \mathcal{F}_t = \bigotimes_{i=0}^{t} \mathfrak{R}^3$$

is sufficiently large for this purpose.

stochastic variable that is independent of $X_t^{(1)}$. The terms a_1 and d_1 denote inverse functions of lognormal cumulative distribution functions. Thus, the size of the re- or devaluation is lognormally distributed.

By choosing the lognormal distribution the authors eliminate jumps in the wrong direction, which could occur if negative values were possible. Furthermore, very small jumps are unlikely, while large jumps are possible.

$X_t^{(2)}$ is a standard uniformly distributed independent stochastic variable,[5] which will determine whether a revaluation or devaluation will occur. This is determined according to Figure 1.

The probability for a revaluation $q(j)$ and $p(j)$ for devaluation are assumed to be Bernoulli-type probabilities:

$$q(j) = k_a\left(1 - \frac{j}{2c}\right)^n \quad \text{and} \quad p(j) = k_d\left(\frac{j}{2c}\right)^n \tag{3}$$

with the natural restriction,

$$\forall j \in [0, 2c]:\ q(j), p(j) \geq 0 \quad \text{and} \quad q(j) + p(j) \leq 1$$

If $n = 0$, the probability will not depend on the position within the band. Thus the probability is evenly distributed over the whole fluctuation area.

The total unconditional probability of a revaluation or devaluation is given as an integral of the probabilities over the whole fluctuation area.

$$p = \int_{[\mathrm{lb},\,\mathrm{ub}]} p(j)\, d\bar{P}(j) \qquad q = \int_{[\mathrm{lb},\,\mathrm{ub}]} q(j)\, d\bar{P}(j) \tag{4}$$

where $\bar{P}$ is a stationary probability measure for the position within the band, $j \in [\mathrm{lb}, \mathrm{ub}]$.

Exchange Rate Movements Including Jumps

The process determining the position of the currency index band ($J_t^{(2)}$), including the possibility of a jump, is defined as follows:

[5] Also independent of $X^{(1)}$ and $X^{(3)}$.

Figure 1 Determination of re- and devaluations using a uniformly [0, 1] distributed random variable ($X^{(2)}$). If A: $X^{(2)} > q(j)$, a revaluation occurs, while if D: $X^{(2)} > 1 - p(j)$, a devaluation occurs.

$$J_t^{(2)} = 1_{A_t^c \in p D_t^c}(X_t^{(2)}) J_t^*(X_t^{(1)}) + 1_{A_t}(X_t^{(2)}) a_2(X_t^{(1)}) + 1_{D_t}(X_t^{(2)}) d_2(X_t^{(1)}) \quad (5)$$

where $A_t = [0, q(J_{t-1}^{(1)})]$ and $D_t = [(1 - p(J_{t-1}^{(1)})), 1]$ when $t > 0$, $A_0 = D_0 = \varnothing$.

Since the location of the index number within the band after a jump is unknown, it is assumed that the location is beta-distributed within the new index band. Thus, a_2 and d_2 are inverse functions of the cumulative beta-distribution function, where the two sufficient distribution parameters are determined to correspond to a priori expectations. Thus, the new position is centered in the middle of the band and the probability of landing outside the range is zero.

The process of the log of the currency index is now easily defined as

$$I = (I_t)_{t \in N} \quad \text{where } \forall t \in N\colon I_t = J_t^{(1)} + J_t^{(2)} \quad (6)$$

The log of the index is the sum of the lower bound and the position in the band. Thus, the currency index process can be written as

$$S = (S_t)_{t \in N} \quad \text{where } S_t = \exp(J_t^{(1)} + J_t^{(2)}) \quad (7)$$

SPECIFICATION OF THE PARAMETER VALUES USED IN THE SIMULATION EXPERIMENTS

The parameters and starting values used in the simulations of the exchange rate movements are defined in Table 1. The width of the index band is set to 6%, which corresponds to the present band used in Finland. In these experiments a sample of 11 evenly distributed initial states that start at the lower and end at the upper boundary are explored. The strength of the mean reverting property is determined using the estimated value from the daily observations of the Finnish currency index in the period 1987–1989. The standard deviation used in the simulations is estimated from the same data. The log of the expected size of the devaluation or revaluation is set to 0.05. The standard deviation around the expected size is assumed to be 0.01. These figures correspond to the authors' view that very small currency realignments are unnecessary, while the realignment usually will be made before the required magnitude grows too large, due to actual or potential speculative pressure.[6]

The case in which the probability of a jump is dependent of the position within the band is parametrized as follows: The probability of a jump as its highest is 0.005 at the boundaries of the band. For a revaluation the maximum

[6]The trend toward smaller realignments can be observed in EMS as well as in Nordic countries. The devaluations used to correct the value of exchange rates were quite large until the middle of the 1980s, but since then they have declined.

Table 1
Parameter Settings Used in the Simulation Experiments

Symbols	Description	Value
Starting value		
x	Relative index position within the band	$x \in [0, 1]$
I_{lb}	Lower bound of the index	97
I_{ub}	Upper bound of the index	103
I_t	Initial position within the band	97–103
Parameters		
b	Strength of the mean reversion property	0.9985
σ	Standard deviation of the error term in the unconstrained autoregressive process	0.001 45
θ	Expected log size of the jump	0.05
δ	Standard deviation of log of the jump	0.01
$\max_j \{p(j) + q(j)\}$	Probability of the jump; j is the relative position within the (log) band	0.005
$E(x\|j)$	Expected relative position of the index value within the new (log) index band after the jump	0.5
Var $(x\|j)$	Variance of the relative position of the index within the new (log) band	0.001

is at the lower bound, and for a devaluation the maximum is at the upper bound. For the rest of the band the probability is determined as a quadratically decreasing function that reaches zero at the other boundary. In the benchmark experiment the overall probability of jumps stays the same, the difference being that the probability for devaluations as well as revaluations will be constant throughout the band. When dependence is assumed, the expected relative value of the index after the jump is in the middle of the new band. The variance of the expected value is set to 0.001. In the benchmark case the expected relative value of the index after the jump is the same as before the jump.

SIMULATION EXPERIMENTS

General Considerations

To evaluate options on the index, the authors started by using the above model to generate a data set. A set of 30,000 exchange rates at the expiration date of the option are produced for each 11 initial states. The initial time to expiration in these simulations is 10 and 90 days.[7] Once the data are given, the values of the currency options are computed.

[7]Initial experiments with 20, 30, and 60 days produced results that were in line with those for the extreme cases. Consequently, these results are not reported.

The strike prices of the options are determined next. For the 11 starting values three corresponding strike prices are defined. Thus, at time 0 the options are either at the money, in the money, or out of the money. The in-the-money and out-of-the-money options at time 0 are defined to have a strike price that is one standard deviation below or above the current rate.

The foreign interest rate is defined as the weighted average of interest rates of the currencies in the basket. The average of daily observations of the three months' currency basket eurorate for the year 1989 was used, which was 9.9%. The domestic interest rate when determined by the model guarantees the elimination of expected speculative profits between the synthetic forward and domestic default-free money market instruments.[8]

However, even in the case of risk neutrality, the uncovered interest rate parity may be violated due to Jensen's inequality. This problem is known as Siegel's (1972) paradox.[9] The convexity problem of nominal interest rates arising from the Jensen's inequality is solved in this model using logarithmic values of the future exchange rates.

Results

The results for two maturities are reported: 90 days, which represents a long time to expiration, and 10 days, which represents a short time. The results for these two maturities are reported in parallel to highlight the effects of the time to expiration.

To make interpretation easier, the main results of this study are reported in graphical form. Since the results depend on the starting position of the exchange rate within the band, the graphs report the outcome with the starting state on the category axis, the first state being the lower border and the eleventh or last state being the upper border of the initial band.

The first results that are of crucial interest for how the options are priced are the domestic interest rates and the volatilities produced by the model. The fact that the exchange rate is not allowed to cross the border of the band unless there is a jump is clearly reflected in the domestic interest rates as seen in Figure 2*a* for the 90-day option and in Figure 2*b* for the 10-day option. An interesting picture emerges if the level of the interest rate in the 90-day case is compared to that in the 10-day case.

---

[8]See Chapter 2 for a discussion of how the domestic interest rates are determined.

[9]Siegel's paradox states that, even in the absence of risk aversion, the efficiency condition in the forward foreign exchange market cannot be that expected nominal profits are zero. This is because nominal profits can be expressed in terms of either currency. It cannot be the case that the forward home-currency price of foreign currency equals the expected future spot rate of foreign currency $F = E(S)$, and the forward foreign price of home currency equals expected future spot price of home currency $1/F = E(1/S)$. Because of Jensen's inequality, expected nominal profits must exist, at least in terms of one of the two currencies.

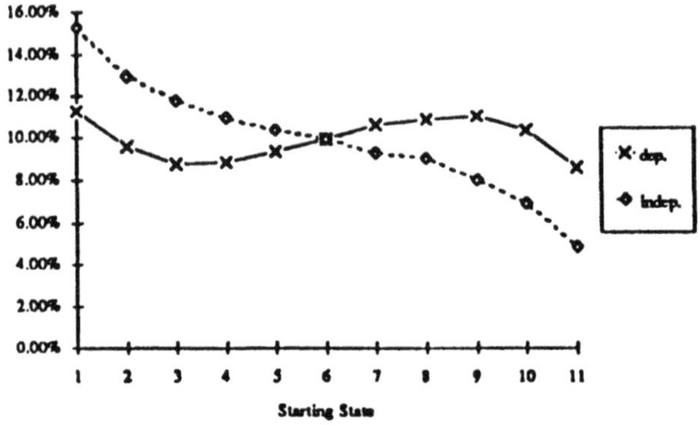

(a)

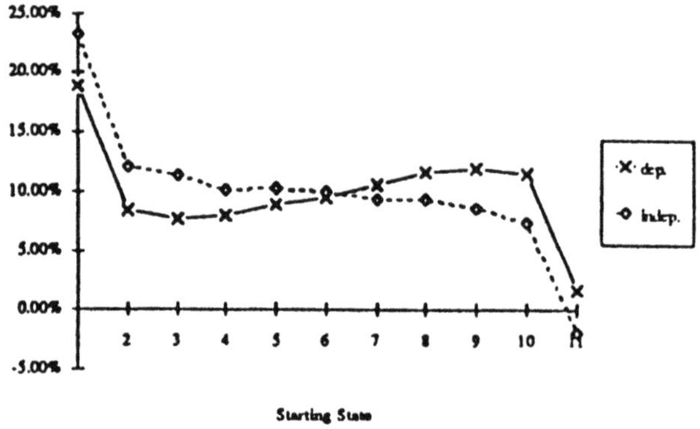

(b)

Figure 2 Domestic interest rates as a function of the starting state within the band: (*a*) Domestic rates, 90 days; (*b*) domestic rates, 10 days.

In general, the border will push the exchange rate in the other direction. At the upper border, this produces an expected appreciation and low domestic rates. This is most transparent in the case in which the jump probability is independent of the exchange rate position. It is seen that a relatively steeply sloping yield curve is required to eliminate expected speculation profits close to the borders of the band.

The main difference between this chapter's main case, in which the probability of a jump depends on the state within the band, and the benchmark case is that the effect of the closeness to the border of the band will be counteracted by an increasing jump probability in the dependent case. The outcome is an S-shaped pattern for the domestic rate, which is almost horizontal.

Figure 3 reports the observed average volatilities. The observed volatilities to a large extent reflect jumps in the band. In the benchmark case these jumps are equally likely and of the same magnitude independently of the exact starting state within the band, which translates into a volatility that is largely independent of the starting state. For the dependent case, however, the size of the jump depends on the state in which it occurs.

Close to the borders the volatility is affected by two counteracting tendencies:

1. The jump probability is higher in the dependent case than in the independent case, which implies a higher volatility for the dependent case.
2. The expected size of the jump is smaller in the dependent case,[10] which implies a lower volatility for the dependent case. It turns out that 2 domi-

[10] The expected size of the jump in the exchange rate at the border is in the independent case a jump in the border, whereas in the dependent case, c should be substracted.

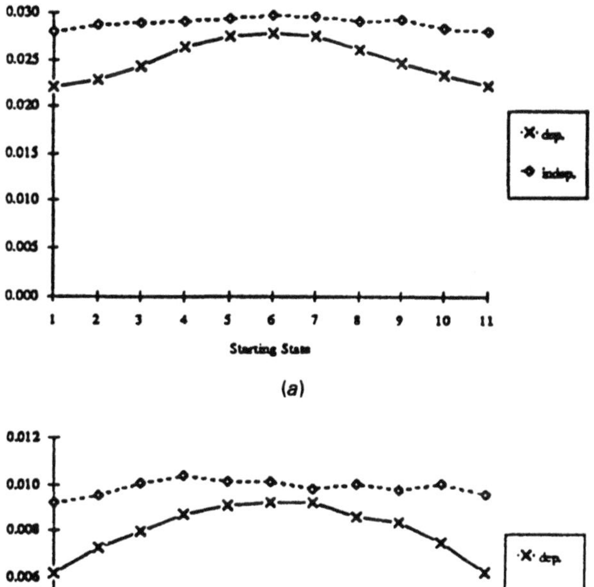

(*a*)

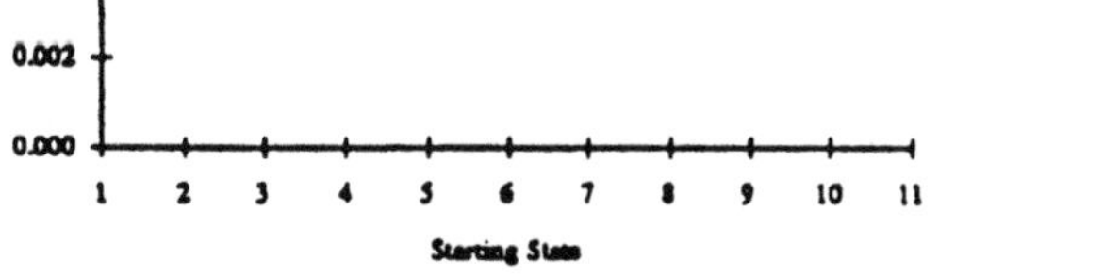

(*b*)

Figure 3 Standard deviation of the exchange rate as a function of the starting state within the band: (*a*) Volatility, 90 days; (*b*) volatility, 10 days.

nates 1 and the volatility is markedly lower close to the borders in the dependent case.

Figure 4 reports the call option prices based on the presented simulation data.[11] Three sets of expiration prices were used: out of the money, at the money, and in the money. The at-the-money options have an exercise price equal to the present exchange rate, the out-of-the-money options have an exercise price one standard deviation (computed ex post) above the present rate, and the in-the-money options have an exercise price one standard deviation below the present rate. In the dependent case the probability of a jump in the wrong direction approaches zero as the exchange rate approaches the border, whereas for the independent case the probability stays on the same level as for all other states within the band.

To be able to focus more directly on the impact of the differences in the second moments of the exchange rate distribution on the expiration date, a new set of option prices with different striking prices were computed. The striking prices in this new case were determined on the basis of the average log value of the exchange rate at the expiration date. This implies that the expiration prices will differ considerably between this study's main case and the benchmark case. However, the deviation produced by the differences in the expected exchange rate[12] on the expiration date is removed. The results based on the adjusted strike are reported in Figure 5. This figure reveals that adjusting the strike price to account for the expected change in the exchange rate will make the differences between the option prices correspond quite closely to the differences in volatilities as displayed in Figure 3 for the at-the-money and the in-the-money cases.

As a summary of the comparison of the option values produced under this specification of the dependence between the location within the band and the jumps produced by re- or devaluations and the option values produced under the assumption of independence, it is concluded that the most notable difference arises because of differences in the expected exchange rate change.

The independence assumption produces the somewhat pathological result

[11]These prices are obtained using the formula

$$C_t(s) = \left. \frac{e^{-r\tau} \sum_{i=1}^{30,000} \max\left(S_{t+\tau}(\omega^i) - X, 0\right)}{30,000} \right|_{S_t = \exp\{s + J_t^{(2)}\}}$$

where τ is time to expiration, i indexes the simulation run, S is the exchange rate, and X the exercise price. This formula gives slightly downward biased option values, due to the fact that the implicit interest rates are path dependent and should be treated as stochastic interest rates. However, the same error is made when currency options are valued using the Garman–Kohlhagen model (1983), instead of the model presented by Grabbe (1983).

[12]The stochastic component in the average as compared to the actual mean or the simulation error is disregarded.

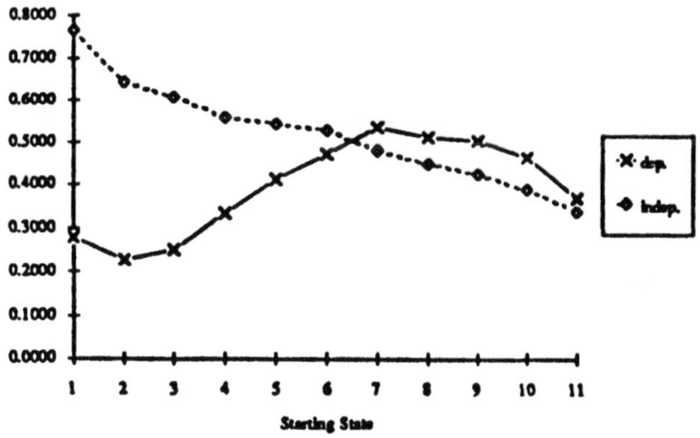

(*a*)

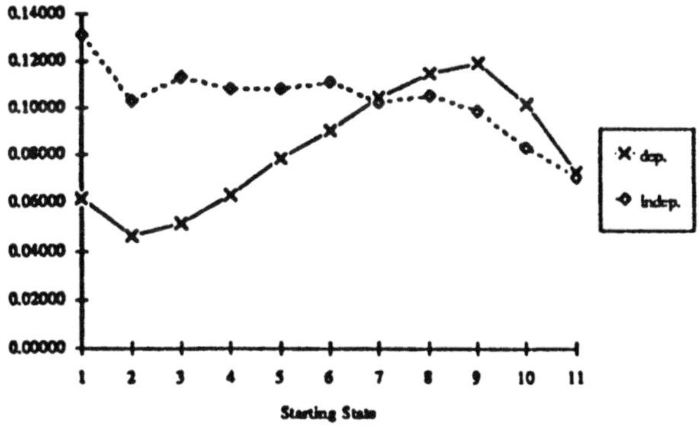

(*b*)

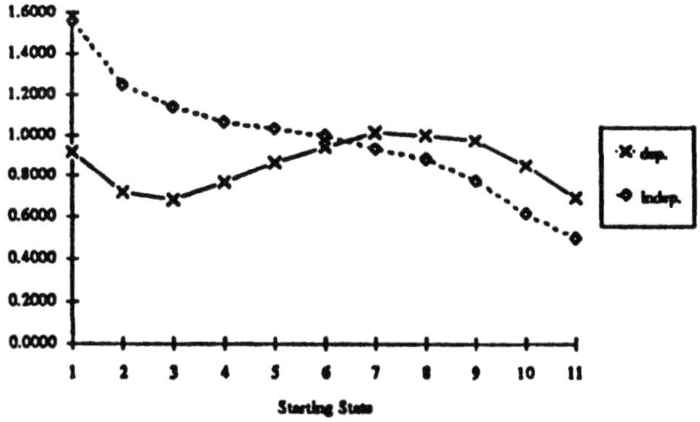

(*c*)

Figure 4 Call option prices as a function of the starting position within the band when the probability of a realignment is dependent vs. independent of where the exchange rate is located within the band: (*a*) Option prices, out-of-the-money, 90 days; (*b*) option prices, out-of-the-money, 10 days; (*c*) option prices, at-the-money, 90 days.

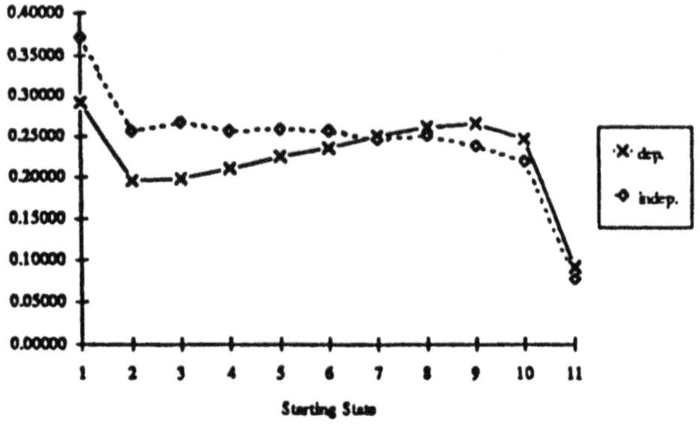

(*d*)

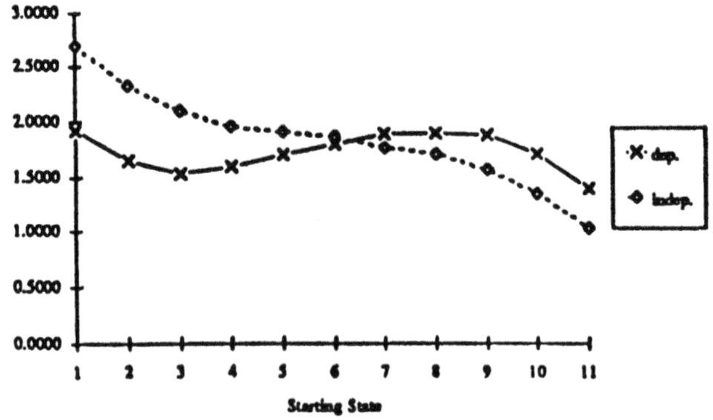

(*e*)

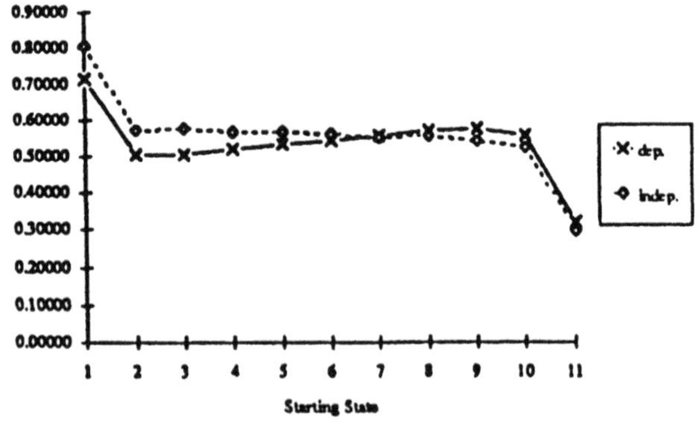

(*f*)

Figure 4 Call option prices as a function of the starting position within the band when the probability of a realignment is dependent vs. independent of where the exchange rate is located within the band (*Continued*): (*d*) option prices, at-the-money, 10 days; (*e*) option prices, in-the-money, 90 days; (*f*) option prices, in-the-money, 10 days.

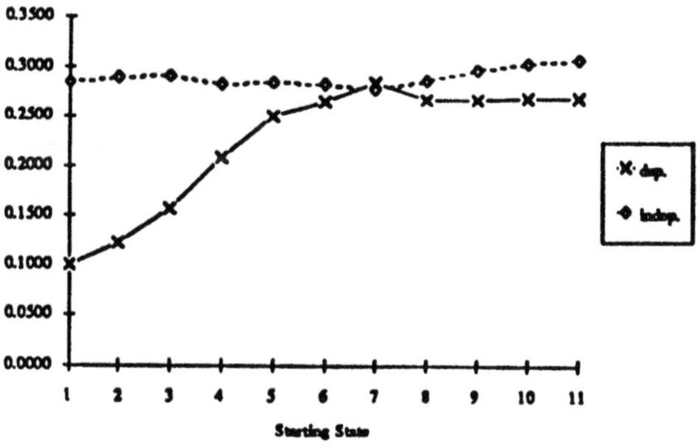

(*a*)

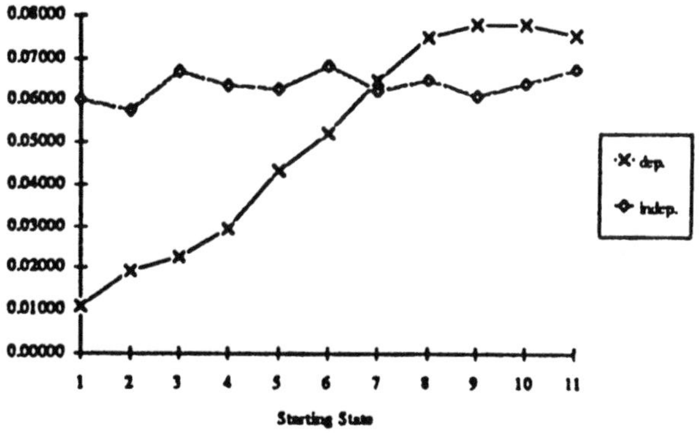

(*b*)

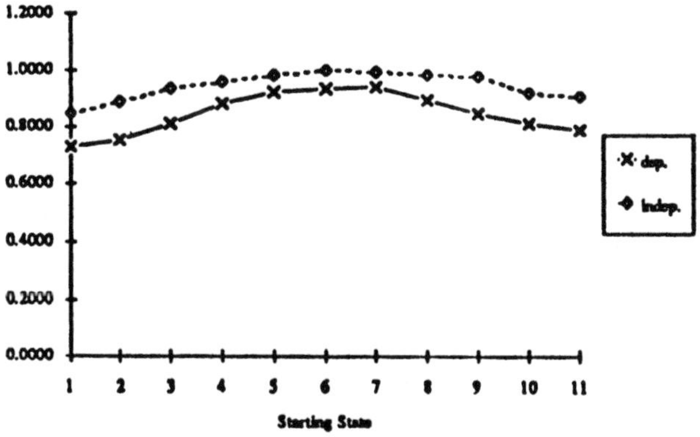

(*c*)

Figure 5 Call option prices as a function of the starting position within the band when the probability of a realignment is dependent vs. independent of where the exchange rate is located within the band. Strike prices adjusted to correspond to the expected change in the exchange rate: (*a*) Option prices, out-of-the-money, adjusted strike, 90 days; (*b*) option prices, out-of-the-money, adjusted strike, 10 days; (*c*) option prices, at-the-money, adjusted strike, 90 days.

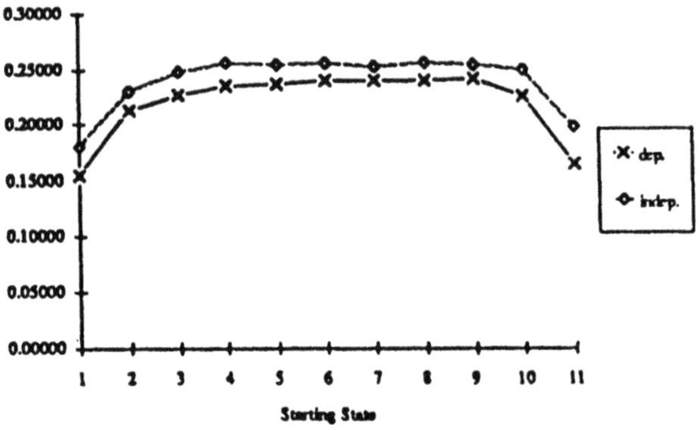

(d)

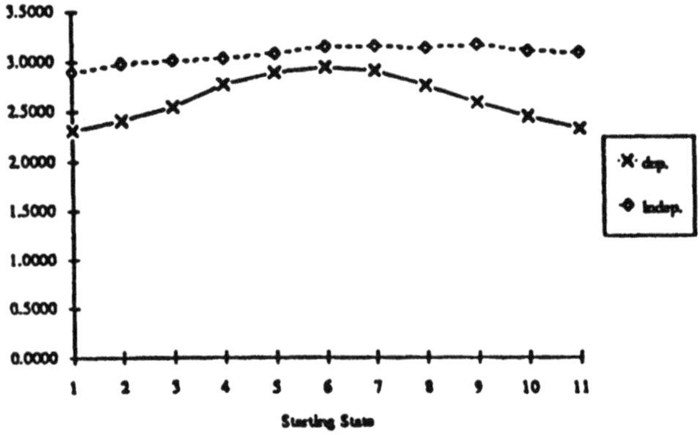

(e)

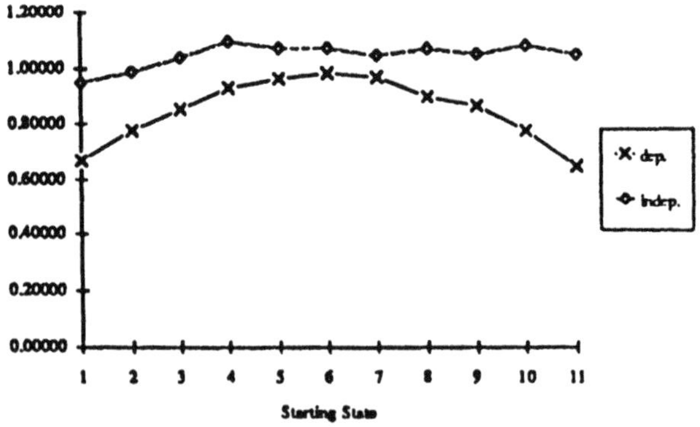

(f)

Figure 5 Call option prices as a function of the starting position within the band when the probability of a realignment is dependent vs. independent of where the exchange rate is located within the band. Strike prices adjusted to correspond to the expected change in the exchange rate (*Continued*): (*d*) option prices, at-the-money, adjusted strike, 10 days; (*e*) option prices, in-the-money, adjusted strike, 90 days; (*f*) option prices, in-the-money, adjusted strike, 10 days.

that the exchange rate must be expected to depreciate when it is close to the lower border and it has to be expected to appreciate when close to the upper border. In general, these results indicate that the shape of the yield curve is quite sensitive to the specific assumptions made about the exact exchange rate dynamics.

Comparisons to the Garman–Kohlhagen Model

Since the most widely used model for pricing exchange rate options is the Garman and Kohlhagen (1983) version of the Black and Scholes (1973) model, it is natural to ask how the prices produced by the present model will differ from those produced by the Garman and Kohlhagen model. The Garman and Kohlhagen model gives the following expression for the value of a call option:

$$C = Se^{-r_f\tau}\Phi(d_1) - Xe^{r_d\tau}\Phi(d_2) \tag{8}$$

where

$$d_1 = \frac{\ln(S/X) + (r_d - r_f + \sigma^2/2)\tau}{\sigma\sqrt{\tau}} \quad \text{and} \quad d_2 = d_1 - \sigma\sqrt{\tau}$$

When applying Eq. (8) to the valuation of the options produced by this simulation experiment, proper values for the input variables have to be selected. Since all input variables other than the volatility normally will be observed, the focus will be on the choice of the volatility measure. The foreign interest rate is taken to be the 9.9% used in these simulations, and the domestic rate is the one produced as a result of these simulations. An analogous choice for the volatility parameter would be the volatility produced by the 30,000 simulation runs.

The other two candidates used in the present chapter are the correct volatility in the case of no restrictions for the autoregressive process, which is called the unconstrained standard deviation[13] (unc.std.) and a simulated proxy for the standard deviation of the truncated process conditional on no jumps, which will be called the in-the-band standard deviation. The Garman–Kohlhagen option prices produced by these standard deviations are given in Figure 6, along with the simulated option values. The figure reveals that the simulated option values

[13]With no constraints the index will follow an AR (1) process. It is easily shown using the formula for the sum of geometric series that the variance of the index k periods from the present will be

$$\sigma^2\frac{1 - b^{2k}}{1 - b^2}$$

where σ^2 is the variance of the error term, k is the number of periods ahead, and b is the autoregressive coefficient in the model $|b| < 1$.

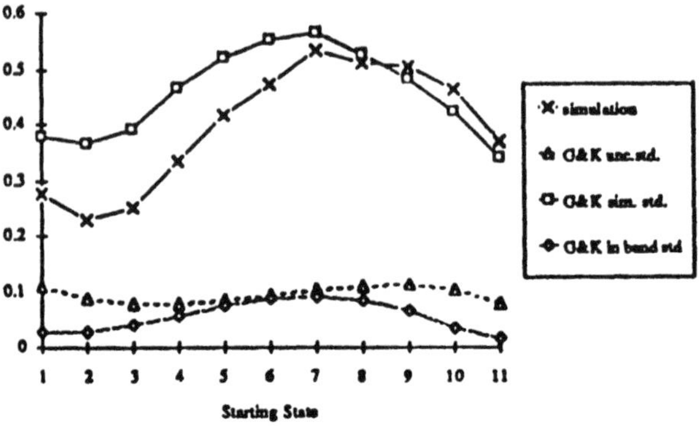

(a)

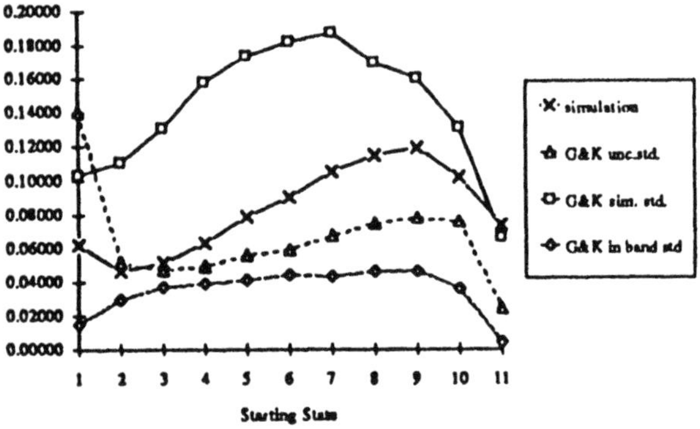

(b)

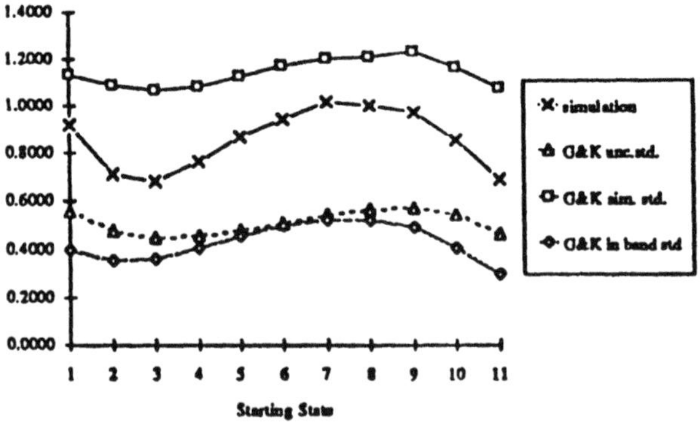

(c)

Figure 6 Simulated call option prices (dependent case) compared to those produced by the Garman–Kohlhagen (1983) model under different estimates for the volatility parameter used as input variable in the Garman–Kohlhagen model: (*a*) Option prices, out-of-the-money, 90 days; (*b*) option prices, out-of-the-money, 10 days; (*c*) option prices, at-the-money, 90 days.

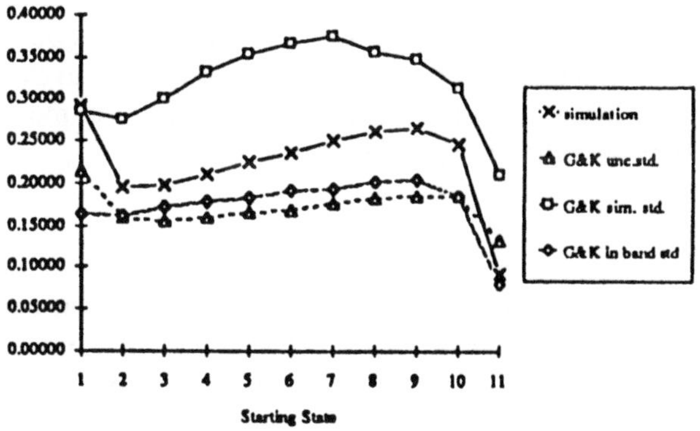

(*d*)

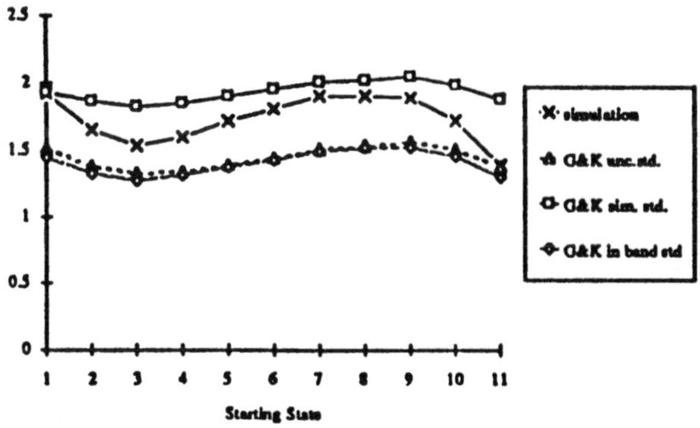

(*e*)

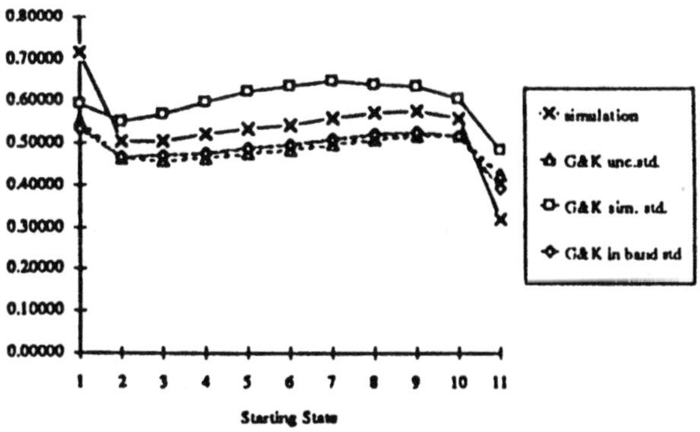

(*f*)

Figure 6 Simulated call option prices (dependent case) compared to those produced by the Garman–Kohlhagen (1983) model under different estimates for the volatility parameter used as input variable in the Garman–Kohlhagen model (*Continued*): (*d*) option prices, at-the-money, 10 days; (*e*) option prices, in-the-money, 90 days; (*f*) option prices, in-the-money, 10 days.

in most cases remain below the Garman and Kohlhagen option value based on the simulated standard deviation, whereas it lies above the option values produced by the other candidates. The simulated volatility tends to overestimate the true value of the option because the standard deviation is more sensitive to extreme values than is the option price itself.

CONCLUSIONS

This chapter has used a simulation model to analyze the consequences of removing the assumption of independence between the jump produced by re- or devaluations and the exchange rate position within the band. A simple form of dependence is introduced that makes the probability of a devaluation, which is set to zero at the lower border, grows quadratically toward the upper border, while the probability of a revaluation, which is set to zero at the upper border, grows toward the lower border.

The results indicate that the expected change in the exchange rate in the independence case will produce unrealistic outcomes. To preclude profitable speculation the exchange rate must be expected to depreciate when it is close to the lower border and to appreciate when close to the upper border. It turns out that these phenomena are avoided if the occurrence of re- or devaluations depends on the location within the band, given a realistic set of parameter values.

The largest difference in the call option values produced by the two models are for out-of-the-money options close to the lower border. The constant probability of an upward jump will drive up the option price in the independent case. In this dependent case it will be driven down by a relatively high probability of a downward jump. The smallest difference was observed for in-the-money options. Even in that case a difference of 25% at its maximum was observed for the 90-day option. Thus, whether independence between the jump and the location within the band is assumed or not is of considerable importance for the pricing of an option on the index.

Finally, when the option values based on these simulation experiments were compared with the option prices calculated with the widely used Garman and Kohlhagen model, the Garman and Kohlhagen model gave rise to over- and underestimation. When the simulated standard deviation was used in the Garman and Kohlhagen model, the prices generally were above the simulated values, but when jumps were disregarded in the standard deviation the reverse turned out to be true. Once again the out-of-the-money options exhibited the most notable differences.

The present simulation model is subject to several apparently unrealistic features. Perhaps the most striking is that de- and revaluations are made dependent on the exchange rate position within the band in a rather simplistic fashion. A more realistic model would derive probability estimates for re- and devaluations from simulated interest rate differentials. That would guarantee realistic interest rate dynamics, which is not the case in the present model.

REFERENCES

Aase, K. 1988. Contingent claims valuation when the security price is a combination of an Ito process and a random point process, *Stochastic Processes and Their Applications* 28:185–220.

Black, F., and M. Scholes. 1973. The pricing of options and corporate liabilities, *Journal of Political Economy* 81:637–654.

Cox, J., and S. Ross. 1976. The valuation of options for alternative stochastic processes, *Journal of Financial Economics* 3:145–166.

Cox, J., S. Ross, and M. Rubinstein. 1979. Option pricing: A simplified approach, *Journal of Financial Economics* 7:229–263.

Garman, M., and S. Kohlhagen. 1983. Foreign currency option values, *Journal of International Money and Finance* 2:231–237.

Grabbe, O. 1983. The pricing of call and put options on foreign exchange, *Journal of International Money and Finance* 2:239–253.

Jarrow, R., and E. Rosenfeld. 1984. Jump risks and the capital asset pricing model, *Journal of Business* 57:337–351.

Merton, R. 1976. Option pricing when underlying stock returns are discontinuous, *Journal of Financial Economics* 3:125–144.

Ross, S. 1976. The arbitrage theory of capital asset pricing, *Journal of Economic Theory* 13:341–360.

Siegel, J. 1972. Risk, interest rates, and the forward exchange, *Quarterly Journal of Economics* 86:303–339.

Chapter 4

Exchange Rate Variations and U.S. Multinational Corporations' Profits: The Case of the 1980s

Luc C. Moens

Because the U.S. dollar remains the prime medium for international trade and investment, its value is a key variable in the world economy. The U.S. dollar exchange rate experienced huge swings in the 1980s, raising the question of the effects of large deviations from purchasing power parity on U.S. industries and firms. The nature and intensity of these effects gives rise to much controversy. Some economists, like Paul Krugman (1989), emphasize the inertia of trade flows in spite of the high volatility of exchange rates, considering that the swings in exchange rates "have had only muted effects on anything real" (Krugman, 1989, p. 37). For others, like Milberg and Gray (1992), the appreciation of the U.S. dollar (1980–1985) had long-lasting unfavorable effects on U.S. tradable-goods industries. Market shares were lost, but, above all, companies have been deprived of a significant amount of internal funds needed for sustained investment in vital areas like innovation, which has obstructed the main engine of growth. In other words, the temporary appreciation of the U.S. dollar had a long-lasting negative effect. This chapter investigates a crucial causal linkage of the latter thesis, and tests whether the operating profits achieved in U.S. tradable-goods industries are negatively correlated with thc U.S. dollar appreciation of the early 1980s.

The nature of the relationship between real exchange rate movements and profits made by multinational corporations (MNCs) is apparently simple. Being by definition the ratio of prices of foreign and domestic goods, both expressed in U.S. dollars (USD), the real exchange rate measures price competitiveness. Its movements are associated with changes in future costs and revenue streams; a combination of accounting (translation) and competitive effects modifies operating profits, and possibly stock market values. However, the relationship between the exchange rate and operating profits is more complicated. First, other factors are involved that may exert divergent influences, including export demand sensitivity, the organizational structure of corporations, the cost structure, the degree of involvement in foreign activities, the intensity of import competition, the degree of substitution between local and imported factors, the import content of inputs, and output and input market structures. Second, the analysis must take into account the ability of MNCs to respond to difficult circumstances, for example, by skillfully managing intracorporate flows. Third, the competitive environment is very different from the textbooks' perfectly competitive markets: MNCs operate in environments characterized by imperfect competition and strategic interactions. Fourth, macroeconomic conditions must be taken into account, in particular, the income effects generated by the economic growth. In sum, the net effect of these influences is more uncertain than a cursory glance might suggest, and it deserves more thorough investigation.

THEORETICAL AND EMPIRICAL BACKGROUND

This work is based on four approaches: the managerial literature, the classical industrial organization, the microeconomics of the MNC, and the new trade theories. The managerial literature has developed the *exposure analysis,* which looks at cost and revenue streams to evaluate a firm's exposure, defined as the extent to which its profitability, net cash flows, and market value are modified as exchange rates change (Flood and Lessard, 1986; Shapiro, 1988; Oxelheim and Wilhborg, 1987; Bodnar and Gentry, 1989; Luehrman, 1990; Jorion, 1990). The analysis of translation exposure, sometimes called accounting or conversion exposure,[1] is not discussed here. This chapter deals mainly with transaction and economic exposures. The translation exposure is driven by changes in the nominal exchange rates, as the U.S. dollar value of contractual cash flows moves one-to-one with these changes. Hedging techniques are available to reduce exchange rate risks associated with both translation and transaction exposures. In contrast, the analysis of economic (or operating) exposure investigates effects of unexpected exchange rate variations on cash flows not captured in present accounting statements, that is, revenues, costs, and profits. Economic exposure is driven by changes in real exchange rates (with probable significant lags) and by competitive conditions prevailing in (input and output) domestic and foreign markets in which the MNC operates.

The classical industrial organization literature provides both a methodology and a wide body of empirical evidence. Many empirical studies belonging to

[1]Under the new rules set out in FASB52 issued in December 1981 by the Financial Accounting Standards Board (FASB), translation gains and losses do not flow through the income statement, but are shown as a direct gain or loss in the owners' equity.

this tradition specify performance indicators as a function of three variables: the ease of collusion, the level of barriers to entry, and the demand conditions (Waterson, 1984). This framework also effectively analyzes performances in open economies and international trade (Pugel, 1980; Jacquemin, 1982).

The microeconomic theory has also provided important contributions, among which are the optimal pricing behavior for oligopoly, the comparative statics for oligopoly (Dixit, 1984; Karikari and Collins, 1988), and the microeconomic analysis of multinational corporations (Horst, 1971; Itagaki, 1981).

The last approach on which this work is based is the *new trade theory*. A prominent contribution is the "pass-through" literature, which analyzes the relationship between exchange rate variations and changes in export and import flows. A host of full-fledged theoretical models attempt to model phenomena as the pass-through effect (Mann, 1986; Dornbusch, 1987; Krugman, 1986) and the hysteresis in trade (Baldwin, 1988).

Before we tackle the empirical issues, a few conceptual and theoretical insights are in order. When the U.S. dollar appreciates, it can be shown that consolidated operating profits (expressed in U.S. dollars) of a representative U.S. multinational corporation are negatively correlated with the conversion losses on foreign earnings, the share of export earnings, the price elasticity of the demand for exports denominated in U.S. dollars, and the proportion of inputs imported by the affiliate. More formally, worldwide U.S. dollar operating profits of a profit-maximizing MNC can be expressed as an implicit function of three sets of variables:

$$\Pi_j = \Pi[S_j(e), S_{-j}(e); e]$$

where the terms in brackets are, successively, the optimal strategy followed by the MNC j, the optimal strategies followed by all the other firms $(-j)$, and the exchange rate itself. The total differentiation of this expression yields three terms: the own effect, the strategic effect, and the direct effect, expressed as

$$\frac{d\Pi_j}{de} = \sum_{i=1}^{N} \frac{\partial \Pi_j}{\partial S_{ij}} \frac{dS_{ij}}{de} + \sum_{i=1;k\neq j}^{N} \frac{\partial \Pi_j}{\partial S_{ik}} \frac{dS_{ik}}{de} + \frac{\partial \Pi_j}{\partial e}$$

where S_{ij} is the strategy (for example, a level of output) adopted by the firm j on the ith market; $i = 1, \ldots, N$ are the different markets, identified here with the currency zones, in which the MNC operates; and $k = 1, \ldots, K$ indexes the firms.

TOWARD AN EMPIRICAL SPECIFICATION

The sustained appreciation of the U.S. dollar during the first half of the 1980s provides a good basis for examining the sensitivity of operating profits to exchange rate variations. To test whether profits are negatively correlated with such appreciation, a set of equations derived from the following general form is estimated:

$$y_{it} = f(R, R\ \Sigma\ \beta_{kit}x_{kit}, Z_t)$$

where y is a measure of operating cash flow (level or rate of return); R is the real exchange rate, introduced as regressor and interacted with firm specific features and/or market structures; and Z is a vector of macroeconomic factors. By pooling time series and cross-sectional observations, a panel of 50 large U.S. multinationals covering the period 1979–1987[2] is created. The companies were selected from lists of the largest U.S. multinationals drawn annually by the magazines *Forbes* and *Business Week*. The energy sector was excluded.

The economic analysis tested four classical models[3]:

(1) $y_{it} = \acute{A} + e_{it}$

(2) $y_{it} = \acute{A}_i + e_{it}$

(3) $y_{it} = \acute{A} + \Sigma\ \beta_k x_{kit} + e_{it}$

(4) $y_{it} = \acute{A}_i + \Sigma\ \beta_k x_{kit} + e_{it}$

The analysis relates mostly to the last two models, which both assume that intercept and slopes are constant over time and that the slopes are identical across companies. The difference lies in the treatment of the intercept. Model 3 is a classical (linear) regression, which ignores the groupwise nature of the observations: The y_{it} are estimated by an ordinary least-squares method under the constraint of identical intercepts. Model 4 is the dummy variable model (with fixed effects) with individual specific constants (that is, the constraint of identical intercepts is relaxed); the software used (LIMDEP) calculates partitioned least-squares estimators. Model 4 becomes a random effects model when the intercept can be written[4] as $\acute{A}_i = \acute{A} + u_i$.

EMPIRICAL RESULTS

Some exploratory work was undertaken by doing preliminary estimations, not reported here. First, the level of consolidated USD operating profits (TP) was

[2]A second panel analysis with a smaller sample of U.S. drug companies (1973–1986) confirmed the results presented here (Moens, 1991).

[3]The estimations were obtained with a software written by William Green (LIMDEP version 5, 1988 and 1989). This choice was justified both by the existence of a version for PC, and by the quality of the output supplied, which includes many tests.

[4]Where $\acute{A}$ is an unknown parameter and the u_i are identically and independently distributed, with a zero mean and a constant variance.

regressed against only one regressor, that is, an index of the exchange rate (real or nominal, composite or not, lagged or contemporaneous). While the coefficients are very significant and the R^2 values are above 80%, the results indicate a positive influence of the exchange rate that clashes with this study's expectations; composite indices and lagged exchange rates exert the biggest influence. This sign recurs after the introduction of a trend as regressor, which yields a positive significant coefficient, thereby confirming the expectations. These results could be attributed to high inflation (a trait of the period covered by the data: inflation reached two-digit numbers from 1979 to 1981 in the United States). The level of profits was deflated by the U.S. consumer price index and ran similar regressions. The positive sign of the exchange rate coefficient then lost its significance (with or without a trend).

These preliminary results have indicated two broad paths for further investigation: first, the setup of a model with distributed lags; second, the necessity to control the effects of macroeconomic growth that may wipe away the negative effects of the appreciation. The first path, the use of distributed lag models, was not followed very far. The period covered by the sample is too short for this type of exercise with annual data. In addition, the use of panel data techniques in such a context raises new issues that were not tackled in this study. The second path, the necessity to control for macroeconomic effects, led to the introduction of other regressors, with the hope that the positive sign obtained in the first rudimentary estimations will disappear in favor of a negative influence of the real exchange rate. The use of deflated profits and the possible introduction of a time trend have already been mentioned. But first and foremost, one must control for the influences of macroeconomic conditions characterizing the United States and its main trade partners. Business cycle conditions vary across countries, with the U.S. economy, going through an expansion unmatched by the other Organization for Economic Cooperation and Development (OECD) countries. In addition, the recession of the early 1980s was much more severe in these countries. The European economy, where a large share of the foreign profits is realized, performed relatively poorly. These conditions justify the bringing in of both an index of industrial production and a relative index of the industrial production in the United States versus its OECD partners or its European partners.

Estimations using the expanded equations have produced mixed results: Both proxies of the aggregate demand conditions wield a significant positive influence, but the coefficients of the exchange rates (real and nominal) and of the (negative) time trend are not statistically significant.[5] On the positive side, the influence of the exchange rate becomes negative in two cases: (1) when both the

[5]Similar results are obtained when the last two years (1986 and 1987) are dropped from the sample to focus the equations on the years of the U.S. dollar appreciation.

index of the U.S. industrial production (IPUSA) and the relative index IPEUR[6] are introduced in addition to the exchange rate; (2) when the total profits are corrected for U.S. inflation: deflated profits are negatively related with the exchange rate. Nevertheless, in both cases, the *t* statistics of the exchange rate coefficient are low.[7]

These preliminary results warrant a few remarks concerning the specification. Overall, two different types of criteria can be used to choose a specification: theoretical and empirical. On the one hand, the economic theory points out the nature of the relationship between the variables at play, either very precisely or in a looser way; on the other hand, the quality of the estimates (sign and statistical significance of the coefficients, goodness of the fit, etc.) must also be taken into account. In the present study, the theory does not point to a specific functional form: The exchange rate influences the operating profits through several channels and within different time runs. The changes in the nominal exchange rate, for example, modify instantaneously and proportionally the USD value of profits denominated in foreign currencies (accounting effect), while changes in the real exchange rates operate through more subtle, indirect, and slower channels. On the empirical side, a simple specification test of log-linearity versus linearity (taken as null hypothesis) was implemented. The lack of a strong theoretical case, the preliminary estimations, and the results of the specification test described led us to emphasize logarithmic specifications (semilog and double log). This choice was confirmed by the better statistical quality of the estimates (in particular, higher *t* statistics) when such nonlinear relationships are assumed.

Table 1 displays the results of two regressions onto the level of worldwide USD operating profits (TP). The functional form adopted is the double-log specification (coefficients are thus elasticities). The model tested assumes fixed effects, identical slopes, and individual intercepts (model 4). The regressors

[6]That is, the index of industrial production in the United States divided by the same index in the European members of the OECD.

[7]The coefficient gets values between 1 and 1.8, while the *t* statistics are between 0.4 and 0.7. The use of a once lagged exchange rate improves the significance level a bit.

Table 1
Model 4 with Fixed Effects; 446 Observations

	R	IPUSA	RIP2	SFAM(R)	R^2
Eq. (1)	−0.14 (0.8)	+2.2***	+1.0*	−0.16 (1.0)	77%
Eq. (2)	−0.18 (1.0)	+2.2***	+1.0*	−0.03 (1.0)	77%

Note. The level of significance of the coefficients are indicated according to the value of the confidence interval (CI): ***CI = 99% for $t > 2.576$; **CI = 95% for $t > 1.96$; *CI = 90% for $t > 1.645$. When the *t* statistic is less than 1.645, its value is in parentheses.

Table 2
Model 4; 449 Observations

Regressor	Eq. (1)	Eq. (2)
R	−.086***	−.026**
IPUSA	+.07***	+.067***
RIP1	+.11 (1.17)	+.11 (1.18)
INTMR	−.02 (1.19)	
IMADR	−.0155***	−.0027***
Constant		−.042 (0.42)

common to the two equations displayed are the real exchange rate (*R*) and indices of industrial production. IPUSA is the industrial production index in the United States and RIP2 is a relative index of industrial production, obtained by dividing IPUSA by the industrial production index in the European OECD countries.

Equation (1) also includes a measure of the international involvement of the corporation (SFAM), while Eq. (2) features an interactive term constructed by multiplying the current real exchange rate by the firms' specific share of foreign assets, averaged over the period.[8] All the signs are as expected, although significance levels are somewhat disappointing. The interactive specification of Eq. (2) is supported, which confirms that the negative effects of the appreciation have been more harmful for corporations with large international involvement.

Table 2 presents results of the regressions onto the rate of return on sales consolidated profits by sales averaged over the period.[9] The statistical model tested is the same, but fixed and random effects models (Eqs. (1) and (2), respectively) are tested. To make further headway in the understanding of the industrial variables at play, a measure of import competition is introduced, in interaction with the real exchange rate, and an adjustment is made for the degree of advertising intensity,[10] under the assumption that product differentiation weakens import competition discipline. The other regressors are the U.S. industrial production index (IPUSA), IPUSA divided by the OECD index (yielding RIP1), and an alternative measure of international involvement (INTMR), the ratio of foreign assets by domestic assets; the latter regressor is interacted with *R*. The signs agree with the predictions: The coefficients of production indices and the exchange rate have the expected signs, and the

[8]Both interacted terms are in log.
[9]The use of other definitions of the rate of return did not bring significant changes.
[10]IMADR is the product of import penetration ratio (at 4-digit industrial level) by the term (1-5ADI)*R*, where *R* is the real exchange rate and ADI the advertising intensity (advertising expenditures divided by sales).

measure of the international involvement wields a positive influence. The results also confirm the negative influence of the adjusted import competition variable. Finally, interactive specifications are supported.

The last set of estimations adopt a somewhat different approach, featuring a composite variable measuring the state of domestic competition (Pugel, 1980). The empirical specification is derived from the definition of the rate of return on sales, that is, the weighted sum of returns in domestic and foreign markets. The weights are, respectively, the share of domestic and foreign sales. If these components are assumed to be some unspecified function, denoted *F* and *G*, of economic variables (including the exchange rate *R*), the return on sales can be expressed as follows: (share of domestic sales) × *F*(state of domestic competition; *R*) + nominal ER × (share of foreign sales) × *G*(state of foreign competition; *R*). In the next step, a composite variable measuring the state of the domestic competition is concocted. First, each MNC's level of domestic market power is measured as follows: concentration ratio × (1 − import penetration) × (advertising intensity + R&D intensity).[11] This composite variable is then inverted to proxy the state of domestic competition and interacted with *R*. In some equations the firm's specific advertising and R&D intensities (respectively, ADIM and RDIM) are entered with different coefficients; in other estimations their coefficients are assumed to be equal (RADIM = ADIM + RDIM is then used).[12] The regressors include, as before, one or two variables meant to control the macroeconomic growth and the movements in the indices of industrial production. The exact specification of the two functions *F* and *G* is unknown, and both linear and log-linear specifications have been estimated.

Table 3 shows the results for the semilog specification, of which several variations were used. Equation (3) redefines *X*1 and *X*2 by deleting the concentration ratio (*C*4) from the definition of the variables. This transformation is made because of the somewhat curious correlations between the concentration ratio and other explanatory variables: It is negatively correlated with the advertising intensity, with the R&D intensity, and with the different measures of foreign involvement. This alteration suppresses the direct effect of the real exchange rate, but an additional negative effect can now be observed through the variable *X*4. Equations (2) and (3) follow closely the simple theoretical framework; most of the signs they yield are as expected, although Eq. (1)

[11]That is, *C*4 × (1 − IMS4) × (ADIM + RDIM). The concentration ratio and the import penetration measure are calculated at the 4-digit level; ADIM and RDIM are, respectively, the firms' specific advertising and R&D intensities, averaged over the period.

[12]The state of foreign competition could not be proxied satisfactorily, given the available data; the use of the domestic measure as a proxy would introduce undesirable multicollinearity.

Table 3
Model 4 with Random Effects; 449 Observations

Regressor	Eq. (1)	Eq. (2)	Eq. (3)
R	−.015 (1.3)	−.032***	
SDC1R	+.009**		
*X*1		−.005 (1.8)	−.003 (1.6)
*X*2		−.003 (1.2)	−.007***
SFSMR	+.0085**		
*X*3		+.02 (1.6)	−.018 (1.4)
IPUSA	+.07***	+.07***	+.067***
RIP1	+.11 (1.2)	+.11 (1.18)	+.14 (1.6)
Constant	−.042 (0.41)	−.042 (0.4)	−.018 (0.2)

Note. The regressors are defined as follows: SDC1R = log(1 − SFSM) log *R* log[ADIM × *C*4 × (1 − IMS4)]; *X*1 = (1 − SFSM) log *R* log[ADIM × *C*4 × (1 − IMS4)] (that is, *X*1 is similar to LSDC1R, with the difference that the share of the domestic assets is not log linearized; *X*2 uses the averaged advertising intensity, while *X*1 uses the R&D intensity; SFSM is the firms' specific share of foreign sales, averaged over the period); *X*2 = (1 − SFSM) log *R* log[RDIM × *C*4 × (1 − IMS4)]; *X*3 = SFSM log *R*; SFSMR = log SFSM log *R*.

exhibits a positive sign for the variable that proxies the degree of international involvement.

CONCLUSIONS

Overall, the results obtained have confirmed the theoretical expectations, although some qualifications must be made. For example, the real exchange rate does not wield a negative influence on worldwide operating profits, denominated in U.S. dollars, when the income effects from unequal macroeconomic growth is not controlled. The degree of international involvement of the MNCs has shown a significant negative influence when regressed on the worldwide operating profits: USD appreciation has caused greater difficulties to firms with large foreign assets (or foreign sales). Nevertheless, the effect has proved unstable (positive or negative, depending on the proxy used) when the measure of international involvement was regressed on the rate of return, confirming the fact that multinational corporations, by their very features, can partially shelter themselves from the negative effects of exchange rate variations. The variable capturing import competition has also been interacted with the exchange rate, and has displayed the negative influence that was expected: The U.S. domestic market shares and profits are not sheltered from the international economy. The last group of equations, featuring a composite term capturing the role of domestic market structure, has given revealing results and confirmed expectations.

Regarding the statistical models, the econometric tests have indicated the superiority of the model with group dummies, which incorporates common regressors and the groupwise nature of the observations. In many cases, the random effects model has not been rejected by the appropriate tests, which means that this model leads to more efficient estimators. However, no striking difference between fixed and random effects models is noted as far as the values of the coefficients and their degree of significance are concerned. The two-way effect model, which allows the intercepts to vary over both individuals and time, has not yielded good results.

There are many possible paths for further research. Innovations on theoretical fronts can be made. The directions for further work are also numerous on the empirical side. Here are a few examples: to investigate in more depth the determinants of the individual firms' responses to exchange rate variations, and to identify groups with similar patterns; to study the influence of exchange rate variations on the intrafirm flows of funds; to test the hypothesis that firms able to price discriminate between national and foreign markets will suffer less from exchange rate variations; and to implement some modern econometric techniques that analyze the causal linkages between time series, in a panel data context or not.

REFERENCES

Baldwin, R. 1988. Hysteresis in import prices: The beachhead effect, *American Economic Review* 78(4):773–785.

Bodnar, G. M., and W. M. Gentry. 1989. Effects of the international economy on domestic industries: Tests using financial data, *Financial Research Center Memorandum No. 106,* Princeton, NJ: Princeton University.

Dixit, A. K. 1984. Comparative statics for oligopoly, *Woodrow Wilson School Discussion Paper No. 81,* Princeton, NJ: Princeton University.

Dornbusch, R. 1987. Exchange rates and prices, *American Economic Review* 77(1):93–106.

Flood, E., and D. R. Lessard. 1986. On the measurement of operating exposure to exchange rates: A conceptual approach, *Financial Management,* 25–36.

Horst, T. 1971. The theory of the multinational firm: Optimal behavior under different tariff and tax rates, *Journal of Political Economy* 79(5):1059–1072.

Itagaki, T. 1981. The theory of the multinational firm under exchange rate uncertainty, *Canadian Journal of Economics* 14(2):276–297.

Jacquemin, A. 1982. Imperfect market structure and international trade: Some recent research, *Kyklos* 35(1):75–93.

Jorion, P. 1990. The exchange-rate exposure of U.S. multinationals, *Journal of Business* 63(3):331–345.

Karikari, J. A., and M. J. Collins. 1988. Exchange exposure and foreign affiliate value in oligopoly, *University of Tulsa Working Paper.*

Krugman, P. 1986. Pricing to market when the exchange rate changes, *NBER Working Paper No. 1926.*

Krugman, P. R. 1989. *Exchange Rate Instability,* Cambridge, MA: The MIT Press.

Luehrman, T. A. 1990. The exchange rate exposure of a global competitor, *Journal of International Business Studies*, 225–242.

Mann, C. 1986. Prices, profits margins, and exchange rates, *Federal Reserve Bulletin*, 366–379.

Milberg, S. William, and H. Peter Gray. 1992. International competitiveness and policy in dynamic industries, *Banca Nazionales del Lavoro Quarterly Review* (March).

Moens, Luc C. 1991. Exchange rate variations and U.S. multinational corporations' profits: The case of the 1980s, Ph.D. thesis, Rutgers University, New Brunswick, NJ.

Oxelheim, L., and C. Wihlborg. 1987. *Macroeconomic Uncertainty and International Risks and Opportunities for the Corporation*, New York: Wiley.

Pugel, T. A. 1980. Foreign trade and U.S. market performance, *Journal of Industrial Economics* 24(2):119–129.

Shapiro, A. C. 1988. *International Corporate Finance*, Cambridge, MA: Ballinger.

Waterson, M. 1984. *Economic Theory of the Industry*, Cambridge, UK: Cambridge University Press.

Chapter 5

Real Exchange Rates and the Sectoral Composition of Output: Some Evidence from Japan

Sadequl Islam

During the last two decades or so many countries have experienced considerable fluctuations in real exchange rates. The appreciation of the U.S. dollar in the early 1980s, followed by its decline since the meeting of G-5 nations in 1985, has generated debates concerning the effects of exchange rate fluctuations on the U.S. manufacturing sector. A number of economists (among others, Marris, 1985; Branson and Love, 1988) have found that appreciation of the real exchange rate has played an important role in "deindustrializing" the U.S. economy. In contrast, Glick and Hutchison (1990) find no significant negative relation between appreciation of the real exchange rate and output growth in tradable sectors of the U.S. economy. They further argue that the relation between movements in the real exchange rate and the sectoral composition of output is unstable over time and varies with underlying monetary and fiscal variables.

The main objective of this chapter is to examine the relation between movements in the real exchange rate and output in the industrial sector and several subsectors of the Japanese economy. Investigation of this relation for Japan would be instructive for several reasons. In the early 1980s persistence of substantial trade surpluses for Japan led to renewed interest in the effects of exchange rate fluctuations on the trade balance. Several features of the Japanese economy have been noted in the literature: a high income elasticity of demand for Japanese exports, compared to that for imports; a small share of manufactured imports in GNP; and official and unofficial import barriers.[1] In recent years, however, a number of changes have taken place in Japan.

Since the mid-1980s, Japan has been liberalizing its imports. The Structural Impediments Initiative (SII) talks between the United States and Japan launched in 1989 are likely to further reduce trade barriers in Japan. Furthermore, since 1986, the growth pattern of the Japanese economy has shifted to growth led by domestic rather than external demand. As a consequence, Japan's trade surplus in nominal as well as real terms has declined considerably since 1986. The implications of these developments for the relation between the real exchange rate fluctuations and the sectoral composition of output, however, is not obvious. For a dynamic economy such as that of Japan, technological and product innovations in the manufacturing sector may outweigh any adverse effect of exchange rate appreciation.

METHODOLOGY AND DATA

Previous studies have examined the effects of real exchange rate movements on the sectoral composition of output by multiple regression analysis. For instance, Branson and Love (1988) have estimated regressions of the log of manufacturing output on current and lagged values of the real dollar exchange rate, the relative price of energy, the unemployment rate, a linear time trend, and a constant. The unemployment rate and the relative price of energy are included to represent business cycles and supply-side effects, respectively. Glick and Hutchison (1990) apply the above model not only to the manufacturing sector but also to nonmanufacturing sectors (such as agriculture, transportation, and construction) and services. These studies, however, do not explore whether variables in the regression model are stationary or not. Many economic time series are known to contain "unit roots" and consequently are nonstationary. In the presence of nonstationary variables, inferences from the traditional regression analysis about the long-term economic relation between variables may be incorrect.[2]

The empirical analysis of this chapter is based on cointegration techniques suggested by Engle and Granger (1987). Two or more variables are said to be cointegrated if individually each is nonstationary but there exists a linear combination of the variables that is stationary. The cointegration technique attempts to find the appropriate linear combination of the variables by estimating a cointegrating regression and then tests whether that linear combination is stationary by applying a unit root test to the residuals from the regression.

---

[1]For discussions in detail on these issues, see Houthakker and Magee (1969) and Lawrence (1987).

[2]The problems of "spurious" regressions due to nonstationary variables are explored by Granger and Newbold (1977).

To detect the presence of unit roots, this chapter applies augmented Dickey–Fuller tests to relevant variables, such as the real exchange rate, the relative price of imports,[3] and the level of output in the industrial sector as well as several industrial subsectors. These tests are also carried out for the first differences of the above variables. Then, in cointegrating regressions, further tests are performed to examine whether the real exchange rate, the relative price of imports, and the level of output in the industrial sector (or in each subsector) are cointegrated.

The real exchange rate (RE) for the yen has been computed by multiplying the nominal effective exchange rate index (NE) by the ratio of the Japanese consumer price index and the industrial countries' consumer price index.[4] The real exchange rate is defined so that an increase implies a real appreciation of the yen. Quarterly data on the nominal exchange rate were obtained from the International Monetary Fund (IMF), *International Financial Statistics, Supplement on Exchange Rates,* 1985, and later issues. The data on the consumer price index were obtained from the IMF, *IFS Supplement on Price Statistics,* 1986, and the Organization for Economic Control and Development (OECD), *Main Economic Indicators.* The relative price of imports has been computed as the ratio of the unit value of imports and the wholesale price index.

This chapter examines the behavior of six output series: total industrial production, manufacturing production, consumer durables, consumer nondurables, intermediate inputs, and fixed investment goods. Output indexes of these series were obtained from the OECD, *Main Economic Indicators,* various issues.

Consistent quarterly data on output in nonindustrial sectors such as services were not available. Accordingly, this chapter focuses largely on the industrial sector and subsectors.

EXCHANGE RATES AND OUTPUT COMPOSITION

It is instructive to examine first the behavior of nominal and real exchange rates and the sectoral composition of output in Japan. Figure 1 shows movements in the nominal (NE) and real (RE) exchange rates during the 1973.1–1991.3 period. Several points are noteworthy. First, the nominal and real exchange rates show considerable fluctuations, the former exhibiting a significant upward trend. The upward trend is pronounced for both from the G-5 meeting in 1985 until the end of 1988. Second, one observes a strong positive correlation between the nominal and real exchange rate changes. This suggests that move-

[3]This chapter uses the relative price of imports rather than the relative price of energy because consistent time series data are available for the former variable. Since Japan imports mainly raw materials and fuel, the relative price of imports is likely to represent better any supply shocks to the economy.

[4]Alternatively, the real exchange rate can be computed using wholesale price indexes or unit labor costs. The time pattern of real exchange rates based on these alternative methods, however, is not likely to be significantly different from that of the real exchange rate used in this chapter.

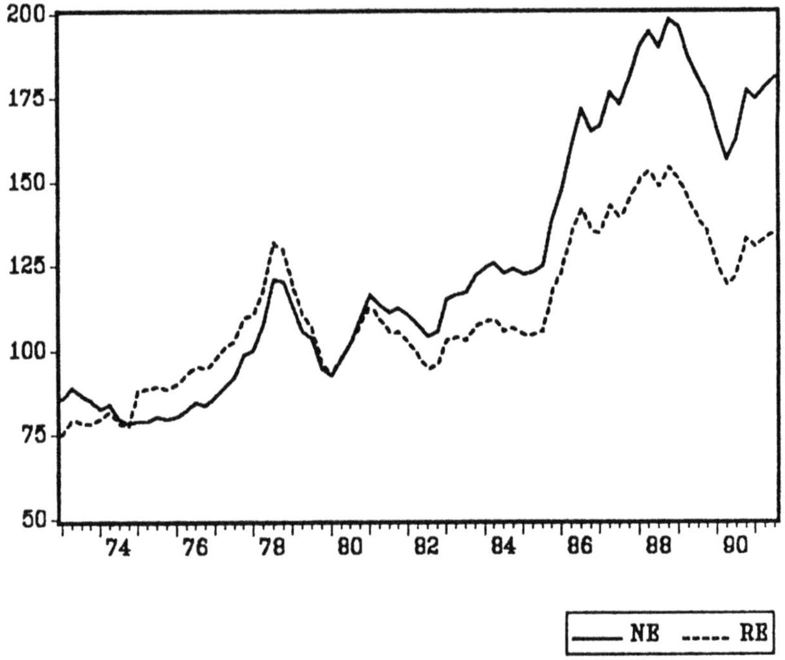

Figure 1 Japan's nominal and real exchange rates (1980 = 100).

ments in the real exchange rate have been dominated by nominal exchange rates rather than by national price levels. Finally, the real exchange rate does not show a clear tendency to return to a constant value. This implies that there have been persistent changes in the exchange rates away from their purchasing-power-parity values.[5]

Over the last two decades or so, the sectoral composition of output has changed significantly in Japan. Changes in output composition measured at current prices, however, differ from those at constant prices. As a percentage of Japan's nominal Gross Domestic Product (GDP), manufacturing production shows a downward trend from 35% in 1970 to 29% in 1988. The share of services (retail and wholesale trade, financial, personal, and government services), in contrast, increased from 37% in 1970 to 52% in 1988. The share of transportation, communication, public utilities, and construction (another non-tradables sector) has been relatively stable in nominal terms at close to 17%. The share of agriculture fell from 6% in 1970 to 2.6% in 1988.

To obtain an accurate picture of the sectoral composition of output, it is essential to examine output shares of each sector at constant prices. The share

[5]The behavior of Japan's real exchange rates has been analyzed by Grauwe (1988).

of services as a percentage of Japan's GDP at 1980 prices increased from 35% in 1970 to 42% in 1988. The share of agriculture and mining, however, declined from 18.1% in 1970 to 6% in 1988. A downward trend is also evident for transportation, construction, and public utilities—from 21% in 1970 to 15.9% in 1988. It is striking to note that the share of manufacturing output at constant prices increased from 26.0% in 1970 to 35.4% in 1988. The discrepancy between nominal and real shares can be attributed to the downward trend in the relative price of manufacturing goods.

COINTEGRATION RESULTS

Before applying cointegration techniques, it is essential to examine whether the relevant series are stationary or nonstationary. This is done with the help of augmented Dickey–Fuller tests of the following forms for any series Y_t:

$$dy_t = a + bT + ry_{t-1} + cdy_{t-1} + e_t \quad (1)$$

$$dy_t = a + ry_{t-1} + cdy_{t-1} + e_t \quad (2)$$

where dy_t is the first difference of y_t, T is a trend, and dy_{t-1} is the first difference of y_{t-1}. Equation (2) is a special of Eq. (1), with no trend. In Dickey–Fuller tests, the coefficient of y_{t-1} is crucial. If the Dickey–Fuller t statistic for this coefficient is smaller, in absolute value, than the reported critical values, one cannot reject the null hypothesis of nonstationarity and the existence of a unit root in Y_t.[6]

The augmented Dickey–Fuller test, indicated in Eq. (1), is applied to the level of a number of series: total industrial production (TP), manufacturing production (MP), consumer durables (CD), consumer nondurables (ND), intermediate inputs (II), fixed investment (FI), the real exchange rate index (RE), and the relative price of imports (RPI). The Dickey–Fuller t statistics and the MacKinnon critical values (provided by the TSP package) are reported in part A of Table 1. At the 5% significance level, the t statistics are less, in absolute value, than the MacKinnon critical value, implying the existence of a unit root and nonstationarity in all the series.

The augmented Dickey–Fuller test, described in Eq. (2), is now applied to the first differences of all the series mentioned above. The results are shown in part B of Table 1. At the 5% significance level, all the t statistics are greater, in absolute value, than the MacKinnon critical value. Accordingly, all the series are stationary at the 5% significance level.

---

[6]There is now extensive literature on unit root tests and methodological problems associated with these tests. See, among others, Cuthbertson et al. (1992, Chapter 5), Hall and Henry (1989, Chapter 2), and Rappoport and Reichlin (1989).

Table 1
Unit Root Tests: 1973.1-1991.3

(A) Variable	Dickey-Fuller *t* statistics	(B) Variable	Dickey-Fuller *t* statistics
TP	−3.21	*d*TP	−3.77
MP	−3.20	*d*MP	−3.80
CD	−2.76	*d*CD	−4.99
ND	−3.34	*d*ND	−8.18
II	−3.33	*d*II	−3.48
FI	−2.22	*d*FI	−3.92
RE	−2.70	*d*RE	−5.26
RPI	−2.43	*d*RPI	−6.73

Significance level	MacKinnon critical value	MacKinnon critical value
1%	−4.09	−3.52
5%	−3.47	−2.90
10%	−3.16	−2.59

Note. *d*TP implies the first differences of TP. Similar interpretation holds for other variables.

The overall results from unit-root tests seem to suggest that while the level of output in the industrial sector or subsectors, the level of the real exchange rate, and the level of the relative price of imports are nonstationary (integrated of order 1), their first differences are stationary (integrated of order zero).[7]

Since the level of output, the real exchange rate, and the relative price of imports are integrated of order 1, it is now useful to explore whether these variables are cointegrated or not. This is done by regressing the level of output in the industrial sector or the subsectors on a constant, the real exchange rate (RE), the relative price of imports (RPI), and a trend and then applying the Dickey-Fuller test to the residuals of the regression.[8]

The cointegrating regression results are reported in Table 2. The coefficients of RE and RPI are negative as expected. However, the coefficient of RE is significant at the 5% level only for consumer durables (CD). The coefficient of RPI is significant for TP, MP, and CD. These results appear to indicate that real appreciation of the yen and rising relative prices of imports have adversely affected output of some industries, such as consumer durables. However, before drawing such an inference it is essential to examine whether residuals of

[7]The unit root test was applied to the six output series in log forms. The results are qualitatively similar: The levels of logged values are nonstationary, but their first differences are stationary.

[8]In contrast to previous studies on the U.S. economy by Branson and Love (1988) and Glick and Hutchison (1990), this chapter does not include the unemployment rate as a business cycle variable. Japan's unemployment is quite low and is largely of structural type. Inclusion of the unemployment rate does not affect the main finding of the chapter.

Table 2
Tests for Cointegration: 1973.1–1991.3

Dependent variable	Independent variables				
	Constant	RE	RPI	Trend	DF statistic
TP	86.22 (10.15)	−.08 (−1.35)	−.17 (−2.02)	1.26 (15.12)	−3.07
MP	86.07 (9.78)	−.09 (−1.33)	−.18 (−2.0)	1.29 (14.88)	−3.05
CD	71.64 (8.94)	−.19 (−3.15)	−.20 (−2.46)	2.10 (26.67)	−2.91
ND	79.43 (22.62)	−.01 (−.22)	−.03 (−.93)	.84 (24.4)	−3.26
II	93.25 (9.40)	−.06 (−.83)	−.20 (−1.97)	1.00 (10.20)	−3.13
FI	85.25 (5.47)	−.18 (1.59)	−.27 (−1.71)	2.00 (13.0)	−2.21

Note. Figures in parentheses are t values. MacKinnon critical values for the Dickey–Fuller test at 1, 5, and 10% levels are −4.93, −4.29, and −3.96, respectively.

the regressions are stationary or not. The last column of Table 2 reports the Dickey–Fuller (DF) t statistics for the residuals of the regressions. It is evident that the DF t statistics are smaller, in absolute value, than the MacKinnon critical value even at the 10% level. This suggests that the residuals in all the regression are nonstationary, implying that the real exchange rate, the relative price of imports, and the level of output are not cointegrated.

The inference that can be drawn is that real exchange rate movements have no systematic long-term relation with changes in output in the industrial sector or subsectors. Consequently, it is unlikely that any significant shift in the sectoral composition of output has been caused by exchange rate movements.

CONCLUSIONS

The real exchange rate for Japan shows considerable fluctuations, with significant appreciations during some years. This chapter has made an attempt to explore whether movements in the real exchange rate along with movements in the relative price of imports have had significant bearings on the sectoral composition of output. The empirical findings suggest that the real exchange rate, the relative price of imports, and the output series are not cointegrated, implying no statistically significant relationship between these variables.

A few points to explain the apparent lack of significant relations between the real exchange rate and the sectoral composition of output deserve to be mentioned. First, exchange rate appreciations may not be fully reflected in prices of tradables if the degree of "pass-through" involving currency appreciations and prices declines (see Sakamoto, 1988). This may happen if Japanese firms, following appreciations of the yen, reduce their export prices in yen terms to maintain their market shares in foreign countries.[9] Second, real exchange rate appreciation may be accompanied by expansionary fiscal policies. In this context, there may not be any shift in the sectoral composition of output away from tradables to nontradables. Finally, dynamic factors, such as technological and product innovations, may counterbalance any adverse effects of real exchange rate appreciations and rising relative prices of imports on the manufacturing sector.

REFERENCES

Branson, W., and J. Love. 1988. U.S. manufacturing and the real exchange rate, pp. 241–270 in R. Marston (Ed.), *Misalignment of Exchange Rates: Effects on Trade and Industry,* Chicago: University of Chicago Press.

Cuthbertson, et al. 1992. *Applied Econometric Techniques,* Ann Arbor: University of Michigan Press.

[9]The strategic pricing behavior of Japanese firms is discussed by Krugman and Baldwin (1987).

Engle, R. F., and C. W. Granger. 1987. Co-integration and error correction: Representation, estimation and testing, *Econometrica* 55:251–276.

Glick, R., and M. Hutchison. 1990. Does exchange rate appreciation "deindustrialize" the open economy? A critique of U.S. evidence, *Economic Inquiry* 28:19–37.

Granger, C. W., and P. Newbold. 1977. *Forecasting Economic Time Series*, New York: Academic.

Grauwe, P. 1988. The long swings in real exchange rates: Do they fit into our theories? *Bank of Japan Monetary and Economic Studies* 6:37–60.

Hall, S. G., and S. G. B. Henry. 1989. *Macroeconomic Modelling*, Amsterdam: North-Holland.

Houthakker, H. S., and S. P. Magee. 1969. Income and price elasticities in world trade, *Review of Economics and Statistics* 51:111–125.

Krugman, P. R., and R. E. Baldwin. 1987. The persistence of the U.S. trade deficit, *Brookings Papers on Economic Activity* 1:1–43.

Lawrence, R. Z. 1987. Japanese imports: Closed markets or minds? *Brookings Papers on Economic Activity* 2:517–548.

Marris, S. 1985. Deficits and the dollar: The world economy at risk, *Policy Analyses in International Economics* 14.

Rappoport, P., and L. Reichlin. 1989. Segmented trends and nonstationary time series (supplement), *The Economic Journal* 99:168–177.

Sakamoto, T. 1988. The Japan–U.S. bilateral trade, *Federal Reserve Bank of San Francisco Economic Review*, 3–13.

Chapter 6

Time-Varying Risk Premia and the Efficiency of the New Zealand Foreign Exchange Market

Dimitri Margaritis and Phay Hoon Teo

One of the most extensively researched topics in international finance literature is the efficiency of the forward market for foreign exchange. Researchers such as Levich (1978), Frenkel (1980), and Tease (1988) reported evidence in support of forward market efficiency. However, a large body of empirical evidence has rejected the forward rate as an unbiased or efficient predictor of the corresponding future spot exchange rate (Frenkel, 1979; Hansen and Hodrick, 1980; Hakkio, 1981; Hsieh, 1984; Hodrick, 1987; MacDonald, 1988; Bailie, 1989; Madsen, 1990).

Results of forward market efficiency in New Zealand are inconclusive. The results by the Reserve Bank of New Zealand (1987) and Szeto and Lattimore (1990) are supportive of forward market efficiency. But Scanlan (1989) and Gibbs, Grimes, and Harrison (1990) found the forward rate to be a biased predictor of the future spot exchange rate. Gibbs et al. also provided empirical evidence in support of a random walk model of exchange rate. This is consistent with the evidence reported by Meese and Rogoff (1983) that none of several economic models tested were able to outperform a random walk model of exchange rates in out-of-sample predictive ability.

Meese and Rogoff suggested that time-varying risk premia could be an important determinant of their findings. In fact, researchers such as Fama (1984), Hodrick and Srivastava (1984), Bilson (1985), Domowitz and Hakkio (1985), and Diebold and Pauly (1988) took the view that the rejection of the unbiasedness hypothesis is due to the existence of a significant number of risk-averse agents in the foreign exchange market. In contrast, Bilson (1981), Longworth (1981), and Cumby and Obstfeld (1984) argued that the rejection of the hypothesis is due to the irrational behavior of the agents. Other explanations of market inefficiency include the nonclearing of financial markets, strong short-term volatility of the fundamentals, speculative bubbles, and central bank intervention (Bomhoff and Koedijk, 1988).

Bomhoff and Koedijk noted at least two reasons why the importance of risk premia in the foreign exchange market was ignored for a long time. The first is that conventional estimates of the degree of risk aversion imply a very small magnitude of risk premium. The second reason is the difficulty in developing a theoretical model of risk premium that is both empirically relevant and tractable. Both arguments appear to have little support in recent studies. First, it has been recognized (see Domowitz and Hakkio, 1985) that conditional on the hypothesis that expectations are rational, a risk premium can reconcile the lack of unbiasedness in predicting future spot rates with market efficiency. Second, Hodrick and Srivastava (1984), Domowitz and Hakkio (1985), Diebold and Pauly (1988), Bomhoff and Koedijk (1988), and Hodrick (1989) have developed theoretical models that generate risk premia in foreign exchange markets. In these models, the risk premia depend on the probability distribution of the future spot rate. The conditional second-order moments of these distributions, like those of other speculative prices, have long been recognized as changing through time (Mandelbrot, 1963; Fama, 1965). Consequently, the exchange rate premium is expected to be time-varying. One of the most popular models of variation in second or higher order moments is the autoregressive conditional heteroscedasticity (ARCH) model of Engle (1982), and its various extensions (such as the ARCH-in mean (ARCH-M) model of Engle, Lilien, and Robins, 1987).

ARCH MODELS

The ARCH model introduced by Engle (1982) has provided a very popular framework for modeling explicitly, time-varying conditional variances of speculative prices. The motivation for this model was provided by the fact that applied researchers, especially in the areas of financial and monetary economics, have found that their ability to forecast varies from one period to another and that there is a clustering of large and small forecast errors (Kmenta, 1986). This behavior reflects the changing uncertainty of speculative prices, as measured by the variances and covariances, through time. The ARCH model and its various extensions is intended to capture this changing uncertainty by explicitly modeling time variation in second or higher order moments.

A linear ARCH (q) model expresses the conditional variance (h_t^2) as a linear function of past squared innovations u:

$$h_t^2 = c_0 + \sum_{i=1}^{q} c_i u_{t-1}^2 \qquad (1)$$

where $c_0 > 0$ and $c_1 \geq 0$. An extension of this model is the ARCH-M model introduced by Engle et al. (1987) in which the conditional mean is an explicit function of the conditional variance (or its parameterization). In this way, changing conditional variances of speculative prices directly affect the expected return on a portfolio (Engle et al., 1987).

The ARCH class of models is ideally suited to modeling exchange rate movements exhibiting volatility, clustering of unpredictable sign, periods of stability, and unconditional distributions with tails fatter than the normal distribution. While bonds and stocks have been found to exhibit some degree of asymmetry in their conditional variance, the two-sided nature of the foreign exchange market diminishes the likelihood of those asymmetries (Bollerslev et al., 1990). Friedman and Vandersteel (1982) state, "one interpretation is that both the trend and volatility of (exchange rate) movements are affected by changing economic and institutional factors."

MARKET EFFICIENCY TESTS

There are two standard tests of the joint hypothesis of rationality and risk neutrality. The first is a test of the unbiasedness of the forward exchange rate (F_t) observed at time t for an exchange at $t + 1$, as a predictor of the future spot exchange rate (S_{t+1}). This can be tested, by estimating a regression equation of the form

$$s_t = \alpha_0 + \alpha_1 f_{t-1} + u_t \tag{2}$$

where lowercase letters indicate natural logarithms of respective variables, u is an error term, and the null hypothesis of unbiasedness is $(\alpha_0, \alpha_1) = (0, 1)$. Given that s and f are nonstationary $I(1)$ processes, a more appropriate specification of the model is given by

$$s_t - s_{t-1} = \alpha_0 + \alpha_1(f - s)_{t-1} + u_t \tag{3}$$

Equation (3) was estimated using nonoverlapping monthly data (as at the 15th of the month) for the post-free float of the exchange rate period May 1985 to June 1990, and nonoverlapping weekly data (Wednesdays) for the period July 1986 to June 1990 for the NZ$/US$ exchange rate as at 9:00 a.m. The source of the spot data is the Reserve Bank of New Zealand (RBNZ) daily database obtained from Reuters data. The forward rate is from the RBNZ internal daily foreign exchange market report.

For the monthly data, Eq. (3) is estimated by ordinary least squares (OLS) as

$$s_t - s_{t-1} = \underset{(1.324)}{-0.016} - \underset{(1.827)}{2.430}(f - s)_{t-1}$$

$$R^2 = 0.053 \quad L = 108.705 \quad \text{SEE} = 0.042 \quad \text{DW} = 2.340$$

$$\text{LM}(19) = 28.062 \quad \text{ARCH}(2) = 9.275 \quad t(60) = -2.578$$

$$F1(2, 60) = 5.872 \quad F2(2, 60) = 1.930$$

where numbers in parentheses are t values of estimated coefficients, L is the log-likelihood value, LM(19) is the Lagrange multiplier test value for autocorrelation to 19th order distributed as χ^2 with 19 df, ARCH(2) is the ARCH test value distributed as χ^2 with 2 df, $t(60)$ is the t-test value for the null hypothesis $\alpha_1 = 1$ with 60 df, $F1(2, 60)$ is the F-statistic value for the null hypothesis $(\alpha_0, \alpha_1) = (0, 1)$ with (2, 60) df, and $F2(2, 60)$ is the F-test value for the random walk hypothesis $(\alpha_0, \alpha_1) = (0, 0)$ with (2, 60) df.

The OLS estimates of Eq. (3) lead us to reject the unbiasedness hypothesis but not the random walk hypothesis at conventional significance levels. Thus, the evidence here indicates that the forward rate is a biased predictor of the future spot rate. In addition, the forward rate contains no information about the future spot rate to be observed one month ahead. The ARCH test value of 9.275, however, indicates the presence of heteroscedasticity in the disturbances and therefore biased test statistics.

Equation (3) is re-estimated using an ARCH(2) model as

$$s_t - s_{t-1} = \underset{(1.949)}{-0.018} - \underset{(2.631)}{2.651}(f - s)_{t-1}$$

$$h_t^2 = \underset{(3.040)}{0.001} + \underset{(0.607)}{0.074}u_{t-1}^2 + \underset{(1.943)}{0.463}u_{t-2}^2$$

$$R^2 = 0.052 \quad L = 115.555 \quad \text{SEE} = 0.042 \quad \text{DW} = 2.344$$

$$\text{Wald } \chi^2(1) = 13.130$$

where Wald $\chi^2(1)$ is the Wald chi-square statistic for the null hypothesis $\alpha_1 = 1$, with 1 df. There is a significant improvement in the log-likelihood value as a result of incorporating ARCH(2) disturbances in the model. The results now indicate a rejection of both the unbiasedness and the random walk hypothesis. The coefficient of the forward-spot differential is negative and significantly different than zero. This is consistent with the results of Fama (1984) and Hodrick (1989). Thus, the forward rate has power to predict (actually mispredict the direction of the change of) the future spot rate when the higher variance (and therefore higher uncertainty) periods are given less weight in the regression. Given rational expectations, the deviation of α_1 from 1 indicates the presence of variation in the premium. This evidence is supported by the significant

ARCH effect, which indicates that a time-varying risk premium has possibly been swept into the disturbance term.

Following Fama (1984), we also estimated an equation of the forecast errors $f_t - s_{t+1}$ on the future change of the spot rate $s_{t+1} - s_t$. The slope coefficient of this regression was significantly greater than 1. This result, in combination with the estimated negative coefficient on the forward premium in Eq. (3), suggests that the variance in risk premia is greater than the variance in expected rates of currency depreciation (Fama, 1984).

Using weekly data, Eq. (3) was estimated by OLS as

$$s_t - s_{t-1} = \underset{(1.316)}{-0.003} - \underset{(1.775)}{2.135}(f - s)_{t-1}$$

$$R^2 = 0.016 \qquad L = 523.205 \qquad \text{SEE} = 0.018 \qquad \text{DW} = 2.292$$

$$\text{LM}(23) = 24.944 \qquad \text{ARCH}(2) = 4.004 \qquad t(198) = 2.606$$

$$F1(2, 198) = -4.840 \qquad F2(2, 198) = 1.647$$

The unbiasedness hypothesis can now be rejected at the 5% and marginally at the 1% level of significance. The random walk hypothesis cannot be rejected at conventional levels. Estimation of a regression of the forecast errors on the future change of the spot rate produced a slope coefficient that was significantly different than zero (but not 1). Thus, the premium component of the forward premium $(f - s)_t$ exhibits variation that affects the forecast error $f_t - s_{t+1}$.

Equation (3) is re-estimated using an ARCH(2) model as

$$s_t - s_{t-1} = \underset{(1.135)}{-0.002} - \underset{(1.751)}{1.808}(f - s)_{t-1}$$

$$h_t^2 = \underset{(5.487)}{0.0001} + \underset{(2.014)}{0.344}u_{t-1}^2 + \underset{(2.137)}{0.237}u_{t-2}^2$$

$$R^2 = 0.015 \qquad L = 534.330 \qquad \text{SEE} = 0.018 \qquad \text{DW} = 2.291$$

$$\text{Wald } \chi^2(1) = 7.391$$

The ARCH results have not altered the conclusions derived from the OLS model. The statistical significance of the ARCH components indicates that a time-varying risk premium has been swept into the disturbance term.

To further investigate the power of the forward premium to predict the future change in the spot rate, Eq. (3) is estimated with a moving average MA(10) error term (note that significant correlations of lower order are hidden in the LM(23) statistic above) as

$$s_t - s_{t-1} = \underset{(2.437)}{-0.003} - \underset{(3.286)}{2.343}(f - s)_{t-1}$$

$$R^2 = 0.086 \qquad \text{SEE} = 0.017 \qquad \text{DW} = 2.003 \qquad t(198) = -4.668$$

The results indicate that the forward rate contains information about the expected future spot rate. They also imply a rejection of the random walk hypothesis.

The second test of the joint rationality and risk neutrality hypothesis is an orthogonality test, that is, a test of whether the agents efficiently process information relevant to exchange rate determination when they make their forecasts. Consider the monetary model of exchange rate determination of Frenkel (1976) and Bilson (1978), which is given by

$$s_t = \beta_0 + \beta_1(r - r^*)_t + \beta_2(y - y^*)_t + \beta_3(m - m^*)_t + \epsilon_t \tag{4}$$

where m is the log of the money supply (M3), r is the 3-month interest rate, y is the log of real income, and asterisks indicate foreign (U.S.) variables. A test of the orthogonality hypothesis can be derived by regressing $s_t - f_{t-1}$ on the relevant information:

$$s_t - f_{t-1} = \gamma_0 + \gamma_1(r - r^*)_{t-1} + \gamma_2(m - m^*)_{t-1} + \gamma_3(y - y^*)_{t-3} + \nu_t \tag{5}$$

and testing the hypothesis $\gamma_i = 0$, $i = 0, 1, 2, 3$. Equation (5) is estimated with monthly data from the Department of Statistics INFOS database for (m, m^*, y^*, r^*) and the RBNZ's economic database for (y, r). Monthly observations on real income were obtained by the application of a cubic-spline interpolation technique to quarterly data. Data on the monetary aggregates and real income were seasonally adjusted either at the source or by the authors (using the SAS X11 procedure). The OLS estimate of Eq. (5) is given by

$$s_t - f_{t-1} = \underset{(1.147)}{1.507} + \underset{(1.185)}{0.002}(r - r^*)_{t-1} + \underset{(1.260)}{0.063}(m - m^*)_{t-1} + \underset{(1.260)}{0.202}(y - y^*)_{t-3}$$

$$R^2 = 0.099 \qquad L = 93.426 \qquad \text{SEE} = 0.045 \qquad \text{DW} = 2.188$$

$$\text{LM}(17) = 20.989 \qquad F(4, 51) = 2.719$$

The F statistic indicates that the joint neutrality and rationality hypothesis cannot be rejected at the 1% (but not the 5%) level. However, when the equation is re-estimated with a correction for MA(4) serial correlation, the results indicate that the interest rate differential has a significant and positive power in explaining the variation in the forecast error over time:

$$s_t - f_{t-1}$$

$$\begin{aligned} = &\ \underset{(0.075)}{0.119} + \underset{(2.602)}{0.003}(r - r^*)_{t-1} + \underset{(0.193)}{0.016}(m - m^*)_{t-1} + \underset{(0.059)}{0.012}(y - y^*)_{t-3} \end{aligned}$$

$$R^2 = 0.275 \qquad \text{SEE} = 0.041 \qquad \text{DW} = 1.794$$

This suggests that investors in the foreign exchange market focus mostly on (or overreact to) movements in the interest rate differential. The positive coefficient on this variable indicates that an increase in the New Zealand interest rates, relative to the U.S. interest rates, gives agents investing in the New Zealand currency exploitable profit opportunities. Note that it is possible that the forward rate will not be an unbiased predictor of the future spot rate, if the interest rate differential reflects differences in expected real returns on bonds (Levine, 1989).

TIME-VARYING RISK PREMIA

The results of the previous section indicate that the behavior of investors in the foreign exchange market is affected by the conditional variance of exchange rates. This is a direct implication of mean-variance optimization behavior by risk-averse agents in the foreign exchange market. Thus, the interest now is to use a model based on the optimization behavior of risk-averse agents to examine the response of exchange rate movements to changing real and monetary uncertainty. More specifically, this study attempts to model the time-varying risk premium in the foreign exchange market and test its ability in explaining movements in the forward rate forecast error.

The time-varying risk premium model uses the intertemporal asset pricing model of Lucas (1982), Hansen and Hodrick (1983), and Hodrick and Srivastava (1984). The risk premium in this model is due to consumption risk. Risk-averse agents prefer assets that help smooth consumption over time. The risk premium will be positive if the covariance of the expected profit from contracting in the forward market with consumption is positive. A time-varying conditional covariance implies a changing risk premium, which can move from positive to negative over time (Kaminsky and Peruga, 1990).

The agents are hypothesized to maximize expected discounted utility over time subject to an intertemporal budget constraint. Following Mark (1985) and Kaminsky and Peruga (1990), the agents' utility function is parameterized by assuming constant relative risk aversion as

$$U(C) = \frac{C^{1-\gamma}}{1-\gamma} \qquad \gamma \geq 0 \tag{6}$$

where C denotes consumption and γ is the coefficient of relative risk aversion. The intertemporal equilibrium condition is given by

$$E_t\left[\left(\frac{C_{t+1}}{C_t}\right)^{-\gamma}\left(\frac{P_t}{P_{t+1}}\right)\left(\frac{S_{t+1}}{S_t}\right)\right] = \left(\frac{F_t}{S_t}\right)E_t\left[\left(\frac{C_{t+1}}{C_t}\right)^{-\gamma}\left(\frac{P_t}{P_{t+1}}\right)\right] \quad (7)$$

where P is the price level and E_t denotes expectations conditional on information at time t. Assuming that the variables in Eq. (7) are jointly log normally distributed, an equation for the expected forecast error is given by

$$E_t(s_{t+1} - f_t) = \theta_t = -\frac{1}{2}\,\mathrm{Var}_t\left(\frac{s_{t+1}}{s_t}\right) - \mathrm{cov}_t\left(\frac{s_{t+1}}{s_t}, \frac{p_t}{p_{t+1}}\right) + \gamma\,\mathrm{cov}_t\left(\frac{s_{t+1}}{s_t}, \frac{c_t}{c_{t+1}}\right) \quad (8)$$

Equation (8) expresses the risk premium (θ_t) as a function of the conditional variance of the spot exchange rate depreciation, the covariance of the exchange rate depreciation with the intertemporal rate of substitution in consumption, and the covariance of the exchange rate depreciation with changes in the purchasing power of money. An increase in the conditional variance of the exchange rate depreciation increases the expected future value of the foreign currency. This will lead to an increase in the demand for future foreign currencies. Thus, the forward rate is expected to increase, leading to a decrease in the risk premium (Kaminsky and Peruga, 1990). However, it should be noted that in theory a hypothesis is needed to establish the link between changes in the variance and changes in the risk premium of either the domestic or the foreign currency. As Frenkel (1988) states, "this requires some idea of what the supply of the foreign asset is relative to the minimum-variance portfolio. The asset whose supply exceeds the minimum-variance portfolio is the one that needs to pay a positive risk premium to be willingly held."

EMPIRICAL RESULTS

First, estimation results are presented from an OLS regression of the forecast error on a constant:

$$s_t - f_{t-1} = \underset{(2.159)}{0.012} \qquad \mathrm{SEE} = 0.044$$

These results show that the ex post returns from a long position in the forward market averaged 15% at annual rates, with a standard deviation of 5% over the sampling period. This finding should be interpreted with caution because sequential Chow tests reveal considerable model instability over time. This instability is presumably due to model misspecification.

Second, assuming that the time path of consumption and prices in Eq. (8) are relatively smooth over time, a regression was estimated of the forecast error on the time-varying conditional variance of the exchange rate depreciation. The conditional variance was generated from an ARCH-M model. The estimated equation is given by

$$s_t - f_{t-1} = \underset{(3.408)}{0.014} - \underset{(3.439)}{0.006h_t^2}$$

$$h_t^2 = \underset{(3.061)}{0.001} + \underset{(0.755)}{0.083u_{t-1}^2} + \underset{(1.791)}{0.393u_{t-2}^2}$$

$$R^2 = 0.087 \qquad L = 115.463 \qquad \text{SEE} = 0.042 \qquad \text{DW} = 2.052$$

The negative sign on the conditional variance (h_t^2) indicates that an increase in the variance of the exchange rate is expected to lower the return from a long position in the forward market, leading to a decrease in the risk premium.

Furthermore, an equation was estimated by regressing the rate of depreciation on the forward premium and the conditional variance as

$$s_t - s_{t-1} = \underset{(1.173)}{-0.010} - \underset{(2.246)}{2.027(f - s)_{t-1}} - \underset{(3.331)}{0.005h_t^2}$$

$$h_t^2 = \underset{(2.792)}{0.001} + \underset{(1.062)}{0.143u_{t-1}^2} + \underset{(2.113)}{0.512u_{t-2}^2}$$

$$R^2 = 0.115 \qquad L = 120.067 \qquad \text{SEE} = 0.040 \qquad \text{DW} = 2.282$$

$$\text{Wald } \chi^2(1) = 11.252$$

The Wald chi-square statistic indicates, once again, rejection of the unbiasedness hypothesis.

In a third attempt, Eq. (8) was tested empirically using different approximations of the covariance terms as determinants of the risk premium. These approximations take the form of movements in the conditional variances of exogenous processes reflecting changes in real and nominal economic uncertainty as in the models of Domowitz and Hakkio (1985), Bomhoff and Koedijk (1988), Hodrick (1989), and Kaminsky and Peruga (1990).

In the Lucas (1982) version of the model considered by Domowitz and Hakkio (1985), the risk premia are shown to be a function of the conditional variances of the forecast errors of the domestic and foreign money supplies. In the Bomhoff and Koedijk (1988) and Hodrick (1989) models, the determinants of the risk premium in the foreign exchange market are nominal (money supply, interest rate) and real (income) uncertainties in both the domestic and the foreign economy.

Since the conditional variances of the exogenous processes driving the risk premium are not directly observed, a two-step estimation procedure is used, as in Hodrick (1989). First, estimates of the conditional variances are generated from a set of linear ARCH models or, more specifically, univariate autoregressive time-series models with ARCH disturbances. Second, the estimated variances are used as regressors in the risk premium equation. To avoid possible errors-in-variables estimation problems, an instrumental variables (IV) approach suggested by Pagan and Ullah (1988) and Park (1990) is used. The squared forecast errors from the ARCH models replace the conditional variances as the explanatory variables in the second-stage equation. The conditional variances are used as instruments. Pagan and Ullah (1988) showed that this estimation procedure produces not only consistent but also robust estimates to possible misspecification of the conditional variances.

The preferred equation is one in which real uncertainty (hy_t) and the interest rate differential are used as determinants of the expected risk premia. The IV estimate of the equation is

$$s_t - f_{t-1} = \underset{(1.648)}{-0.074} + \underset{(2.090)}{0.058}(r - r^*)_{t-1} + \underset{(1.328)}{0.030}hy_t$$

The results from this regression as well as those of other regressions using different combinations of explanatory variables indicate that the data provide little support for the underlying theoretical models of risk premia determination. These results are consistent with the empirical findings of Hodrick (1989).

CONCLUSIONS

The presence of a risk premium in the foreign exchange market provides an alternative way to examine the proposition that the forward rate is an unbiased predictor of the future spot rate, without sacrificing the notion of market efficiency (Domowitz and Hakkio, 1985). In this chapter, an attempt was made to empirically reconcile the market efficiency hypothesis by distinguishing between an inefficient market and a time-varying premium. The empirical results suggest that there is a time-varying risk premium in the foreign exchange market. However, the attempt to model the risk premium in the context of asset price theory has not received strong empirical support by the data. In future work, it would be worthwhile to re-examine this issue in the context of a multivariate asset pricing model. It should also be kept in mind that a potentially serious problem in modeling the variability of risk premia is the existence of a peso problem. If this affects the forward market, it will also affect the spot market. To cope with this problem, it will be necessary to introduce a learning process in the exchange rate model.

REFERENCES

Bailie, R. T. 1989. Econometric tests of rationality and market efficiency, *Econometric Reviews* 8:151–186.

Bilson, J. F. 1978. The current experience with floating exchange rates: An approval of the monetary approach, *American Economic Review* 68:392–397.

Bilson, J. F. 1981. The speculative efficiency hypothesis, *Journal of Business* 54:435–451.

Bilson, J. F. 1985. Macroeconomic stability and flexible exchange rates, *American Economic Review* 75:62–67.

Bollerslev, T., R. Y. Chou, N. Jayaraman, and K. F. Kroner. 1990. *ARCH Modelling in Finance: A Selective Review of the Theory and Empirical Evidence, with Suggestions for Future Research,* Research Paper.

Bomhoff, E. J., and K. G. Koedijk. 1988. Bilateral exchange rates and risk premia, *Journal of International Money and Finance* 7:205–220.

Cumby, R. E., and M. Obstfeld. 1984. International interest rate and price level linkages under floating exchange rates: A review of recent evidence, pp. 121–154 in J. F. Bilson and R. C. Marston (Eds.), *Exchange Rates: Theory and Practice,* Chicago: University of Chicago Press.

Diebold, F. X., and P. Pauly. 1988. Endogenous risk in a portfolio balance rational expectations model of the deutschemark dollar rate, *European Economic Review* 32:27–53.

Domowitz, I., and C. S. Hakkio. 1985. Conditional variance and the risk premium in the foreign exchange market, *Journal of International Economics,* 19:47–66.

Engle, R. F. 1982. Autoregressive conditional heteroskedasticity with estimates of the variance of U.K. inflation, *Econometrica* 50:987–1008.

Engle, R. F., D. M. Lilien, and R. P. Robins. 1987. Estimating time-varying risk premia in the term structure: The ARCH-M model, *Econometrica* 55:391–407.

Fama, E. F. 1965. The behaviour of stock market prices, *Journal of Business* 38:34–105.

Fama, E. F. 1984. Forward and spot exchange rates, *Journal of Monetary Economics* 14:319–338.

Frenkel, J. A. 1976. A monetary approach to the exchange rate: Doctrinal aspects and empirical evidence, in J. A. Frenkel and H. G. Johnson (Eds.), *The Economics of Exchange Rates,* Reading, MA: Addison-Wesley.

Frenkel, J. A. 1979. Tests of rational expectations in the foreign exchange market, *Southern Economic Journal* 46:1083–1101.

Frenkel, J. A. 1988. Recent estimates of time-variation in the conditional variance and in the exchange rate premium, *Journal of International Money and Finance* 7:115–125.

Frenkel, J. A. 1980. The demand for intervention reserve under pegged flexible exchange rate regimes, in D. Bigman and D. Taya (Eds.), *The Functioning of Floating Exchange Rates,* Cambridge, MA: Ballinger.

Friedman, D., and S. Vandersteel. 1982. Short-run fluctuations in foreign exchange rates. *Journal of International Economics* 13:171–186.

Gibbs, D., A. Grimes, and I. Harrison. 1990. Exchange rate predictions: Forward rates versus a random walk, *Reserve Bank of New Zealand Research Note No. 90/2.*

Hakkio, C. S. 1981. Expectations and the forward exchange rate, *International Economic Review* 22:663–678.

Hansen, L. P., and R. J. Hodrick. 1980. Forward exchange rates as optimal predictors of the future spot rates: An economic analysis, *Journal of Political Economy* 88:829–853.

Hansen, L. P., and R. J. Hodrick. 1983. Risk averse speculation in the forward foreign exchange market: An econometric analysis of linear models, pp. 113–142 in J. A.

Frenkel (Ed.), *Exchange Rate and International Macroeconomics*, Chicago: University of Chicago Press.

Hodrick, R. J. 1989. *The Empirical Evidence on the Efficiency of Forward and Futures Foreign Exchange Markets*, New York: Scientific and Technical Book Service.

Hodrick, R. J. 1989. Risk, uncertainty, and exchange rates, *Journal of Monetary Economics* 23:433–457.

Hodrick, R. J., and S. Srivastava. 1984. An investigation of risk and return in forward foreign exchange, *Journal of International Money and Finance* 3:5–30.

Hsieh, D. A. 1984. Tests of rational expectation and no risk premium in forward exchange market, *Journal of International Economics* 24:129–141.

Kaminsky, G., and R. Peruga. 1990. Can a time-varying risk premia explain excess returns in the forward market for foreign exchange? *Journal of International Economics* 28:47–70.

Kmenta, J. 1986. *Elements of Econometrics*, 2d ed., New York: Macmillan.

Levich, R. M. 1978. Further results on the efficiency of markets for foreign exchange, pp. 58–80 in The Federal Reserve Bank of Boston, *Managed Exchange Rate Flexibility: The Recent Experience*, Boston: Federal Reserve Bank of Boston.

Levine, R. 1989. The pricing of forward exchange rates, *Journal of International Money and Finance* 8:163–179.

Longworth, D. 1981. Testing the efficiency of the Canadian–U.S. exchange market under the assumption of the risk premium, *Journal of Finance* 36:43–49.

Lucas, R. E. 1982. Interest rates and currency prices in a two-country world, *Journal of Monetary Economics* 10:335–360.

MacDonald, R. 1988. *Floating Exchange Rates: Theories and Evidence*, Scranton, PA: Urwin Hyman.

Madsen, J. B. 1990. Is the forward market still inefficient, *Working Paper No. 195*, Australian National University.

Mandelbrot, B. 1963. The variation of certain speculative prices, *Journal of Business* 36:147–165.

Mark, N. C. 1985. On time-varying risk premia in the foreign exchange market, *Journal of Monetary Economics* 16:3–18.

Meese, R. A., and K. Rogoff. 1983. Empirical exchange rate models of the seventies: Do they fit out of sample? *Journal of International Economics* 14:3–24.

Pagan, A., and A. Ullah. 1988. The econometric analysis of models with risk terms, *Journal of Applied Econometrics* 3:87–105.

Park, J. W. 1990. Changing uncertainty for time-varying risk premia in the term structure of nominal interest rates, *INSEAD Working Paper No. 90/35/Ef.*

Reserve Bank of New Zealand. 1987. The New Zealand foreign exchange market: Some efficiency aspects, *Reserve Bank of New Zealand Bulletin*, 93–103.

Scanlan, M. H. 1989. Testing for bias, efficiency and normality in New Zealand dollar exchange rates, *Auckland University Working Paper.*

Szeto, K. L., and R. Lattimore. 1990. The efficiency of the New Zealand foreign exchange market, *Lincoln University Working Paper.*

Tease, W. J. 1988. Speculative efficiency and the exchange rate: Some evidence since the float, *The Economic Record* 64:2–13.

Chapter 7

European Monetary Integration: Theoretical Issues and Practical Implementations

André Fourçans

Several strategies for the European Monetary Union can be envisaged. But before evaluating these strategies, one must ask whether it is economically justifiable to seek a Monetary Union, that is, to establish a single currency for Europe. The following section studies the conceptual background of the question, without relating it directly to the European problem.

The next section concentrates on European monetary integration per se. After the new treaty signed in December 1991 the objective is clear: to create a single currency. What strategy, then, should be adopted to implement it? What are the main economic problems associated with the transition toward integration, and how should they be treated? What degree of fiscal policy coordination is necessary? What part should the ecu play in the process? The concluding section sets forth the absolute necessity for close coordination of monetary policies as well as the need for a European Central Bank, with the main measures to be adopted for doing so.

ONE CURRENCY FOR EUROPE?

Advantages of a Single Currency

The role of money. The use of money diminishes information and transaction costs of trade. As a unit of account, medium of exchange, and store of value, money demonstrates a high economic and social productivity. It reduces uncertainty and costs associated with economic activity by reducing resources

I thank Michele Fratianni, John Pattison, and participants at the ITFA conference (Marseilles, 2 June 1991) for helpful comments on an earlier draft.

necessary to acquire, process, and stock information and to pursue production and transaction activities (Brunner and Meltzer, 1971). These advantages increase with the currency domain (Mundell, 1961).

More concretely, a single-currency system facilitates comparison of international prices and costs without having to generate and collect information relative to actual and future exchange rates and to different rules and regulations about exchange controls. A single currency eliminates exchange rate uncertainties as well as transaction costs due to the exchange of monies. It suppresses the socially unproductive activities resulting from exchanging one currency for another. A multicurrency world, with (potential or real) exchange risk, constitutes an obstacle to market integration (Kenen, 1976).

A single currency versus fixed exchange rates. A fixed exchange rate system demonstrates some, but only some, attributes of a single-currency system. Even by supposing perfectly fixed exchange rates (that is, without any expectations of parity changes), a single-currency system still possesses one main advantage: It eliminates the socially unproductive costs of exchanging one money for another.

In the real world, adjustments of parities exist within a fixed-exchange rate system. Of course, a single currency eliminates these risks. It also suppresses all the risks associated with the possible occurrence of exchange controls and other rules or regulations concerning the exchange of currencies. It therefore leads to a better allocation of international funds. Yet, if a single currency gets rid of nominal exchange rate fluctuations, it does not eradicate real exchange rate changes due to disparities in relative prices and costs between countries. But real exchange rate variations would be less than with a fixed (or flexible) but adjustable exchange system, since they would not be affected by expectations about the relative stability of each currency (Lehment, 1984).

Another important difference between a fixed- and a single-currency system resides in the type of monetary management that each implies. In the first case, monetary policy coordination is necessary to maintain the fixed-rate system. In the single-currency system, one, and only one, monetary policy must be conducted. If the different countries of the area agree on the policy objective, the latter is institutionally easier to obtain in a single-currency system than in a system whereby different monetary policies need to be coordinated (Christie and Fratianni, 1978).

An increased mobility of goods and production factors. A widening of the currency area due to a monetary union leads to a better allocation of resources. Consumer welfare is increased by a sharpening of the competition thus created, with the traditional advantages of such an occurrence (on prices, product quality, and innovation). Production costs decrease due to more freedom in trade, economies of scale, and optimal choice of investment. Hence, there are gains in employment and growth.

Arguments Against a Single Currency

Loss of one degree of freedom: exchange rate adjustments. A single currency (or irrevocably fixed rates) would render short-run economic adjustments more difficult insofar as nominal exchange rate changes are eliminated. Because nominal exchange rates are more flexible than prices and wages, it would be easier to correct imbalances by a change in parities than by a change in prices and wages. This case is defendable in the short run. In the longer run, the adjustment of nominal exchange rates to eliminate fundamental imbalances in the economy could aggravate the situation insofar as the parity variation (in a flexible or a fixed but adjustable exchange system) would be used as a substitute for the necessary change in policies (budgetary, fiscal, interest rates, etc.), or insofar as the policy would be implemented too late and in a more difficult situation. Furthermore, a single currency diminishes the amount of adjustments implied by real shocks compared to a flexible or adjustable fixed-rate system. The latter may lead to supplementary adjustment due to monetary shocks that stimulate flows of capital (Lehment, 1984).

Loss of one degree of freedom: independence of monetary policy. A single currency implies the loss of national monetary sovereignty. In a currency area all countries have the same ex post, if not ex ante, inflation rate. The transition from the ex ante to the ex post inflation rate may lead to an unemployment rise if wages do not adjust in the higher inflation countries. This risk exists in any anti-inflationary process, whatever the cause.[1] Yet, it must be added, the anti-inflationary costs have largely been paid by most of the European countries (Bailey et al., 1987) (the exception being some of the southern countries).

Monetary independence does not automatically mean an increase in efficiency. The real efficiency constraint appears to be the degree of openness of the economy, rather than the exchange rate regime per se, especially when financial flows are free to move (Frenkel and Goldstein, 1988). And flexible exchange rates do not protect from changes in relative prices between countries. This implies internal adjustments, whether in fixed or flexible rates (or with a single currency); only the speed of adjustment can vary. If monetary policy has no long-run influence on employment and growth, a plausible occurrence, it is obvious that the problem of monetary independence to achieve the goals of lasting full employment and growth becomes irrelevant.

Undesirable regional consequences. A currency area may entail undesirable regional consequences if compensatory measures are not taken. Demonstration effects, or a centralized wage setting process whereby wages would evolve at the same pace whatever the productivity gains of each region, would lead to an

[1]In other words, whether the inflation rate decrease results from the establishment of fixed exchange rates and a single currency, or from restrictive national economic policies in a flexible exchange rate system.

increase in unemployment in the periphery (Christie and Fratianni, 1978). In this case, a redistributive policy could be established between the different regions (or countries), from the richer to the poorer peripheral zones. The aid should be conceived so as to accelerate productivity gains in the unfavored regions and to alleviate social costs through income redistribution.

There is also the possibility that, through a decrease in information and transaction costs, as well as through lower banking risks, a single currency would accelerate the movements of physical capital and labor between regions. Even though the new allocation of production factors so induced would be economically efficient for the area as a whole, it would occur at the expense of some regions. Here too, redistributive income policies and/or incentives (be they fiscal or other) could help alleviate the problem.

WHAT KIND OF EUROPEAN MONETARY UNION? HOW TO ESTABLISH IT?

To better understand these questions, it is first necessary to establish where the European Monetary System (EMS) stands and its implications.

The EMS and Its Results

After almost 15 years in operation, one can say that the EMS has reached its first objective reasonably well: to stabilize exchange rates between European currencies. The goal of a stable monetary zone has been satisfactorily achieved, even though several adjustments of parities were implemented.

Most economists feel that the German Bundesbank dominance over the EMS explains this new stability (for example, Sarcinelli, 1986; Giavazzi and Giovannini, 1988). Fratianni and Von Hagen (1990a, b) disagree with that view and offer empirical tests rejecting German dominance, yet showing the Bundesbank independence in pursuing its own policy goals.

Despite this disagreement, it is true that, via the constraint imposed by the EMS, the authorities of the various countries have learned to consult each other on their main economic and monetary policies and to make more decisions in common. Decisions on realignments of exchange rates are now largely made together. The same argument can be defended, though to a lesser extent, about short-term interest rate policies.

The EMS appears to have stabilized exchange-rate expectations and thereby to have increased the credibility of (relatively) fixed parities, with its positive consequences on intracommunity trade and resource allocation. Yet, reinforcement of the EMS raises several questions.

The Reinforcement of Monetary Integration and Its Problems

An "inconsistent quartet." With the free movements of financial capital and the elimination of nontariff barriers to trade, a challenge must be faced. The

European zone must reconcile (1) full capital mobility, (2) free trade, (3) fixed exchange rates, and (4) autonomous national monetary policy. Theory as well as experience suggests that this quartet is inconsistent; at least one has to give way (Padoa-Schioppa, 1988).

Via the EMS constraint, monetary policies are already close enough, be it through coordination or dominance of Germany policy. With the increasing liberalization of the flow of capital, goods, services, and resources, more coordination will be unavoidable with the liberalization of 1993. If not, one can expect the EMS to work erratically, at least less satisfactorily than during its first phase. If monetary policies are not well coordinated, fixed exchange rates will have to give way.

The anchor and burden of adjustment questions. Some economists (for example, Giavazzi and Giovannini, 1988; Schinasi, 1989) argue that a well-managed and well-defined nominal anchor is necessary for international monetary orders to be successful. The same authors generally consider that the past success of the EMS is due to the deutsche mark (DM) role as an anchor to the system. Other countries have thus to adjust their policies to Germany's, even though the policies are inconsistent with their national objectives. The burden of adjustment is therefore asymmetric and falls more heavily on the weaker currency countries. If the proponents of this view are right, the DM will have to keep on fulfilling that function and asymmetry is the price to pay. If the Bundesbank is not the dominant player, but pursues its own policy goals of low inflation (as Fratianni and Von Hagen suggest) it does not make much economic difference (though it would politically) to the future working of the EMS: Other countries will have to follow monetary policies on the same lines to attain the goal of fixed exchange rates with complete liberalization within the Community.

In that case, could the DM be considered an anchor? This seems to be a semantical question of little relevance. If one admits that the Bundesbank will never accept inflationary policies (a reasonable hypothesis in view of historical experience), and if the Community wants to maintain fixed exchange rates with free movements of funds and resources, each country's monetary policy will have to be geared toward price-level stability.

Is there a need for fiscal policy coordination? On one hand, one can argue that the stronger the monetary integration, the greater the fiscal discipline will be, due to market constraints. With fixed exchange rates and perfect capital mobility a country's budget deficit is financed by issuing debt on the capital market (money financing is assumed to be prohibited). If the deficit is too high, the country will not be able to finance it, or at a higher interest rate. This cost constraint is supposed to discipline countries in their fiscal policies, and hence lead to implicit and sufficient coordination (Padoa-Shioppa, 1988). On the other hand, it is possible to argue that free capital mobility on a large financial market renders the financing of deficits easier, and so introduces another degree of freedom in fiscal management, which could diminish incentives to maintain budget deficits within reasonable limits. Furthermore, if a large country or a combination of countries follow a lax fiscal policy, there would be a flow of savings out of the other countries and an interest-rate rise for the monetary zone as a whole, with its consequences on investment and growth.

During the transition period toward monetary union, it seems reasonable to establish some fiscal policy discipline so as to avoid external imbalances. A growing budget deficit in one country (especially a large country) may entail an interest rate rise that, even if it does not last, may induce a flow of capital that would put pressures on exchange rates and jeopardize their fixity, which is one of the main objectives of monetary integration (before complete monetary union is obtained, of course). It seems that a minimal degree of fiscal coordination is desirable, but without the need for strong central rules and regulations.

A Critical Review of the Treaty on European Monetary Union

In view of the above economic background, the Treaty on European Monetary Union (1991) and the proposal of the Delors Committee (Delors, 1989), which served as the background for the Treaty, are analyzed. More specific proposals, such as the parallel currency approach, are also analyzed.

The final objective: one currency for Europe. The EMU Treaty and the Delors Report agree on the main goal: to establish a single currency (the ecu) in the final stage of monetary union. This choice means that they recognize that the benefits of a single currency outweigh its costs. Yet, the Delors Report postponed the establishment of this currency until monetary union is completed, without the slightest hint as to the possible date for such an outcome, a strategy that opened the door to unlimited delays. Fortunately, the Treaty has become more specific on that matter since, by 1 January 1999, a single currency will presumably be put in place. Yet, only countries with an inflation rate generally in line with the best performers in Europe and a budget deficit contained within certain limits will be allowed to enter the union.[2] It is doubtful whether the single currency would be established if only, let us say, three or four countries meet the test, which may appear very rough to some countries, at least rougher than would seem necessary. There is therefore still some uncertainty as to this supposedly "deadlock" date. It must also be added that Great Britain may decide, through an option out clause, not to enter the EMU. All in all, even if the Union is created in 1999, it is doubtful that it will involve all European countries; therefore, one can expect it to constitute a partial EMU. This being

[2]More precisely, a country's deficit should not exceed 3% of its GNP, a country's public debt should be no more than 60% of GNP, inflation should not exceed that of the three best-performing members states for the prior year by more than 1.5 percentage points, and interest rates should not exceed the three best-performing countries in the previous year by more than 2 points. Members are admitted after a qualified majority vote. New members may be admitted every two years through the same voting rule.

said, it must be added that, if all went very well, the currency union could be created as soon as January 1997 since leaders could, by agreement based on a weighted majority vote, initiate it with at least seven member states prepared to go ahead (as long as they meet the above-mentioned economic test). Here again, if that road were chosen, the currency union would not be complete.

What symmetry of adjustments and what fixity of exchange rates? As was seen earlier, if the Bundesbank never deviates, at least in the long run, from a relatively stable price-level goal, the European system with fixed exchange rates and complete capital mobility can function only if all countries agree on the same goal. Otherwise, the inconsistent quartet problem will arise. This means closer coordination of monetary policies and, to bring about such coordination, the establishment of a European central bank (Euro-Fed) is of paramount importance.

An agreement on that matter also exists. The Treaty (and the Delors Report) says explicitly that the price stability goal must be the goal of the future European central bank. Yet, the European Monetary Institute, which should be created by 1 January 1994 (the second stage of the move to EMU) and which should be a beginning of the future central bank, is far from being that. Its monetary powers are small and it more resembles the already existing Committee of Governors of the nations' central banks than a future European central bank.

A major question, eluded in the Treaty and the Delors Report, must be investigated: Should the current exchange-rate limits be quickly narrowed, or is it better to wait until a single currency exists and until then maintain the status quo? It will be necessary for all currencies to enter the EMS and for all to be subjected to the same limits. This being said, it is difficult to say whether a fast narrowing (in the long run this narrowing is unavoidable, at the latest, the day when the single currency is established) of exchange-rate limits would ease integration or would render it more difficult.

With free capital mobility, exchange-rate pressures and the risk of exchange-rate fluctuations increase. To avoid realignments, intervention mechanisms and monetary cooperation become of paramount importance. Exchange-rate limits that are too narrow could entail the need for numerous realignments and thus jeopardize the system's credibility, as long as strong cooperation has not yet been established. On the other hand, to avoid realignments, more narrow bands could induce (oblige?) monetary authorities to accelerate the convergence and coordination measures; in that case, the pace toward the Euro-Fed and monetary union would be increased.

Fiscal and "regional" policies. The Delors Report emphasizes the need for strong fiscal policy coordination in terms of deficit financing, government expenditure, and taxes. It suggests the establishment of medium-term objectives. In the final stage of monetary union, the Report proposes that binding rules be established. The final Treaty is a little less stringent, but does remain rigorous in that respect. The economic criteria for entering the union are rather strict and may block the entry of some important countries. Yet, as was discussed earlier, in terms of the prerequisite for EMU, the need for fiscal policy coordination is probably less strong than that which implicitly emerges from the Treaty.

If the proposals for regional policies and financial redistribution are justified, they appear to be overstated as far as fiscal policies are concerned. They probably reflect central bankers' fears of having to finance budget deficits through money creation in case of lax fiscal policies. This fear is understandable, but during the transition period, it is more related to the policy mix within each country than to the policy coordination problem between member states. When the single currency is created, this problem disappears and what is important is to severely limit, or even forbid, any monetary financing of each country's deficit by the European central bank. This constraint seems to be accepted by member states and is part of the Treaty.

The ecu and the parallel currency strategy. The Delors Report and the Treaty reject the ecu–parallel currency as a means of accelerating the pace of the monetary union process for two main reasons: first, because it would add another source of money creation that could jeopardize price stability, and second, because it would further complicate the already difficult coordination of national monetary policies. Inflationary risk can easily be avoided by having the ecu created only through substitution with national monies (Alphandéry and Fourçans, 1984a, b). There is no reason for this procedure to entail more complexity within the monetary policy-coordinating process (see also Mayer, 1986).

When the ecu basket of currencies is converted into a new fully fledged parallel currency, it is obvious that its issue should be controlled and regulated by a European central bank (see Alphandéry and Fourçans (1984a, b) and Basevi et al. (1975) for parallel currency strategies).

If the institutional approach toward union of the Treaty works well a priori, the ecu (as a basket of currencies or as a complete currency in itself, like the "hard ecu") as a parallel currency is not a necessary condition of the integration process. However, there are still uncertainties as to the date when all countries would be part of the EMU. The widely agreed on date of 1999 for a single currency fully shared would be more credible if the role of the ecu was reinforced. It would constitute a force for monetary and financial integration that would help accelerate the move of all countries toward union. It is regrettable that the Treaty did not incorporate that idea.

CONCLUSION: TOWARD A EUROPEAN CENTRAL BANK

Whatever the date, the EMU is created (1997? 1999?) and whatever the number of countries that enter the Union, the approach chosen means more monetary coordination during the transition period, and, at the latest when a single currency is created, the establishment of a European central bank. From the beginning of the EMS, and especially from the start of the 1980s, monetary coordination has been improved. With the new capital mobility, this coordination must be reinforced. How (without entering into the technical details of the process, which are not the object of this chapter), and what main lines should be followed?

Two main strategies can be implemented (Guitian et al., 1988). First, by agreeing on the price-stability objective, each country could set up growth objectives for its internal money sources in line with internal price stability and real growth, with further agreement not to sterilize international reserves to maintain fixed exchange rates. The second strategy could consist of fixing a money growth objective for the Community as a whole, in view of the expected real growth of all the countries taken together. The monetary rule could (should?) be adjusted, for example, to velocity changes, financial innovations, and structural changes in production supply. In both strategies a common decision-making process is necessary. To ease the implementation of such a process the establishment of a common policy body, that is, the European central bank, would be very welcome. And if one adds the desire to develop the ecu, and therefore the need to manage its issue, there is another reason for setting up such an institution.

From the terms of the Maastricht Treaty, the European central bank will be created only a few months before currency union is established. The European Monetary Institute, to be set up as of 1 January 1994, will have limited monetary powers; its role will be to lay the groundwork for blending the various national currencies into the single currency, but it will not have any of the instruments of a central bank.

As far as the European central bank is concerned, all the questions related to its precise role and development, its management and its degree of independence with respect to each member-state and to the European political systems must be asked and answered (Fourçans, 1989; Thygesen, 1989). In that respect, a monetary constitution with simple and clear rules must be implemented and agreed upon by the different member states.

REFERENCES

Alphandéry, E., and A. Fourçans. April 1984a. L'ecu: stratégie pour une Europe en crise, *Revue Banque*, 397–402.

Alphandéry, E., and A. Fourçans. June 1984b. How to create single European currency, *The Financial Times*.

Bailey, R. W., C. Bordes, M. J. Driscoll, and M. O. Strauss-Kahn. 1987. Monnaie, demande globale et inertie des rythmes d'inflation dans les principaux pays européens, *Economie Appliquée* 3:483–538.

Basevi, G., et al. 1975. The All Saints Day manifesto for European Monetary Union, *The Economist*.

Brunner, K., and A. Meltzer. 1971. The use of money: Money in the theory of an exchange economy, *American Economic Review* 61:784–805.

Christie, H., and M. Fratianni. 1978. European Monetary Union: Rehabilitation of a case and some thoughts for strategy, in M. Fratianni and T. Peeter (Eds.), *One Money for Europe,* New York: Macmillan.

Delors, J. 1989. Report on economic and monetary union in the European community, *European Communities.*

Fourçans, A. 1989. Une banque centrale pour l'Europe, *Le Monde.*

Fratianni, M., and J. Von Hagen. 1990a. The European Monetary System ten years after, *Carnegie-Rochester Conference Series* 32:173–242.

Fratianni, M., and J. Von Hagen. 1990b. German dominance in the EMS: The empirical evidence, *Open Economies Review* 1:67–88.

Frenkel, J., and M. Goldstein. 1988. The International Monetary System: Developments and prospects, *International Monetary Fund Working Paper.*

Friedman, M. 1984. Currency competition: A skeptical view, in P. Salin (Ed.), *Currency Competition and Monetary Union,* Amsterdam: Martinus Nijhoff.

Giavazzi, F., and A. Giovannini. 1988. Modèles du SME: l'Europe n'est-elle qu'une zone deutsche mark? *Revue Economique* 3:641–666.

Guitian, M., M. Russo, and G. Tullio. 1988. Policy coordination in the European Monetary System, *F.M.I. Occasional Paper 61.*

Kenen, P. 1976. Capital mobility and financial integration, *Princeton Studies in International Finance,* 39.

Lehment, H. 1984. Freely flexible exchange rates or a common currency? A new look at the issue, in P. Salin (Ed.), *Currency Competition and Monetary Union,* Amsterdam: Martinus Nijhoff.

Mayer, H. 1986. Private ecus potential macroeconomic policy dimensions, *BIS Economic Papers,* No. 16, Bank for International Settlements.

Mundell, R. 1961. A theory of optimum currency areas, *American Economic Review* (September):657–665.

Padoa-Schioppa. 1988. The European Monetary System: A long-term view, in F. Giavazzi, J. Micossi, and M. Miller (Eds.), *The European Monetary System,* Cambridge, UK: Cambridge University Press.

Sarcinelli, M. 1986. The EMS and the International Monetary Systems: Toward greater stability, *Banca Nazioniale del Lavoro Quarterly Review* (March):57–84.

Schinasi, G. 1989. European integration, exchange rate management, and monetary reform: A review of the major issues, *International Finance Discussion Papers,* Board of Governors of the Federal Reserve System, No. 364.

Thygesen, N. 1989. On the prospects for a European central bank, in M. de Cecco and A. Giovannini (Eds.), *A European Central Bank,* Cambridge, UK: Cambridge University Press.

Treaty on European Monetary Union, Maastrich (Dec. 1991).

Part Two
Capital Markets

Chapters 8–14 examine capital markets in developed and developing countries. They study the optimal capital structure in a dynamic competitive model, whether diversification in international capital markets is beneficial, international co-movement of capital markets, the benefits and problems of defeased debt in international capital markets, deregulation of financial institutions, capital flight and the "round tripping" effect of debt–equity swaps, and the effect of emerging capital markets on economic development.

In Chapter 8, Dilip Ghosh determines the optimum leverage of a firm in terms of the payout maximization and utility maximization hypotheses, by using the income-generating process in a dynamic environment with debt and equity accumulation. In Chapter 9, Krishnan Dandapani and Jerry Haar examine the benefits of diversifying in international equity markets in terms of different performance measures during the 1987–1990 period. In Chapter 10, Teppo Martikainen, Ilkka Virtanen, and Paavo Yli-Olli use a multimarket model of Finnish securities to show that several Finnish stocks have significant Swedish risk components. In Chapter 11, Emiel Owens and Ronald Singer discuss the potential financial consequences of an in-substance defeasance transaction by evaluating potential levels of wealth transfer among bond and stockholders of a defeased corporation. In Chapter 12, William Dowling and George Philippatos examine the question of whether scale economies existed in the U.S. S&L industry when it was deregulated in the early 1980s. In Chapter 13, M. T. Varizi and Hossein Shalchi test empirically the relationship between round-trip capital flight and its several possible determinants for the most highly indebted Latin American countries for the 1980–1989 time period. Chapter 14 by Edgar Ortiz presents a synthetic model that highlights the importance of the equity and bond markets on economic activity and the role that the government plays in the mobilization of resources for economic development.

Chapter 8

Optimal Leverage of a Dynamically Competitive Firm

Dilip K. Ghosh

In their seminal work, Franco Modigliani and Merton Miller (1958) established the proposition that there was no optimum leverage for a perfectly competitive firm. Durand (1952, 1959) (whose original view was further clarified and certainly upheld in the most convincing fashion by Modigliani and Miller) and Brewer and Michaelson (1965) questioned the realism and adequacy of the postulates behind the Modigliani–Miller analysis.[1] But, soon after those criticisms, numerous studies (for example, Hirschleifer, 1966; Stiglitz, 1969, 1973; Fama and Miller, 1972; Baron, 1974; Hamada, 1969; Rubinstein, 1973) reestablished the validity of the celebrated result under more general and less restrictive conditions. In their original work, Modigliani and Miller (1958) pointed out that if the firm's cost of borrowing fell short of the investors' cost of borrowing, then the value of the firm would rise with an increase in its debt. Baumol and Malkiel (1967) also contended that a firm was not leverage-indifferent if investors incurred transaction costs in arbitrage activities. A few years later, Stiglitz (1972) showed that if debt capital was traded in markets in which equity investors held superior prospect on the firm's performance to that of the firm's creditors, then a sufficiently high level of debt could induce a drop in the value of the firm. Rubinstein (1973) demonstrated that if security markets were partially segmented and that if debt was traded in a separate market where

---

The author expresses his sincere appreciation to Stephen Bowman, Robert Sherman, Vincent Wu, and Shyamasri Ghosh for their useful comments and constructive criticism. For a more detailed analysis on this question, see Ghosh (1992a, b).

[1]Durand (1952, 1959) was indeed the first person to demonstrate, as Chen (1978a, b) correctly pointed out, that the value of a firm is independent of its capital structure under the net operating income theory of market valuation.

traders were more risk averse than investors in the firm's equity capital, then the value of the firm and its debt level were inversely related. Having introduced corporate income taxes and bankruptcy costs in tandem, however, several authors (such as Baxter, 1967; Jensen and Meckling, 1976; Kim, 1978; Turnbull, 1979, 1981; Lee and Barker, 1977; Kraus and Litzenberger, 1973; Scott, 1976; Robichek and Myers, 1965; Bierman and Thomas, 1972) proved the existence of the optimum capital structure for a firm.

Most of the studies mentioned above examined issues in static analytical frameworks. Using a multiperiod model, Scott (1976) introduced the dynamic analysis on this issue. Later, Brennan and Schwartz (1978) used the dynamic stochastic optimization technique, adopted by Merton (1971), to analyze corporate income taxes, valuation, and optimal capital structure. In this chapter, the dynamic framework, as adopted by Merton (1971), Scott (1976), and Brennan and Schwartz (1978), is used, but unlike in those studies, here the analytical vehicle is the optimum control theory of Pontryagin et al. (1962). Following Modigliani and Miller by taking their paradigm of perfect competition in which taxes, the agency costs, and other distortionary factors are absent, we establish the same results quite correctly obtained by Chen and Kim (1979), DeAngelo and Masulis (1980), Taggart (1980), Barnea, Haugen, and Senbet (1981), and others without making use of any of their distortionary factors.

Under these market conditions, an attempt is made to determine or define optimum leverage of a firm in terms of two different objective functions by using the income-generating process in a dynamic environment with debt and equity accumulation. First, it is postulated that the firm's operational objective is to maximize the net payout of the firm, subject to the perpetual maintenance of its capital mix that admits to intertemporally sustainable maximum net payout. This objective is consistent with the traditional literature wherein optimum capital structure refers to the capital mix that maximizes the value of the firm. The value of the firm is simply the sum of the discounted stream of payout of dividends (see, for instance, Lintner, 1956, 1963). Here net payout is the surplus that the firm generates, part of which is kept for the betterment of its capital structure and the remaining part is paid out to investors as dividend. In the analysis to follow, it is shown that in the dynamically optimum situation capital structure is held constant (as no betterment of capital structure is possible at the optimum point), and hence maximization of net payout is equivalent to maximization of dividend. The second objective postulated was that investors desire to maximize their utility level over time, where utility is a function of net payout. Both these objectives have been nicely utilized by Sau (1969), whose work is based on two papers by Lintner (1956, 1963). Consistent with this new approach, under both scenarios of different objective goals, as adopted here, the optimal value of the debt/equity ratio of the firm that maximizes the chosen objective function is determined and, interestingly, it is shown that payout maximization and utility maximization yield identical optimal capital structure in the dynamic analytical framework.

ANALYTICAL STRUCTURE

Net Payout Maximization

Consider a firm that operates in a perfectly competitive market with no distortion or artificial contrivance, and generates the income at time t ($V(t)$) by utilizing two types of capital assets, debt $D(t)$ and equity $E(t)$, where debt capital is measured by its number (underlying the value in terms of which V and E are expressed), but $V(t)$ and $E(t)$ are measured in the same unit (say, dollars). The income-generating process is as follows:

$$V(t) = F[E(t), D(t)] \tag{1}$$

where for any scale factor $\gamma > 0$, $\gamma V(t) = F[\gamma E(t), \gamma D(t)]$, and $F_i(\cdot) > 0$, $F_{ii}(\cdot) < 0$ for $i = E(t), D(t)$, and (F_{ij}) is a negative-definite matrix. Accordingly, if both equity and debt capital are increased by the same percentage, then the firm's income also increases equiproportionately, but the firm's income increases at successively lower and lower rates with every increase in capital alone. With these simple restrictions on the income-generating process, one can reduce Eq. (1) to

$$V(t)/D(t) = f[E(t)/D(t)] \tag{2}$$

where $f'(\cdot) > 0$ and $f''(\cdot) < 0$. That is, income of the firm per unit of debt increases with the equity/debt ratio at diminishing rates. Note that the income-generating function here is different from that of Sau (1969) in which

$$V(t) = F(K \equiv E + P_D D)$$

where P_D is the price of debt capital and P_E is the price of equity capital (here assumed equal to 1, by standard normalization).[2] The income-generating structure has been chosen, as in Eq. (1), to bring the capital structure to the forefront, but later in this chapter, it is shown that the Sau (1969) framework can also demonstrate the optimal capital mix by working out an additional constrained maximization.

Now consider the total retained earnings $R(t)$ and the amount of earnings the firm pays out at each instant of time t, ($X(t)$). By definition,

$$V(t) = R(t) + X(t) \qquad (\equiv \beta f(E/D) + X) \tag{3}$$

$R(t)$ is the firm's internal source of the reinvestible equity ($\equiv \beta f(E/D)$, where β is the plowback ratio), and so the firm's equity accumulation can be expressed as

[2]Since, by normalization, $P_E = 1$, E is both the dollar value of equity capital as well as the number of equity capital instruments. That means E/D is also the equity debt ratio in numerical terms.

$$\frac{dE(t)}{dt} = R(t) - bE(t) \tag{4}$$

where b measures the rate of depletion of equity capital (if $b > 0$; when $b < 0$, it is a case of increase in equity capital). Similarly, if the debt capital changes exogenously at the rate a, then the following equation is used:

$$\frac{dD(t)}{dt} = aD(t) \tag{5}$$

Equations (4) and (5) together define the dynamics of the firm's income generation. The differentiation of E/D with respect to time t and some simple algebraic manipulations of Eqs. (2)–(5) yield

$$f(E/D) = X(t)/D(t) + (a + b)E(t)/D(t) + \frac{d(E/D)}{dt} \tag{6}$$

Equation (6) shows that the income of the firm per unit of its debt equals the sum of total payout, the value required to maintain its equity/debt ratio, and the net growth in its equity/debt ratio. In view of relation (2), Eq. (6) is shown graphically in Figure 1, where the horizontal axis measures the equity/debt ratio E/D and the vertical axis measures the income of the firm per unit of its debt V/D and the net payout plus increases in the level of equity per unit of debt $\{(X(t)/D(t)) + [d(E/D)/dt]\}$. The curve $f(E/D)$ represents the income of the firm and the ray $(a + b)(E/D)$ measures how much of the firm's income is required to keep its capital structure intact at each level of its equity/debt ratio. So, for any chosen equity/debt ratio of the firm, the vertical distance between the $f(E/D)$ curve and the $(a + b)(E/D)$ ray gives what can be paid out to investors and used for net increase in equity per unit of debt, and this is what is being exhibited by the humped curve *OGSU*. A close examination of Eq. (6) and Figure 1 reveals unmistakably that if the equity/debt ratio is $(E/D)^+$, and if that equity/debt ratio is maintained over time (that is, $d(E/D)/dt = 0$), then *OM* is the maximum and intertemporally sustainable payout for investors. Notice now that at $(E/D)^+$, the slope of $f(E/D)$ is equal to $a + b$. That is,

$$f'(E/D) = a + b \quad \text{for } E/D = (E/D)^+ \quad \text{and} \quad \frac{d(E/D)}{dt} = 0$$

At this margin the rate of gain in the income of the firm equals the rate of dilution of equity per unit of debt. At $E/D = (E/D)^{**}$, one can visualize $X(t)/D(t) + d(E/D)/dt = 0$, which means that if E/D is held constant at this equity/debt ratio, then capital structure can be perpetually maintained, but payout for investors will be zero. Obviously, this is an unacceptable situation for investors, and thus $(E/D)^{**}$ is inferior to $(E/D)^+$. If maximization of net payout is the goal of the firm, which in turn means the maximization of the net worth of the

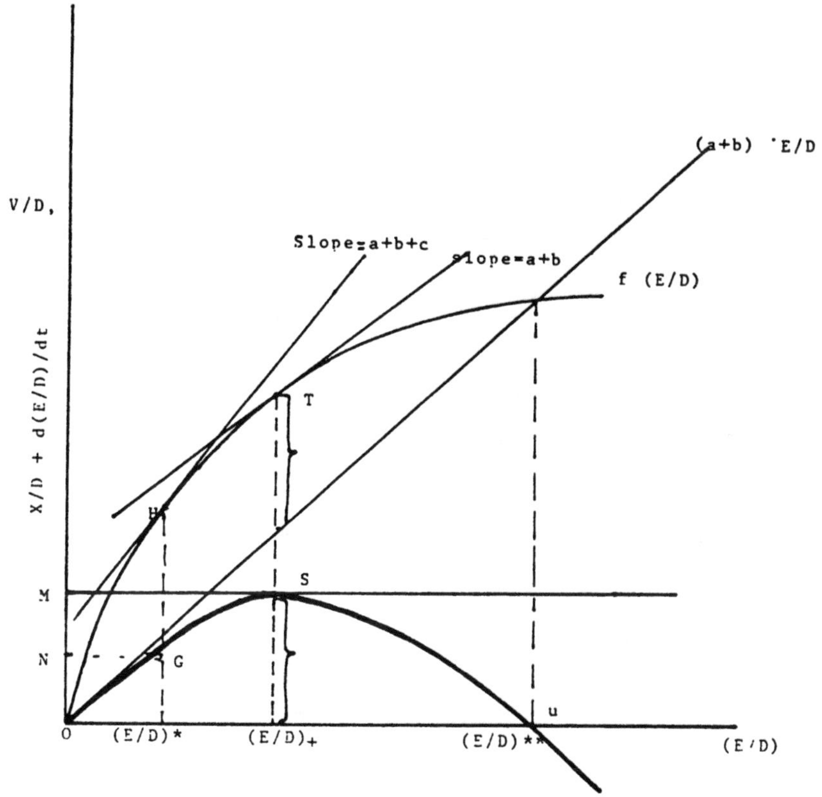

Figure 1

firm, then the equity/debt ratio $(E/D)^+$ is better than any other equity/debt ratio, and hence is the optimum capital structure of the firm.

So far net payout has been kept undiscounted. It is appropriate, therefore, that the discount rate c is introduced in the intertemporal optimization framework. The problem now is as follows:

$$\max \int_0^T (1 - \beta) f(E/D) e^{-ct}\, dt$$

subject to

$$\frac{d(E/D)}{dt} = \beta f(E/D) - (a + b)(E/D)$$

$$0 \leq \beta \leq 1 \quad \text{and} \quad E(T)/D(T) \geq (E/D)_T$$

Here $T(0 < T < \infty)$ is the end of the time horizon.[3] Following Pontryagin's optimum principle (Pontryagin et al., 1962), we then have the Hamiltonian:

$$He^{ct} = (1 - \beta)f(E/D) + \mu[\beta f(E/D) - (a + b)(E/D)]$$

where μ is the dynamic multiplier (shadow price of capital accumulation), and the equation denotes the discounted value (that is, present value) of earnings of the firm. The canonical equations defining the optimality condition are then

$$\frac{d(E/D)}{dt} = \beta f(E/D) - (a + b)(E/D)$$

$$\frac{d\mu}{dt} = (a + b + c)\mu - (1 - \beta + \mu\beta)\frac{df(E/D)}{dt}$$

$$\beta \text{ maximizes } (1 - \beta + \mu\beta) \text{ subject to } 0 \leq \beta \leq 1$$

The dynamical system given by these necessary optimality conditions does not reduce to a system of differential equations since β is an upper semicontinuous correspondence in μ, and not a function in μ.[4] As a result, the dynamical system is represented by

$$\frac{d(E/D)}{dt} = \beta f(E/D) - (a + b)(E/D)$$

$$\frac{d\mu}{dt} = (a + b + c)\mu - \max(1, \mu)f'(E/D)$$

$$\beta = 1 \quad \text{for } \mu > 1 \qquad \beta = 0 \quad \text{for } \mu < 1 \qquad 0 \leq \beta \leq 1 \quad \text{for } \mu = 1$$

It is now obvious that $d\mu/dt = 0$ if and only if

$$\mu = \max(1, \mu)\frac{f'(E/D)}{a + b + c}$$

[3] In this finite time horizon situation, the transversality condition

$$\mu(T)e^{-cT}[E(T)/D(T) - (E/D)_T] = 0 \quad \text{and} \quad \mu(T)e^{-cT} \geq 0$$

must hold. In the infinite time horizon case, the problem is easier, and the transversality condition is simply

$$\lim_{t\to\infty} e^{-ct}\mu(t)(E(t)/D(t)) = 0$$

[4] That β is an upper semicontinuous correspondence in μ is obvious from the following: $\beta = 1$ when $\mu > 1$, $\beta \in [0, 1]$ when $\mu = 1$, and $\beta = 0$ when $\mu < 1$. The dynamics can be easier with this understanding of the correspondence.

Therefore, for $\mu \geq 1$, $d\mu/dt = 0$ if and only if $E/D = (E/D)^*$, as in Figure 1, where $f'(E/D) = a + b + c$. The curvature of $f(E/D)$, as already specified, implies

$$0 < (E/D)^* < (E/D)^+ < (E/D)^{**}$$

One can find furthermore that

$$\left.\frac{d\mu}{d(E/D)}\right|_{\frac{d\mu}{dt} = 0} = \frac{f''(E/D)}{a + b + c} < 0 \quad \text{for } \mu < 1$$

The phase diagram in Figure 2 portrays the dynamics of capital accumulation (or decumulation) and the shadow price of capital (μ). One can see in this diagram that $[(E/D)^*, 1]$ is a saddle point in the $(E/D, \mu)$ space since the stable branches are unique here, which proves that $(E/D)^*$ is the unique and optimum value of equity debt ratio for the firm.

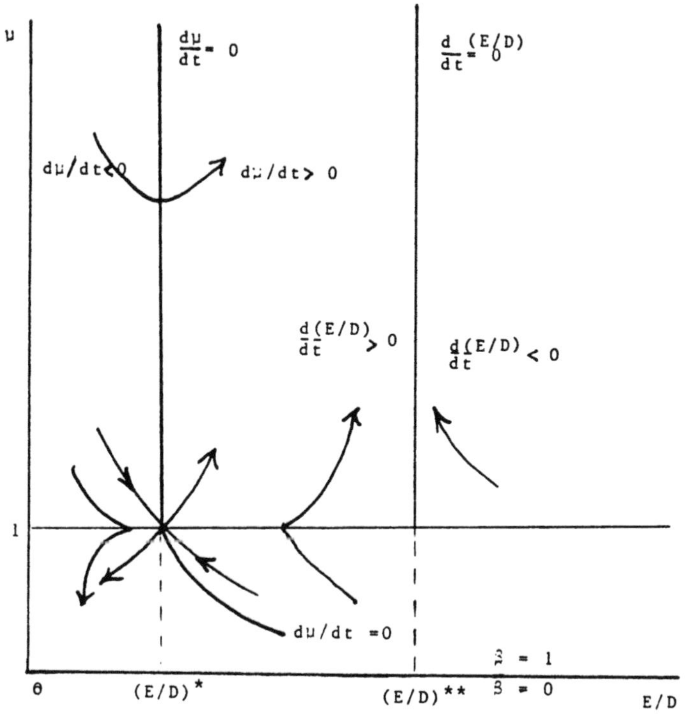

Figure 2

Utility Maximization

In this section, consider that the investors' objective is to maximize their utility over time, where utility is a function of payout of the firm (that is, $U = U[X(t)/D(t)]$). The static and instantaneous utility function of shareholders is intertemporalized, as envisaged by Lintner (1956, 1963); Baumol (1962) and Sau (1969) use the same utility function. The maximization problem, already rooted so well in the existing literature, can then be expressed as follows:

$$Y = \int_0^\infty U(X/D)e^{-ct}\,dt \tag{7}$$

subject to

$$\frac{d(E/D)}{dt} = f(E/D) - X/D - (a + b)(E/D)$$

$$(E/D)_{t=0} = (E/D)_0 \qquad f(E/D) > X/D > 0$$

and $X(t)/D(t)$ is continuous. This means that investors maximize utility under the constraint of the dynamics of equity accumulation, as defined in Eq. (6), initial equity/debt ratio of the firm is given, and payout to investors is positive, but cannot exceed the income of the firm. Assume that utility function is increasing at a diminishing rate:

$$U'(X/D) > 0 \quad \text{and} \quad U''(X/D) < 0$$

In the traditional literature, value maximization is the standard objective; but here we soon find that since at the optimum point utility maximization is equivalent to value maximization, this analytical structure, although operationally different, is not really different from the traditional apparatus. The problem now is to find the time profile of X/D for which the utility integral is dynamically maximized. To do so let us form the following intertemporal maximand:

$$L = \{U(X/D) + \lambda[f(E/D) - X/D - (a + b)(E/D)]\}e^{-ct}\,dt \tag{8}$$

where λ is the dynamic Lagrange multiplier, which means that it is the shadow price of incremental equity per unit of debt, measured in terms of utility. The expression $U(X/D) + \lambda[f(E/D) - X/D - (a + b)(E/D)]$ in Eq. (8) is thus the imputed value of earnings per unit of debt; thus, L stands for the imputed present value of earnings of the firm. As we indicated earlier, we are also engaged in value maximization via this constrained dynamic utility optimization. Following the optimum control principle of Pontryagin et al., we obtain the optimality when the following conditions hold:

$$\frac{\partial L}{\partial (X/D)} = 0 \tag{9}$$

which yields $U'(X/D) = \lambda$, and

$$\frac{\partial L}{\partial (E/D)} = \frac{d\lambda e^{-ct}}{dt}$$

which results in the following expression after a slight algebraic manipulation:

$$f'(E/D) + \frac{d\lambda/dt}{\lambda} - (a + b + c) = 0 \tag{10}$$

Equation (9) states that at the dynamic optimum point, the marginal utility of investors is equal to the shadow price of equity accumulation. In simpler terms, equality between marginal utility and marginal productivity of equity capital defines the necessary condition for optimality. Equation (10) expresses the zero-profit situation (which is the ultimate result of arbitrage in perfectly competitive markets so well recognized by Modigliani and Miller (1958)) for holding equity capital per unit of debt. Here, $f'(E/D)$ measures the marginal productivity of equity per unit of debt, the term $(d\lambda/dt)/\lambda$ is the capital gain, and $a + b + c$ is the loss due to growth of debt, equity depletion and interest rate (rate of discount).

From Eq. (9), one can derive

$$\frac{d\lambda/dt}{\lambda} = \frac{-z[d(X/D)/dt]}{X/D} \tag{11}$$

where $z = -(E/D)[U''(X/D)/U'(X/D)] > 0$ is the celebrated Arrow–Pratt measure of relative risk aversion.[5] Now, the substitution of Eq. (11) into Eq. (10) results in the following expression:

$$\frac{d(X/D)}{dt} = z^{-1}[f'(E/D) - (a + b + c)](X/D) \tag{12}$$

Following the dynamic optimization principle, as outlined in Pontryagin et al. (1962), one can now find that X/D and E/D are intertemporally optimal at $(X/D)^*$ and $(E/D)^*$, respectively, if they satisfy the differential Eqs. (12) and (6). If $d(X/D)/dt = 0$ and $d(E/D)/dt = 0$, that is, if X/D and E/D are held constant with respect to time, then

$$f'[(E/D)^*] = a + b + c \tag{13}$$

[5]See Arrow (1970) and Pratt (1964). In this instance, z is also the elasticity of marginal utility for investors.

and

$$(X/D)^* = f[(E/D)^*] - (a + b)(E/D)^* \tag{14}$$

Now examine Eqs. (12) and (6) more closely. Equation (12) shows that

$$\frac{d(X/D)}{dt} \gtreqless 0 \quad \text{if } f'(E/D) \gtreqless a + b + c \text{ or } (E/D)^* \gtreqless E/D$$

Similarly, one can find that

$$\frac{d(E/D)}{dt} \gtreqless 0 \quad \text{if } f(E/D) - (a + b)E/D \gtreqless X/D$$

Figure 3, which is extracted from Figure 1, depicts the loci of $d(X/D)/dt = 0$ and $d(E/D)/dt = 0$, and the intersection of these loci defines the optimum, that is, the utility-maximizing payout $(X/D)^*$ and equity/debt ratio $(E/D)^*$. The

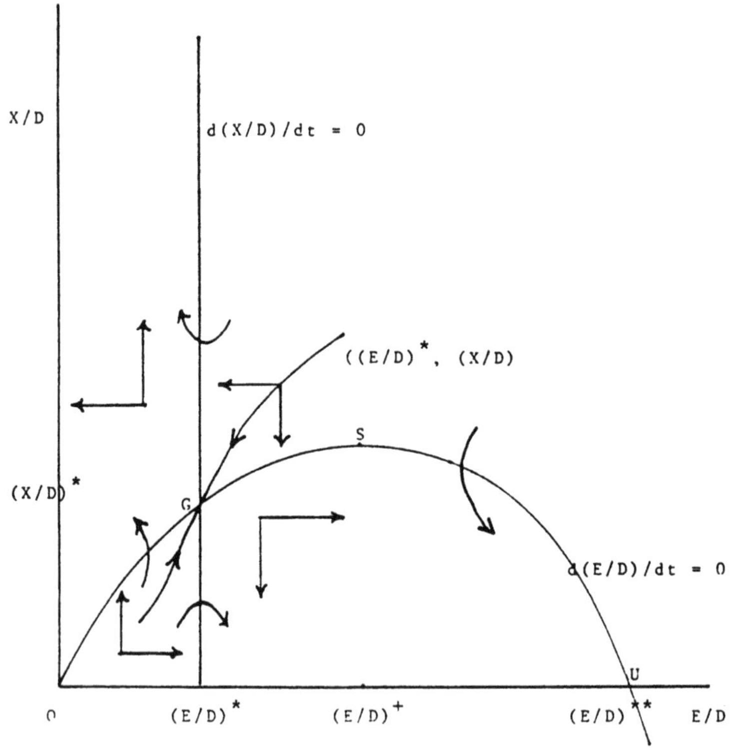

Figure 3

phase diagram (Figure 2) portrays the dynamics of X/D and E/D. Because the vertical axis represents X/D and the horizontal axis represents E/D, the humped curve here obviously represents $d(E/D)/dt = 0$. At $E/D = (E/D)^*$, when Eq. (13) is satisfied, $d(X/D)/dt = 0$; here it is represented by the vertical line GH, the perpendicular on $(E/D)^*$. Obviously, at the point G on the humped curve $OGSU$ where the perpendicular GH (at the point $(E/D)^*$ on the E/D axis) intersects it, the slope is c (see Figure 1).

The coordinates of this intersection define the optimum configuration. The loci $d(X/D)/dt = 0$ and $d(E/D)/dt = 0$ bring out four distinct zones, and in these zones, movement of X/D and E/D is indicated by a pair of arrows. It is clear now that if initial equity/debt ratio is equal to $(E/D)^*$, then this capital structure is optimally invariant over time. However, if initial capital structure is different from the optimum structure, it will converge toward the optimum structure by moving down the stable branches of the saddle point.[6] That is,

$$\lim_{t \to \infty} X(t)/D(t) = (X/D)^*$$

and

$$\lim_{t \to \infty} E(t)/D(t) = (E/D)^*$$

It is now clear that the utility-maximizing equity/debt ratio is exactly equal to the payout-maximizing equity/debt ratio. This means that no matter what objective function is chosen, optimal capital structure is identical in the intertemporal optimization framework.

REFERENCES

Arrow, K. 1970. *Essays in the Theory of Risk Bearing*, Chicago: Markham.

Barnea, A., R. A. Haugen, and L. W. Senbet. 1981. Market imperfections, agency problems, and capital structure: A review, *Financial Management* 10(2).

Baron, D. P. 1974. Default risk, homemade leverage, and the Modigliani–Miller Theorem, *American Economic Review*.

[6]The stability is obtained by the Taylor expansion around the coordinates of $(X/D)^*$ and $(E/D)^*$.

$$\frac{d(X/D)}{dt} \approx \frac{(X/D)^* f''(E/D)}{z(X/D)}[(E/D) - (E/D)^*]$$

$$\frac{d(E/D)}{dt} \approx -[(X/D) - (X/D)^*] + c[(E/D) - (E/D)^*]$$

The eigenvalues of these equations are real and of opposite sign; hence, the stability is unquestionably established.

Baumol, W. J. 1962. On the theory of expansion of the firm, *American Economic Review*.

Baumol, W. J., and B. Malkiel. 1967. The firm's optimal debt–equity combination and the cost of capital, *Quarterly Journal of Economics* 91(4).

Baxter, N. 1967. Leverage, risk of ruin, and the cost of capital, *Journal of Finance* 22(3).

Bierman, H., and J. Thomas. 1972. Ruin considerations and debt issuance, *Journal of Financial and Quantitative Analysis* 7(1).

Brennan, M. J., and E. J. Schwartz. 1978. Corporate income taxes, valuation and the problem of optimal capital structure, *Journal of Business*.

Brewer, D. E., and J. B. Michaelson. 1965. The cost of capital, corporation finance and the theory of investment: Comment, *American Economic Review*.

Chen, A. H. 1978a. A theory of corporate bankruptcy and optimal capital structure, in J. Bicksler (Ed.), *Handbook of Financial Economics*, Amsterdam: North-Holland.

Chen, A. H. 1978b. Recent developments in the cost of debt capital, *Journal of Finance*.

Chen, A. H., and E. H. Kim. 1979. Theories of corporate debt policy: A synthesis, *Journal of Finance*.

DeAngelo, H., and R. Masulis. 1980. Optimal capital structure under corporate and personal taxation, *Journal of Financial Economics*.

Durand, D. 1952. Cost of debt and equity funds for business: Trends and problems of measurement, *Conference on Research in Business Finance*, New York: National Bureau of Economic Research.

Durand, D. 1959. Cost of capital, corporation finance and the theory of investment: Comment, *American Economic Review*.

Fama, E. F., and M. H. Miller. 1972. *The Theory of Finance*, New York: Holt, Rinehart & Winston.

Ghosh, D. K. 1992a. Optimum capital structure redefined, *Financial Review*.

Ghosh, D. K. 1992b. Capital structure and dividend policy in a unified intertemporal optimization framework, mimeo.

Hamada, R. S. 1969. Portfolio analysis, market equilibrium, and corporation finance, *Journal of Finance*.

Hirschleifer, J. 1966. Investment decision under uncertainty: Applications of the state-preference approach, *Quarterly Journal of Economics* 80(2).

Jensen, M. C., and W. H. Meckling. 1977. Theory of the firm: Managerial behavior, agency costs and ownership structure, *Journal of Financial Economics*.

Kim, E. H. 1978. A mean variance theory of optimal capital structure and corporate debt capacity, *Journal of Finance*.

Kraus, A., and R. H. Litzenberger. 1973. A state-preference model of optimal financial leverage, *Journal of Finance*.

Lee, W. Y., and H. H. Barker. 1977. Bankruptcy costs and the firm's optimal debt capacity: A positive theory of capital structure, *Southern Economic Journal*.

Lintner, J. 1956. The cost of capital and optimal financing of corporate growth, *Journal of Finance* 11(1).

Lintner, J. 1963. Optimal dividends and corporate growth under uncertainty, *Quarterly Journal of Economics*.

Merton, R. C. 1971. Optimum consumption and portfolio rules in a continuous time model, *Journal of Economic Theory*.

Miller, M. H. 1988. The Modigliani–Miller propositions after thirty years, *Journal of Economic Perspectives* 2(4).
Modigliani, F., and M. H. Miller. 1958. The cost of capital, corporation finance and the theory of investment, *American Economic Review.*
Modigliani, F., and M. H. Miller. 1959. The cost of capital, corporation finance, and the theory of investment: Reply, *American Economic Review.*
Pontryagin, L. S., V. G. Boltyanskii, R. V. Gamkrelidze, and E. F. Mishchenko. 1962. *The Mathematical Theory of Optimal Processes,* New York: Wiley.
Pratt, J. 1965. Risk aversion in the small and in the large, *Econometrica.*
Robichek, A. A., and S. C. Myers. 1965. *Optimal Financing Decisions,* Englewood Cliffs, NJ: Prentice-Hall.
Ross, S. A. 1977. The determination of financial structure: The incentive signalling approach, *Bell Journal of Economics.*
Rubinstein, M. 1973. A mean-variance synthesis of corporate financial theory, *Journal of Finance.*
Rubinstein, M. 1973. Corporate financial policy in segmented security markets, *Journal of Financial and Quantitative Analysis.*
Sau, R. K. 1969. The optimal rate of investment in a firm, *Journal of Finance* 24(1).
Schwartz, E., and R. Aronson. 1967. Some surrogate evidence of the concept of optimal financial structure, *Journal of Finance* 22(1).
Scott, D. 1972. Evidence on the importance of financial structure, *Financial Management* 50(2).
Scott, D. 1976. A theory of optimal capital structure, *The Bell Journal of Economics and Management Science.*
Scott, D. 1977. Bankruptcy, secured debt, and optimal capital structure, *Journal of Finance.*
Stiglitz, J. 1969. A re-examination of the Modigliani–Miller theorem, *American Economic Review.*
Stiglitz, J. 1972. Some aspects of the pure theory of corporate finance: Bankruptcies and takeovers, *The Bell Journal of Economics and Management Science.*
Stiglitz, J. 1973. Taxation, financial policy, and the cost of capital, *Journal of Public Economics.*
Stiglitz, J. 1974. On the irrelevance of corporate financial policy, *American Economic Review* 64(6).
Taggart, R. A. 1980. Taxes and corporate capital structure in an incomplete market, *Journal of Finance.*
Turnbull, S. M. 1979. Debt capacity, *Journal of Finance* 34(4).
Turnbull, S. M. 1981. Debt capacity: Erratum, *Journal of Finance* 36(1).

Chapter 9

Is Diversification in International Capital Markets Beneficial? Issues, Evidence, and Prospects

Krishnan Dandapani and Jerry Haar

The 1980s marked a decade of significant change and transformation in global financial markets. An increase in investor sophistication, advancements in electronics and communication technology, the breakdown of national and international investment barriers, and the development of international investment instruments, such as the American Depository Receipt, have indeed changed the landscape of the global market place. Additionally, improvements in the operations of stock exchanges, the comprehensive revisions in security law, and improved accounting and auditing standards have had far-reaching impacts as well. One of the most striking and far-reaching developments of the last decade was the tremendous growth of portfolio investment in emerging equity markets. And the trend continues. Developing countries in Asia and Latin America have embarked on domestic economic reforms, including liberalizing foreign portfolio investment conditions and privatizing state-owned companies. Developing country equity markets have evolved during this time from virgin territory to an increasingly well-developed arena of global finance. In addition to the facts mentioned above, several others explain this explosive growth: notably the trend toward measuring portfolio managers' performance against international indexes as well as local benchmarks; the large and increasing amount of funds at the disposal of institutional investors in the United States, Europe, and Japan, presently estimated in excess of US $3 trillion along with a long-term orientation of these investors; and the profitability performance of emerging markets, which has outperformed most developed market benchmarks during the last five years.

Not all emerging equity markets, let alone foreign stock markets in general, have performed well. This poses an interesting research question of particular relevance to both personal and institutional investors: Is international diversification beneficial, and if so, what is the optimal method of achieving its benefits? Various researchers, most notably Lessard (1974), Stapleton and Subrahmanyan (1977), and Jacquillat and Solnik (1977/78), have examined these questions with widely varying conclusions. The essence of the prior studies is that the diversification benefits seem to depend on the degree of international market segmentation/integration, the degree of correlation/co-movements among the markets, the impact of exchange rates, and other selected factors. Developing upon previous research work, this chapter examines the benefits of diversifying in international equity markets, with special attention to the different performance measures in selected equity markets of the world from 1987 to 1990.

ISSUES IN INTERNATIONAL DIVERSIFICATION

Problems in Global Investing

Global investing, attractive as it appears, is fraught with complexities and difficulties that dissuade potential investors from diversifying their portfolios internationally. To begin with, there are, of course, unfamiliar investment practices. These may be of a regulatory and/or tax nature, and when combined with another intervening factor, varied accounting rules, increase the perceived risk for the investor. Additionally, many local firms authorized to have their shares traded in foreign markets are required to comply with local standards set for filing financial statements; however, these firms invariably would not be able to meet the high standards set by the U.S. Securities and Exchange Commission.

In addition to government regulations, taxes, and problems of political instability, factors such as multiple currencies and currency appreciation/depreciation further compound the difficulties of international portfolio diversification. There are other less important, yet nonetheless, annoying problems (such as the difficulty in getting financial statements and in buying shares due to the varying time zones) that can cause complications in global investing.

Advantages of Global Investing

There are a number of advantages to global investing. The most important is the broader choice of securities. There are a variety of industrial groups, companies, and mutual funds worldwide whose composition, competitiveness, and overall attractiveness within the global financial markets are particularly appealing to both personal and institutional investors. Another advantage for the investor is reduced risk through diversification. Slower growth or recession in the home market with its concomitant decline in portfolio worth can be cushioned or protected completely through investments in countries whose economies are growing at high levels. Global investing also enables the investor to take advantage immediately of certain periods of fast growth in other economies. Spain, Mexico, and Chile in the late 1980s are examples of fast-growth countries whose equity markets were viewed as very attractive to foreign investors. Finally, for the participating host countries, global investing presents a mechanism for attracting stable and long-term capital. The debt explosion of the early to mid 1980s thoroughly convinced both public and private borrowers and lenders of the need for equity—foreign and domestic—rather than debt as the principal means by which to stimulate economic growth and development.

Methods of Global Investing

Three principal methods of global investing attract international investors: direct purchase of shares, American depository receipts, and mutual funds.

Direct purchase of shares. There are over 25,000 foreign companies' shares that one can invest in, but 80% of the foreign shares do not qualify for purchase on margin. Therefore, one cannot borrow against them. One can, however, identify some super achiever shares and take advantage of that. Most U.S. brokers do not handle foreign stock transactions of less than $10,000. By some estimates $100,000 is the minimum size of a portfolio necessary to diversify adequately.

Unfortunately, these transactions are difficult. To begin with, the settlement process in certain markets, like Spain and Italy, can take as long as 15 days. Additionally it is difficult to get delivery of stock certificates and to keep track of foreign stock performance. Orders are subject to size requirements and fees can be very high.

American depository receipts (ADRs). ADRs are certificates for shares of foreign corporations on deposit with a large (non-U.S.) bank affiliated with a major financial institution. ADRs, denominated in U.S. dollars, offer investors an alternative within their home markets to investing in foreign markets. ADRs enable the investors to receive all the dividends and capital gains and are exchangeable with the underlying securities. (For a detailed description of ADRs, see Haar et al. (1990).) ADRs were developed in 1927, and there was a surge of ADRs in the 1980s as the non-American stock markets boomed. Tables 1 and 2 list the top 25 ADRs in the United States and ADRs from Latin America.

One of the advantages of ADRs is that investors who understand the operations, performance, and attractiveness of a foreign firm can invest in that company without having to purchase equities in the firm's home markets. Other advantages are the fact that ADRs comply with the SEC's strict reporting requirements, the market for ADRs is highly liquid, and most ADR prices are widely available. ADRs are not without problems, however. Among these are the difficulty in securing information about the company, the fact that ADR prices may not be available, and the fact that ADRs may be thinly traded.

Table 1
Top 25 ADRs Traded on U.S. Exchanges
(May 1991, ranked by volume)

Name of security	Volume of shares traded (millions)	Value ($ in millions)
Telefonos de Mexico S.A. C.V. Ser A	350.0	849.0
Telefonos de Mexico S.A. C.V. Ser L	37.0	1012.9
Glaxo Holdings PLC	23.1	929.4
Royal Dutch Petroleum Co.	19.4	1593.5
Saatchi & Saatchi Co. PLC	17.3	18.4
ADT Ltd.	12.7	163.6
Hanson PLC	11.8	229.1
Grand Metropolitan PLC	10.5	290.7
Unilever N.V.	10.3	858.1
Reuters Holdings PLC	8.9	375.1
Ericsson Telephone Co. "B" shares	8.8	273.3
Smith Kline Beecham PLC "A" shares	8.0	484.1
Telefonica de Espana S.A.	4.4	128.0
B.A.T. Industries PLC	3.6	43.3
Imperial Chemical Industries PLC	3.3	273.5
British Petroleum Company PLC	3.1	224.1
Norsk Hydro A/S	2.9	86.4
Tubos de Acero de Mexico	2.9	27.8
Philips N.V.	2.7	43.7
British Airways PLC	2.7	78.9
WPP Group PLC	2.5	16.1
The News Corp. Ltd.	2.5	34.1
Empresa Nacional de Electricidad S.A.	2.3	51.3
British Telecommunications PLC	2.1	141.2
Repsol S.A.	2.1	51.6

Source: Bank of New York.

Mutual funds. Out of the more than 1000 equity funds in the United States, approximately 100 funds invest exclusively outside the United States. The advantages of these kinds of funds are their professional management and their diversification benefits. These equity funds include both growth and income funds and are equally divided in terms of the number of funds and their availability. Among these funds are the following:

(1) **Global funds:** These funds invest anywhere in the world as well as in the domestic markets. The funds shift monies between domestic and foreign markets as dictated market needs, although most managers tend to split the holdings equally.
(2) **International funds:** These funds invest in any country outside the United States.

(3) **Regional funds:** Investment in one particular region or part of the world such as the Pacific Basin Fund is the object of these funds.
(4) **Single country funds:** For investors who are comfortable with one country and its currency trends, these are viewed as the ideal funds. By 1989 there were 20 in existence, namely Australia, Brazil, Canada, Chile, France, Germany, Switzerland, Iberia, Indonesia, Italy, Japan, Korea, Malaysia, Mexico, Scandinavia, South Africa, Spain, Taiwan, Thailand, and the United Kingdom. Only five of these funds are open-end. The oldest is the Japan Fund, established approximately 29 years ago. Funds of countries rich in natural resources, such as Australia and Canada, have been deemed good inflation hedges.

The question of whether country funds are better than direct portfolio investment is debatable. For some markets, such as South Korea and Taiwan, country

Table 2
Latin American ADRs

	Where traded	Ratio	When issued
Mexico, unsponsored			
Cifra	OTC	1 : 1	na
Industria Electrica de Mexico (IEM)	OTC	1 : 1	na
Telmex	Nasdaq	1 : 1	na
Mexico, sponsored			
Tasma	Amex	1 : 1	1964
Grupo	OTC	1 : 2	1989
Corp. Industrial San Luis Series A	OTC	1 : 1	1990
Corp. Industrial San Luis Series A-1	OTC	1 : 1	1990
Corp. Industrial San Luis Series A-2	OTC	1 : 1	1990
EPN	OTC	1 : 1	1990
Grupo Synkro	OTC	1 : 1	1990
Tolmex B Shares	OTC	1 : 1	1990
Tolmex (convertible bond)	144A	1 : 1	1990
Empaques Ponderosa	144A	1 : 4	1991
Femsa	144A	1 : 1	1991
Grupo Gigante	144A	1 : 1	1991
Internacional de Ceramica	144A	1 : 1	1991
Internacional de Ceramica	OTC	1 : 1	1991
Ponderosa Industrial	OTC	1 : 1	1991
Telmex Series L	NYSE	1 : 2	1991
Vitro	144A	1 : 1	1991
Chile, sponsored			
Compania de Telefonos de Chile (CTC)	NYSE	1 : 17	1990
Venezuela, sponsored			
Sivensa	OTC	1 : 3	1991

Note. ADR issues as of 15 October 1991. na, not available; 144A, private placement.
Source: Euromoney Supplement (Nov. 1991).

funds are the only authorized channels of investment because of government restrictions on foreign investment. These funds also enable the foreign investor to avoid difficulties associated with inadequate information and cumbersome settlement and repatriation procedures. Malaysia, Thailand, and the Philippines have granted some closed-end funds certain tax and other benefits, as they are viewed as long-term stable investors.

For the invested country, also, this has certain benefits. These funds represent significant capital transfers when debt, particularly that of less developed countries, becomes overwhelming. Additionally, this form of foreign investment is portfolio in nature; therefore, it does not create the problem of foreign control. The investments from closed funds tend to stay invested in the country, unlike other direct investment, which may be withdrawn in times of trouble or peril. Most of the single-country funds are registered in the United States or the United Kingdom, even though some may be registered outside the United States in a tax haven such as the Cayman Islands.

The principal advantages of fund investing are professional management, security of exchange listing, and regulation. The disadvantages are that sometimes most country funds trade at a discount from net asset value because of weak economic fundamentals, poor market performance, few foreign investment restrictions, and greater perceived risk. High annual expenses, which can range from 0.7 to 3.0% of net asset values, are clearly a disadvantage. Additionally, foreign countries impose varying percentages of withholding tax on dividend income. It is also difficult for the investor to "make a killing" in the market by identifying a stock with superior performance. Finally, there are restrictions on capital repatriation, fewer disclosure requirements, and currency fluctuations.

Deciding on a fund or the best source for investing internationally is a difficult task. It depends primarily on the individual investor's situation, based on the considerations outlined above. Clearly, economic outlook, stock market performance, exchange rate, and political stability are major risk factors to consider.

EVIDENCE OF BENEFITS OF INTERNATIONAL DIVERSIFICATION

Hypothesis

In this segment we evaluate the benefits of international diversification for a recent time segment. The American stock markets have dominated the world for a long time and have historically represented about 35 to 60% of the world capitalization over the last few decades. Investing in international markets has traditionally been hampered due to a variety of impediments, such as fluctuations in foreign currencies, lack of information regarding tax and regulatory aspects, communication and language problems, transaction and commission costs, lack of depth, liquidity and breadth of international markets, and absence of market makers. Hence, most investors have confined their investments to the U.S. markets.

However, with the development of theoretical models of portfolio sections, and other academic research and normative rules establishing the advantages of diversification, the usefulness of international equity markets to diversity risk was explored. The earliest rigorous work in this area can be traced to Grubel (1968), Levy and Sarnat (1970), Grubel and Fadner (1971). These studies established the large potential gains to be achieved relative to domestic diversification. Lessard (1974) showed that only a small proportion of the variance of national portfolios is common in an international context, and considerable risk reduction can be accomplished through international investing. He also showed that the industry dimension is much less important than the national dimension and is a less important part of the diversification strategy as well. Jacquillat and Solnik (1977/78) show that while there are tremendous gains to be realized from international diversification, multinational companies are a poor tool for accomplishing this end.

The implications of these studies for the current work are that the one optimal method of accomplishing internal diversification is by investing in world stock indices. The difficulty in testing the benefits of international diversification arises due to the unavailability of accurate data on international investments. There were less than five active country funds as of 1985, and usage of country stock market indices would be analogous to buying a country fund.

Another aspect to consider in international investment is the role of exchange rates. The effect of exchange rate influence on international diversification seems mixed. Levy and Sarnat (1975) found substantial influence emanating from exchange rate fluctuations, while many other researchers have found that in the context of international portfolios, exchange risk matters much less than would be expected. But, as Solnik (1988) points out, this could be due to the countries and the time period covered and whether the exchanges were fixed or flexible. Recent studies by Solnik (1984) and Adler and Simon (1986) show a weak correlation between stock indices and currency movements. The implication of these studies for our work is that the influence of the exchange rate has to be minimized for meaningful interpretation of our results.

Another potential problem with international diversification is the measurement of gains from diversification and using the evidence to develop profitable trading rules. Madura and Abernathy (1985), using a more recent data set, examine the gains from international diversification. Using stock market indices from eight countries for the period January 1978 through 1981, they show that while there are considerable advantages to be gained from international diversification, the potential gains shown in several studies from an ex post analysis do not reveal the whole picture for constructing useful trading or investment strategies.

One persistent problem is that the ex ante efficient portfolios do not necessarily turn out to be ex post efficient. Therefore, in this study we develop the theme of using ex post data for ex ante strategies and show how trading strategies could be developed under such an evaluation procedure. Classifying the data into different time segments, we test whether the efficient set in one period could be used to develop profitable trading strategy in subsequent periods.

Methodology

Based on the prior studies, we evaluate the performance of the selected equity markets of the world during the time period January 1987 through January 1990. Well-diversified stock indices were chosen as valid and representative indicators of a country's capital markets. The data for constructing the return series are obtained from *Barrons,* wherein the weekly prices of the equity indices are reported. For simplicity of analysis, it is assumed that the indices capture all the returns and risks inherent in investing in a particular country.

The data are analyzed from the perspective of an American investor, and we compare the various investment strategies with the benchmark portfolio—investing 100% of the funds in the U.S. index represented by the *Standard & Poors 500 Index*. In the initial stages of the analysis we used the perfect capital markets assumptions; however, we found that these assumptions can be relaxed without the loss of generality. The benchmark portfolio is compared with other investments, such as investing in equal proportions of the foreign market. The many problems that exist in overseas investment are also addressed. We use data from the following countries: Australia, Belgium, Canada, France, Hong Kong, Italy, Japan, the Netherlands, Singapore, Sweden, Switzerland, United Kingdom, United States, and West Germany.

The prices of the indices are converted to return series and, using their respective currencies, converted into dollar returns. From this currency, we adjust for the risk-free return, which is the corresponding weekly U.S. Treasury Bill rate with seven-day maturity. Having performed this procedure for each index, we compute mean returns and the standard deviations using the standard formulas mentioned below.

In the next stage of analysis the portfolios are evaluated using the standard portfolio performance measures. The standard measures of portfolio evaluation used in this study are the Sharpe, Jensen, and Treynor measures of performance, which are widely used in the assessment of well-diversified mutual funds.

Finally, the performance of these indices over different time segments is evaluated. For this purpose we separate the time horizon into six segments of six months each, and evaluate the performance of the indices over these time intervals. Based on the prior time segment's risk/return level, the portfolios are classified into three groups: low risk, intermediate risk, and high risk. This information, which is based on the indices' performance during the previous time segment, is utilized to form an ex ante portfolio during the subsequent time segment. The benchmark portfolios used for comparison are the policy of investing in the U.S. market alone to earn the rate of return of the *Standard & Poors 500.*

The classification on the basis of risk into low-, intermediate-, and high-risk categories during the prior time segment, and making a diversified investment in the subsequent period, follow the procedure advocated by Madura and Abernathy (1985). We use the standard measures of portfolio evaluation of the Sharpe, Jensen, and Treynor indices on such portfolios and evaluate their performance.

Analysis of Results

The risk-adjusted performance of the different countries using the Sharpe measure of portfolio evaluation is reported in Table 3. Table 4 illustrates the risk-adjusted performance using the Treynor measure of portfolio performance. Table 5 reports the performance measure using the Jensen index. In general, our results show that there is considerable gain in investing internationally; however, there is no single portfolio combination or trading rule that consistently outperforms the prudent strategy of spreading investment in all countries, suggesting a strong form of efficiency. Our results are similar to those of Logue (1982) and Madura and Abernathy (1985) in predicting ex ante efficient investment using ex post performance. None of the ex post efficient portfolios consistently turns out to be the optimal portfolio ex ante, indicating the inherent difficulty in building profitable trading strategies.

PROSPECTS

The prospects for diversification in international capital markets appear bright, indeed. In examining emerging markets—a relatively recent phenomenon—the total capitalization of 30 of these tracked by the International Finance Corporation's Emerging Market Database grew from $85.6 billion in 1980 to more than $700 billion in 1991, while the number of companies listed more than doubled to almost 12,000 during this period. These emerging markets have performed as well or better than those of more established markets over the last seven years. To illustrate, in 1989 alone, in U.S. dollar terms, the five markets with the highest price increases were Turkey, up 300%; Argentina, up 136%; Taiwan, up 95%; Thailand, up 85%; and Greece, up 67%. In contrast, Japanese stocks increased by 12% and U.S. stocks by 25%. In fact 10 of the 19 emerging markets monitored in depth by the International Finance Corporation outperformed the U.S. stock market's banner year of 1989.

The boom in emerging markets is just beginning. It is true that things have cooled since the late 1980s. The inflated premiums to net asset value that many country funds enjoyed over the last several years have fallen. However, a positive reversal of fortune has indeed begun. Taiwan, Brazil, Chile, and Mexico are all markets whose stock prices outperform those in the United States, the United Kingdom, and Japan by a wide margin.

Table 3
Risk-Adjusted Performance Measured by the Sharpe Index

Country index	1987	1988	1989
Australia	−0.121	0.010	0.223
Belgium	−0.180	0.166	0.436
Canada	0.067	−0.038	0.183
France	−0.243	0.343	0.226
Hong Kong	−0.089	0.016	0.282
Italy	−0.204	0.224	0.023
Japan	0.100	0.261	0.184
Netherlands	−0.219	0.077	0.337
Singapore	−0.116	−0.048	0.278
Sweden	−0.088	0.243	0.149
Switzerland	−0.063	0.187	0.150
United Kingdom	−0.063	0.058	0.101
United States	−0.193	0.018	0.137
West Germany	−0.041	−0.039	0.424

Regional attractiveness will vary as well. Asia funds were very attractive for a while, then Latin America; and during the past year and a half Eastern European funds, especially those in Hungary, Poland, and Czechoslovakia, have received wide attention. However, fund managers, corporate financing specialists, and asset traders have been rethinking the opportunity and profits envisioned in Eastern Europe since Communism died. Much, they believe, has proven to be illusive. Privatization, the belief in market-oriented forces, and management reform have not truly taken hold in that part of the world. Elsewhere in the world, it remains to be seen whether a postsanctioned South Af-

Table 4
Risk-Adjusted Performance Measured by the Treynor Index

Country index	1987	1988	1989
Australia	−0.00954	−0.00090	0.01720
Belgium	−0.02797	−0.02584	0.06235
Canada	0.00545	−0.00132	0.01311
France	−0.01779	0.06553	0.03266
Hong Kong	−0.03320	0.20461	0.03210
Italy	−0.02916	−0.03834	0.01126
Japan	0.01117	−0.01995	−0.10797
Netherlands	−0.01182	−0.01001	0.01895
Singapore	−0.04007	−0.00327	−0.07887
Sweden	−0.00645	0.02122	0.01604
Switzerland	−0.00466	−0.00848	0.01092
United Kingdom	−0.00471	0.02901	−0.03086
United States	−0.00811	0.00032	0.00283
West Germany	−0.00325	−0.00729	−0.06452

Table 5
Risk-Adjusted Performance Measured by the Jensen Index (Alpha)

Country index	1987	1988	1989
Australia	−0.00145	0.00037	0.00396
Belgium	−0.00449	0.00477	0.00671
Canada	0.01562	−0.00110	0.00176
France	−0.00508	0.00744	0.00955
Hong Kong	−0.00611	0.00038	0.00670
Italy	−0.00552	0.00588	0.00060
Japan	0.00898	0.00561	0.00463
Netherlands	−0.00285	0.00455	0.00496
Singapore	−0.00829	−0.00118	0.00627
Sweden	0.00093	0.00646	0.00297
Switzerland	0.00197	0.00470	0.00246
United Kingdom	0.00274	0.00164	0.00597
United States	0.00000	0.00000	0.00000
West Germany	0.00297	−0.00180	0.01312

rica, especially in light of the decline in gold prices, will prove to be as attractive as many investors and traders had earlier thought.

In general, with a fluid emerging market situation in Latin America and Asia, the prospects overall should prove to be attractive for investors. Latin America is especially promising. Emerging from the debt decade of the 1980s, countries in the region are adopting privatization, market reform, and fiscal and monetary measures that have produced very positive impacts on capital markets. As illustrated in Table 6, Chile, Venezuela, and Mexican funds have doubled or tripled since their initial listing.

CONCLUSION

Interest in international investments is increasing worldwide as technology makes the world a truly global marketplace. In our research, we have identified and examined the relevant issues, prospects for growth, and benefits derived from international diversification. In general, our results suggest that during the time period examined, a U.S. investor would have gained substantially by investing in the international equity market. Our results are confirmed by Cumby and Glen (1990) who also examine the performance of 15 U.S.-based internationally diversified mutual funds for the period 1982–1988 and conclude that the funds outperform investing domestically in the United States.

Nevertheless, their results show that mutual funds, as successful as they are, still do not outperform the international equity index. The many different portfolios we constructed outperformed the risk-averse strategy of investing domestically in the United States. While the different performance measures suggest different rank ordering of countries in order of returns, we can state equivocally that the returns for international investments are higher, even after adjusting for

Table 6
Latin American Funds

Launch date	Fund	Initial amount	Recent value ($ m)
	U.S. closed-end funds		
Jun 81	Mexico	120.0	497.0
Apr 88	Brazil Fund	150.0	143.0
Mar 89	New World Investment Fund	62.5	148.0
Sep 89	Chile Fund	74.7	207.7
Aug 90	Mexico Equity & Income Fund	70.0	100.0
Oct 90	Emerging Mexico Fund	55.8	95.7
Dec 90	Latin America Investment Fund	58.3	107.8
Oct 91	Argentina Fund	5.8	—
	International closed-end funds		
Oct 87	Equity Fund of Brazil	87.5	96.3
Jul 89	Equity Fund of Latin America	114.5	309.3
Nov 89	Genesis Chile Fund	60.0	214.0
Nov 89	Sovereign High Yield Investment Co.	80.0	100.0
Feb 90	Five Arrows Chile Fund	75.0	181.8
Feb 90	GT Chile Growth Fund	100.0	311.0
Jul 90	Latin American Investment Trust	75.0	118.0
Aug 90	First Mexico Income Fund	60.0	79.0
Dec 90	Latin American Capital Appreciation Fund	72.0	72.0
Apr 91	Mexican Horizons Investment Co.	25.3	28.8
Apr 91	Baring Puma Fund	60.0	104.0
Apr 91	Genesis Condor Fund	12.0	20.0
May 91	Venezuela High Income Fund	57.5	100.0
Aug 91	South America Fund	64.0	64.1
Sep 91	Latin America Capital Fund	47.0	—
Oct 91	Latin American Extra Yield Fund		
	Open-end funds		
Nov 87	Brazilian Investment Co.	0.0	61.2
Dec 89	Mexican Investment Co.	30.0	66.4
Dec 90	Schroder Latin America Fund	7.0	18.0
Feb 91	Argentinian Investment Co.	0.0	55.1
Apr 91	GT Latin America Fund	11.7	30.2
Jul 91	BEA/Vestcorp Latin American Debt Fund	4.7	10.6
Aug 91	GT Latin America Growth Fund	100.0	—
Sep 91	Latin American Companies Trust	10.0	—
Sep 91	Mexico Liquid Assets Fund	32.0	—

Source: Euromoney (Nov. 1991).

transactions and commission costs. In essence, the benefits from international diversification are real and substantial. Consequently, the future development of vehicles to promote international investments appears to hold great promise.

REFERENCES

Adler, M., and D. Simon. 1986. Exchange risk surprises in international portfolios, *Journal of Portfolio Management* 12(2):44–53.

Cumby, R. E., and J. D. Glen. 1990. Evaluating the performance of international mutual funds, *The Journal of Finance,* 497–521.

Grubel, H. G. 1968. Internationally diversified portfolios, *American Economic Review,* 1229–1314.

Grubel, H. G., and K. Fadner. 1971. The interdependence of international equity markets, *The Journal of Finance* 26(1):89–94.

Haar, J., K. Dandapani, and S. P. Haar. 1990. The American depository receipt (ADR): A creative financial tool for multinational companies, *Global Finance Journal,* 163–171.

Jacquillat, B., and B. Solnik. 1977/78. Multinationals are poor tools for diversification, *Journal of Portfolio Management* 4(2):8–12.

Lessard, D. R. 1974. World, national and industry factors in equity returns, *The Journal of Finance* 29(2):379–391.

Levy, H., and M. Sarnat. 1970. International diversification of investment portfolios, *American Economic Review,* 668–675.

Levy, H., and M. Sarnat. 1975. Devaluation, risk, and the portfolio analysis of international investments, in Elton and Gruber (Eds.), *International Capital Markets,* New York: North Holland.

Logue, D. E. 1982. An experiment in international diversification, *Journal of Portfolio Management* 9(1):22–27.

Madura, J., and G. Abernathy. 1985. Playing the international stock diversification game with an unmarked deck, *Journal of Business Research* 13:465–471.

Solnik, B. 1984. Stock prices and monetary variables: The international evidence, *Financial Analysts Journal* 40(2):69–73.

Solnik, B. 1988. *International Investments,* Reading, MA: Addison-Wesley.

Stapleton, R. C., and M. G. Subrahmanyan. 1977. Market imperfections, capital market equilibrium, and corporate finance, *Journal of Finance* 32(2):307–319.

Chapter 10

International Co-movements of Capital Markets: Evidence from Two Scandinavian Stock Markets

Teppo Martikainen, Ilkka Virtanen, and Paavo Yli-Olli

International asset pricing and portfolio diversification have reached increasing attention in the empirical research of finance. This is because most of the national capital markets have experienced rapid deregulation and integration in recent years. This development has enhanced the efficiency in the international allocation of capital. Numerous studies have investigated relationships between the average returns of different stock markets. In an early paper, Makridakis and Wheelwright (1974) investigated the short-term stability of the relationships between 14 stock market indices and reported that the co-movements of international stock exchanges seem to be random processes. Similar conclusions have been drawn by Hilliard (1979). However, most studies provide results suggesting a higher level of stability and stronger co-movements of international stock markets (see, for example, Ibbotson et al., 1982; Philippatos et al., 1989; von Furstenberg and Jeon, 1989; Meric and Meric, 1989; Grinold et al., 1989; Jeon and von Furstenberg, 1990; Malkamäki et al., 1991).

In the context of the international CAPM, a typical approach has been to study the sensitivities of individual assets to a worldwide market portfolio (for a test based on the consumption CAPM, see Wheatley, 1988). As suggested by Solnik (1977), an efficient way to test for market segmentation and integration would be to specify the type of imperfection that might create it and to study its specific impact on portfolio optimality and asset pricing. Assuming this specific imperfection to be due to the inability of a group of investors to trade in a subset of securities as a result of portfolio restrictions imposed by some governments, Errunza and Losq (1985) defined the conditional market risk based on return behavior of different stock markets. Some empirical evidence of mild segmentation of the world's capital markets was reported. Their results were further extended by Bradfield (1990) for South African markets. He found that a large proportion of shares in the Johannesburg Stock Exchange appeared to be influenced by the movements in the New York Stock Exchange, but only a small proportion of stocks were influenced by the U.K. and Japanese stock markets. In general, the proposed multimarket model seemed to provide useful information about the risk characteristics of individual South African stocks. Hietala (1988) reported relatively low betas for Finnish securities with respect to a worldwide market portfolio. Recently, Martikainen et al. (1991) found that Finnish securities have significant Swedish risk components, whereas the association between Finnish and U.S. returns was weaker. A significant part of the cross-sectional variation of the international risk components of the investigated Finnish companies could be attributed to industry differences across the investigated firms. An analysis of the underlying restrictive assumptions in this model is offered by Gultekin et al. (1989).

In addition to the international market models, the usefulness of the international Arbitrage Pricing Model (APM) by Solnik (1983) has also been researched intensively. Cho et al. (1986) studied the existence of international common factors in the APM using interbattery factor analysis. Their results indicated that the number of common factors between a pair of countries ranged from one to five, depending on the level of their economic integration. Recently, Yli-Olli et al. (1990) investigated the common factors in the Finnish and Swedish stock markets. They found two or three stable factors generating stock returns in these two neighboring countries. Their results were further extended by Booth et al. (1991), who reported that two of these Scandinavian factors could be regarded as worldwide in nature, being important in the U.S. stock market as well.

THE PURPOSE AND STRUCTURE OF THE STUDY

This study investigates the level of segmentation of the Finnish stock market to the Swedish stock market using the multimarket model suggested by Errunza and Losq (1985). Due to the rapid deregulation of the Finnish stock market, this is an important task to carry out. In Finland the relative importance of other stock markets in generating the risk characteristics of listed firms may be especially high because of thin trading in the Helsinki Stock Exchange, and because of the considerably increased direct investments of Finnish companies abroad. As an open country that carries on foreign trade to a great extent, Finland is highly dependent on the overseas establishment and macroeconomic conditions. On the other hand, the Finnish stock market has generally been regarded as being very different than the major exchanges of the United States, Japan, and Western Europe. It is a very small market composed of generally thinly traded stocks. This thin trading may lead to significantly biased market-based estimates of systematic risk (see, for example, Berglund et al., 1989). In this context, the use of Swedish data, where the trading is clearly more frequent by nature, might be useful when measuring the systematic risk of Finnish securities. In addition, it has been suggested that efficiency of the Finnish stock market is not especially high (see, for example, Virtanen and Yli-Olli, 1987 and Booth et al., 1992). This being the case, the return behavior of the Finnish stock market may be very different from that of the more developed stock markets (compare Mathur and Subrahmanyam, 1991).

In addition, we investigated whether the risk components obtained by the multimarket model contain incremental information with respect to the systematic risk components obtained by the APM. Chen (1983) discovered that the CAPM based on national systematic risk estimates did not produce incremental information with respect to the APM systematic risk components on the U.S. stock market. His results were strongly supported by Östermark (1989), who used a somewhat similar approach on Finnish and Swedish stock markets. This chapter extends these two studies by investigating a two-factor CAPM, where the risk components are produced by market returns of two neighboring capital markets.

METHODOLOGY

The traditional equilibrium model presented in finance literature, the Capital Asset Pricing Model (CAPM), assumes that the expected return of a stock is linearly related to its systematic risk, where the systematic risk of the security is defined to be the covariance of the asset return with the return of the market portfolio divided by the variance of the market portfolio return. Traditionally, betas have been measured using a simple bivariate regression, that is, Sharpe's (1964) market model:

$$\underline{R}_i - \text{Á}_i + \text{Ã}_i\underline{R}_m + \underline{\text{Ÿ}}_i \qquad (1)$$

where random variables are denoted by underlining the symbols of the variables. In the above model, $\underline{R}_i$ represents the return of security *i*, Á_i is the intercept term for a security *i*, Ã_i is the measure for systematic risk, beta, of a security *i*, $\underline{R}_m$ is a return of a national stock market index, and $\underline{\text{Ÿ}}_i$ is the idiosyncratic risk of security *i*. Thus, the model assumes that the return of an individual stock is a function of the return of the national stock market.

To investigate the Swedish risk components of Finnish securities, a multimarket model in the spirit of Errunza and Losq (1985) is used in this chapter. To obtain tractable expressions for the risk components of individual assets' Finnish market risk, Swedish market risk, and idiosyncratic risk, the vectors of returns of Finnish and Swedish markets are orthogonalized. Here this means removing the effect of a Swedish index from the index describing the behavior of the Finnish stock market, which can be done by using the following simple bivariate regression:

$$\underline{R}_m(\text{FIN}) - \text{Á} + \text{Ã}\underline{R}_m(\text{SWE}) + \underline{\text{Ÿ}} \qquad (2)$$

where $\underline{R}_m$(SWE) represent the returns of the Swedish market, and $\underline{R}_m$(FIN) the return of the Finnish market. The residual term $\underline{\ddot{Y}}$ is the part of the Finnish returns with Swedish returns removed. In the following, let us note the residual term in Eq. (2) with $\underline{R}_m$(FIN − SWE). The multimarket model can now be expressed as

$$\underline{R}_i = \acute{A}_i + \tilde{A}_{1i}\underline{R}_m(\mathrm{SWE}) + \tilde{A}_{2i}\underline{R}_m(\mathrm{FIN} - \mathrm{SWE}) + \underline{\ddot{Y}}_i \qquad (3)$$

In the following, the above model is referred to as the Scandinavian market model for Finnish securities. The components of risk for a security i can be obtained considering the expression for the variance of the returns of a security i:

$$\mathrm{Var}(\underline{R}_i) = \tilde{A}_{1i}^2\mathrm{Var}[\underline{R}_m(\mathrm{SWE})] + \tilde{A}_{2i}^2\mathrm{Var}[\underline{R}_m(\mathrm{FIN} - \mathrm{SWE})] + \mathrm{Var}(\underline{\ddot{Y}}_i) \qquad (4)$$

The multimarket model makes it possible to investigate the level of segmentation across the two Scandinavian stock markets in terms of individual securities. First, assume the Finnish and Swedish markets to be totally integrated. The second term in Eq. (3), $\tilde{A}_{2i}\underline{R}_m$(FIN − SWE), does not produce significant incremental information with respect to the first term, $\tilde{A}_{1i}\underline{R}_m$(SWE), when the returns of individual assets are investigated. Making an assumption concerning partial segmentation across the two investigated markets, both of the two terms should be significant in the return-generating process of individual assets.

In addition to testing the applicability of the multimarket model, its incremental significance with respect to the asset sensitivities obtained by testing the APM is investigated in this study. The APM, originally formulated by Ross (1976), predicts that on the perfectly competitive and frictionless stock markets the stock return is a linear function of a certain number, say k, economic factors (see Roll and Ross, 1980, pp. 1076–1082). To test the arbitrage pricing theory, two main alternative approaches have been presented. The first is used to estimate the unknown factors and asset sensitivities to these factors simultaneously by factor analysis. Without theory, a decision on how many factors to extract from the data must be made subjectively or by statistical criteria. When the systematic components of the risk are obtained, the risk premia are then estimated using cross-sectional regressions. The second approach tries to specify a priori, on the basis of the theory, the general factors that explain pricing in the stock market (see, for example, Chen et al., 1986 and Martikainen and Yli-Olli, 1990 on Scandinavian data). In this approach, time-series regressions are run for each series of stocks (portfolios) to estimate each stock's (portfolio's) sensitivities to macroeconomic variables. Then the risk premia are estimated by running cross-sectional regressions.

In this study the exploratory factor analysis approach is used to estimate the APM's unknown factors and asset sensitivities to these factors. In the first stage, the following factor analysis model is estimated:

$$\underline{R}_i = E(\underline{R}_i) + b_{i1}\underline{F}_1 + b_{i2}\underline{F}_2 + \cdots + b_{ik}\underline{F}_k + e_i \tag{5}$$

where $E(\underline{R}_i)$, $i = 1, 2, \ldots, n$, is the expected return of the stock i; $\underline{F}_j$, $j = 1, 2, \ldots, k$, are unobserved economic factors; b_{ij} is the sensitivity of the security i to the economic factor j; and $\underline{e}_i$ are the idiosyncratic risks of the stocks. Ross (1976) has shown that if the number of stocks is sufficiently large, a linear risk-return relationship between expected returns and asset sensitivities can be written. In this study, the risk-return relationship is tested using the following ordinary least squares (OLS) regression:

$$E(\underline{R}) = \lambda_0 + \lambda_1\underline{b}_1 + \lambda_2\underline{b}_2 + \cdots + \lambda_k\underline{b}_k + \underline{\grave{I}} \tag{6}$$

where λ_0 is a constant riskless rate of return (the common return on all zero-beta stocks) and λ_j, $j = 1, 2, \ldots, k$, represents, in equilibrium, the risk premium for the jth factor.

In the next stage, the part of expected returns unexplained by the APM risk components, that is, $\underline{\grave{I}}$, is explained by the risk components produced by the Scandinavian market model. Thus, the following cross-sectional regression is finally run:

$$\underline{\grave{I}} = \gamma_0 + \gamma_1\underline{\tilde{A}}_1 + \gamma_2\underline{\tilde{A}}_2 + \underline{\grave{I}}' \tag{7}$$

where $\underline{\grave{I}}$ is the residual term from regression (6), that is, the part of expected returns not explained by the APM systematic risk components; $\underline{\tilde{A}}_1$ represents the Swedish risk component of the Scandinavian market model in (3), and $\underline{\tilde{A}}_2$ is the Finnish risk component of the Scandinavian market model, after first controlling for the average returns of the Swedish stock market. Thus, the main focus in estimating (7) is to discover whether the risk components produced by the Scandinavian market model offer incremental information content with respect to the APM systematic risk components in explaining the cross-sectional variation of expected stock returns.

THE DATA

Monthly stock returns from the Helsinki Stock Exchange for January 1980 to December 1986 are used in this study. These individual asset returns are collected from a data base originally introduced by Berglund, Wahlroos, and Grandell (1983). This study's sample consists of 28 firms that have had their ordinary shares listed for the entire research period. The price indices used in the study are closing values for each month. The prices are corrected for splits, new issues, etc., assuming that dividends are reinvested with zero transaction cost. The returns for each month are determined as first differences of the natural logarithms of these price indices. The market index in use for the Helsinki Stock Exchange is the value-weighted market index collected from the same data base. For Swedish returns, a market index published by a Swedish journal, *Affarsvärlden,* is in use.

A TEST OF THE SCANDINAVIAN MARKET MODEL ON FINNISH SECURITIES

To obtain some preliminary evidence on the relationships of the returns on the investigated stock markets, the following time-series OLS regressions between the market returns are first run:

$$R_{mt}(\text{FIN}) = \text{Á} + \tilde{\text{A}}R_{mt}(\text{SWE}) + \ddot{\text{Y}}_t \quad (8)$$

$$R_{mt}(\text{FIN}) = \text{Á} + \tilde{\text{A}}R_{mt-1}(\text{SWE}) + \ddot{\text{Y}}_t \quad (9)$$

Table 1 presents the results of these regression analyses. The two markets seem to be positively related to each other. The strongest relationship between the two markets is found in model (8), that is, between the Finnish and Swedish stock markets when the returns are measured from the same month.

To produce evidence on the appropriateness of the so-called multimarket model in Finland, a market model extended to the Swedish stock market is tested next. The nondiversifiable risk components of this model are presented in Table 2. The results of that table are based on the following model:

$$R_{it} = \text{Á}_i + \tilde{\text{A}}_{1i}R_{mt}(\text{SWE}) + \tilde{\text{A}}_{2i}R_{mt}(\text{FIN} - \text{SWE}) + \ddot{\text{Y}}_{it} \quad (10)$$

where $\underline{R}_m$(SWE) represents the returns of the Swedish stock market, and R_{mt}(FIN − SWE) the return of the Finnish market orthogonalized with respect to the returns of the Swedish market, that is, the residual term from the regression $R_{mt}(\text{FIN}) = \text{Á} + \tilde{\text{A}}R_{mt}(\text{SWE}) + \ddot{\text{Y}}_t$. Typically, when estimating betas, portfolios have been preferred to single securities. In this study, however, time series of single securities are used, due to the small number of listed securities in the Helsinki Stock Exchange.

Table 1
Regression Analysis Estimates of Market Returns
(*t* values in parentheses)

Model	Constant	Coefficients	R^2	F	
Eq. (8)	0.0156 (3.530)***	0.2250 (2.864)**	0.092	8.200**	$N = 83$
Eq. (9)	0.0167 (3.667)***	0.1852 (2.304)*	0.062	5.307*	$N = 82$

*Significant at .05 level, **significant at .01 level, ***significant at .001 level.

Table 2
Results of the Scandinavian Market Model and Traditional National Market Model (1) for Finnish Stocks

Firm	Sweden	Finland	Total	Traditional market model
Effoa	0.0011	0.0504	0.0515	0.0415**
Kesko	0.0674**	0.2081***	0.2755	0.2636***
Ford	0.0043	0.1137**	0.1180	0.0909***
Stockmann	0.0648*	0.1501***	0.2149	0.1992***
Talouskauppa	0.0036	0.0650*	0.0686	0.0682***
Tamro	0.0614*	0.0206	0.0819	0.0449**
Enso	0.0130	0.0614*	0.0743	0.0732***
Fiskars	0.0020	0.1768***	0.1787	0.1499***
Huhtamäki	0.0625**	0.3697***	0.4322	0.4293***
Instru	0.0352 +	0.2208***	0.2560	0.2547***
Kajaani	0.0790**	0.1992***	0.2783	0.2607***
Kemi	0.0042	0.0625*	0.0667	0.0666***
Kymi	0.0145	0.3031***	0.3176	0.3149***
Lassila	0.0209	0.0689*	0.0898	0.0864***
Lohja	0.0363*	0.4707***	0.5070	0.5063***
Nokia	0.0688**	0.4218***	0.4906	0.4878***
Otava	0.0016	0.0169	0.0184	0.0125
Partek	0.0656**	0.3346***	0.4002	0.3955***
Rauma	0.0203	0.3322***	0.3525	0.3510***
Rosenlew	0.0040	0.0809***	0.0849	0.0843***
Schauman	0.0270(−)	0.0653*	0.0923	0.0375*
Serla	0.0011	0.1791***	0.1802	0.1707***
Sokeri	0.0152 +	0.2277***	0.2549	0.2547***
Trikoo	0.0116	0.0550*	0.0667	0.0657***
Tamfelt	0.0049	0.0965**	0.1014	0.1007***
Tampella	0.0190	0.0487*	0.0677	0.0635***
Wärtsilä	0.1102***	0.3078***	0.4180	0.3961***
Yhtyneet	0.0927***	0.3159***	0.4086	0.3943***

Note. Systematic risk measures obtained by

$$\tilde{A}_{1i}^2 \mathrm{Var}[\underline{R}_m(\mathrm{SWE})]$$

and

$$\tilde{A}_{2i}^2 \mathrm{Var}[\underline{R}_m(\mathrm{FIN} - \mathrm{SWE})]$$

*Significant at .05 level; **significant at .01 level; ***significant at .001 level; +, significant at .10 level; (−), negative.

The first column in Table 2 presents the systematic risk components of securities (in percentage of the total risk associated with the variability of the returns of a security in question) appointed to the Swedish market index. For 12 securities the estimated beta coefficient for Swedish markets has been significantly different from zero. In only one case, Schauman, has beta been negative. Thus, the results clearly support the segmentation hypothesis of Finnish and Swedish security markets. Swedish risk components seem to be important in the return-generating process of Finnish stocks.

The second column in Table 2 contains information about the part of total risk associated with the general return of the Finnish market after first controlling for the behavior of the Swedish stock market. All of the estimated betas have expected positive signs, and almost all are statistically different from zero. These results give support to the so-called mild segmentation hypothesis. There seems to exist significant incremental information in Finnish market returns after removing the part associated with Swedish market returns.

A COMPARISON OF APM AND SCANDINAVIAN MARKET MODEL

In this section the empirical results of the APM and multimarket model are compared. Specifically, the incremental significance of the risk components produced by the multimarket model are compared to those of the APM. The next step in the empirical analysis is to test the APM using the factor analysis procedure to identify the number of factors affecting equilibrium returns. In earlier studies, this procedure has been problematic because the number of factors discovered depends, for example, on the size of the groups of securities one deals with. The estimation of factors can be carried out by different factor analytic methods. In this study, the initial factor extraction is carried out by the principal component method based on the covariance matrices of monthly stock returns; thereafter, a varimax rotation is applied.

In this study, two-, three-, and four-factor solutions were first derived for Finnish returns. The selection of these factor solutions was based on earlier findings by Yli-Olli et al. (1990) and Booth et al. (1991) indicating that no more than four common factors exist in the Finnish stock market. The cumulative proportions of total variance (of the unrotated factor patterns) are presented in Table 3. The figures of cumulative proportions in Table 3 reveal that the first factor accounts for 23.9% of the total variation of Finnish security returns during the research period, while 47% of this variation can be explained by the first four factors appearing in descending order of variance. The results are of about the same order as those reported by Yli-Olli et al. (1990). The slightly

Table 3
Cumulative Proportions of Total Variance Explained

Factor			
1	2	3	4
0.239	0.334	0.404	0.470

Table 4
Regression Analysis Estimates
(*t* values in parentheses)

Number of factors	Constant	Factor 1	2	3	4	R^2	F
2	0.0160 (2.878)**	0.0069 (0.724)	0.0153 (1.870)+	—	—	0.126	1.808
3	0.0161 (2.933)**	0.0051 (0.581)	0.0173 (2.179)*	0.0033 (0.472)	—	0.185	1.816
4	0.0153 (2.119)*	0.0153 (1.863)+	0.0062 (0.685)	0.0173 (2.089)*	0.0038 (0.530)	0.217	1.590

Note. Dependent variable: average monthly return for security; independent variables: factor loadings ($k = 2$–4).

*Significant at .05 level; **significant at .01 level; ***significant at .001 level; +, significant at .10 level.

higher cumulative proportions of total variance reported by Yli-Olli et al. may be due to the longer estimation period used in this chapter.

The following step involves examining the effect of factor loadings, that is, systematic risk components of the APM, on equilibrium returns. In cross sections the dependent variable is the monthly mean return and the independent variables are factor loadings from factor analysis. The risk-free rate of return is not restricted, but estimated from the stock returns, assuming the intercept term to represent this return. The OLS regression coefficients are the estimated risk premia. In factor analysis there is no absolute meaning to the signs of the parameters or the scaling of the factors; the signs of regression coefficients are also arbitrary. Therefore, only the statistical significance of regression coefficients is relevant, instead of their numerical values. The results of the cross-sectional test of the APM are presented in Table 4. The results in Table 4 support 1–2 priced factors in the APM in the Finnish stock market. However, the R^2 and F values of the regressions are low, indicating that a significant proportion of the cross-sectional variation of expected returns cannot be explained by the risk components of the APM.

Finally, to discover whether the risk components of the Scandinavian multi-market model offer incremental information with respect to the estimated APM risk components, the part of expected returns unexplained by the APM risk components, that is, the residual term of the *c* cross-sectional regressions shown in Table 4, is explained by the risk components produced by the Scandinavian market model. The results of this incremental information content analysis are reported in Table 5. The results in Table 5 are clear. The international risk components of the Scandinavian market model do not offer incremental information with respect to the APM risk components when explaining the

Table 5
Regressions Analysis Estimates
(t values in parentheses)

Number of factors in the APM	Constant	$\tilde{A}_{1i}\underline{R}_m$(FIN − SWE)	$\tilde{A}_{2i}\underline{R}_m$(SWE)	R^2	F
2	−0.0016	0.0036	−0.0065	0.022	0.275
	(−0.391)	(0.624)	(−0.673)		
3	−0.0007	0.0030	−0.0086	0.033	0.426
	(−0.188)	(0.540)	(−0.921)		
4	−0.0010	0.0025	−0.0051	0.013	0.168
	(−0.263)	(0.457)	(−0.545)		

Note. Dependent variable: residual term of the cross-sectional APM; independent variables: Scandinavian market model risk components.
*Significant at .05 level; **significant at .01 level; ***significant at .001 level; +, significant at .10 level.

cross-sectional variation of expected returns in the Finnish stock market. This can be seen from the statistically insignificant t values of the regression coefficients, and from the low R^2 and F values of the models.

CONCLUSIONS

This study focused on the level of segmentation of the Finnish stock markets to Swedish stock markets and was carried out by exploiting an internationally extended market model for Finnish stocks and the APM originally developed by Ross (1976). The multimarket model of Finnish securities revealed that several Finnish stocks have significant Swedish risk components. The results supported the mild-segmentation hypothesis of the two investigated Scandinavian stock markets.

When analyzing the incremental information of the Scandinavian market model risk components with respect to the APM, in explaining the cross-sectional variation of expected returns, the multimarket model parameters did not produce incremental information content. In this context, this chapter extends the earlier work by Chen (1983) and Östermark (1989), who discovered that traditional market model betas did not offer incremental information with respect to the systematic risk components of the Arbitrage Pricing Model.

Because of the recent deregulation and integration of the world's capital markets, the results obtained here should be applied to other stock markets as well. In addition, the effects of certain macroeconomic changes, such as inflation, demand for money, industrial production, and interest rates, should be considered in terms of the time-series variation of the systematic risk components of the multimarket model. Finally, the level of firm-specific characteristics, such as profitability, financial leverage, operating leverage, and growth, should be investigated with respect to the cross-sectional variation of the systematic risk components of the multimarket model, because these four components can be regarded as theoretical determinants of systematic risk (see, for example, Martikainen, 1992, and the literature cited therein).

REFERENCES

Berglund, T., B. Wahlroos, and L. Grandell. 1983. The KOP and UNITAS indexes for the Helsinki Stock Exchange in the light of value weighted index, *Finnish Journal of Business Economics* 32(1):30–41 (in Swedish).

Berglund, T., E. Liljeblom, and A. Löflund. 1989. Estimating betas on daily data for a small security market, *Journal of Banking and Finance* 13(1):41–64.

Booth, G. G., T. Martikainen, I. Virtanen, and P. Yli-Olli. 1991. On the common factors in the arbitrage pricing model: International evidence from U.S. and Scandinavian stock markets, Paper presented to the Joint International Meeting of TIMS XXX–SOBRAPO XXIII, Rio de Janeiro, Brazil, 1991.

Booth, G. G., J. Hatem, I. Virtanen, and P. Yli-Olli. 1992. Stochastic modeling of security return: Evidence from the Helsinki Stock Exchange, *European Journal of Operational Research* 56(1):98–106.

Bradfield, D. J. 1990. An extended market model for non-USA markets, Paper presented at the 12th Triennial Conference on Operations Research, IFORS, Athens, Greece, 25–29 June 1990.

Chen, N. F. 1983. Some empirical tests of the theory of arbitrage pricing, *Journal of Finance* 38(5):1393–1414.

Chen, N. F., R. Roll, and S. A. Ross. 1986. Economic forces and the stock market, *Journal of Business* 59(3):383–403.

Cho, D. C., C. S. Eun, and L. W. Senbet. 1986. International arbitrage pricing theory: An empirical investigation, *Journal of Finance* 41(2):313–329.

Errunza, V., and E. Losq. 1985. International asset pricing under mild segmentation: Theory and test, *Journal of Finance* 40(1):105–124.

Grinold, R., A. Rudd, and D. Stefek. 1989. Global factors: Fact or fiction, *Journal of Portfolio Management,* 79–88.

Gultekin, M., B. Gultekin, and A. Penati. 1989. Capital controls and international capital market segmentation: The evidence from the Japanese and American stock markets, *Journal of Finance* 44:697–718.

Hietala, P. T. 1988. Super premiums in the Finnish stock market, *Finnish Economic Papers* 1(2):148–171.

Hilliard, J. E. 1979. The relationship between equity indices on world exchanges, *Journal of Finance* 34(1):103–114.

Ibbotson, R. C., R. C. Carr, and A. W. Robinson. 1982. International equity and bond returns, *Financial Analyst Journal* 38:61–83.

Jeon, B. N., and G. M. von Furstenberg. 1990. Growing international co-movements in stock price indexes, *Quarterly Review of Economics and Business* 30(3):15–30.

Makridakis, S. G., and S. C. Wheelwright. 1974. An analysis of the inter-relationships among the world stock exchanges, *Journal of Business Finance and Accounting* 1(1):195–215.

Malkamäki, M. J., T. Martikainen, and J. Perttunen. 1991. On the riskiness of the world's stock markets, *European Journal of Operational Research* 53(3):288–296.

Martikainen, T. Stock returns and classification pattern of firm-specific financial variables: Empirical evidence with Finnish data, *Journal of Business Finance and Accounting* (in press).

Martikainen, T., and P. Yli-Olli. 1990. A test of the arbitrage pricing model using accounting information, *Economics Letters* 34(1):55–59.

Martikainen, T., I. Virtanen, and P. Yli-Olli. 1991. Further evidence on international asset pricing: On the level of segmentation of the Finnish stock market to Swedish and U.S. stock markets, Paper presented to the Joint International Meeting of TIMS XXX–SOBRAPO XXIII, Rio de Janeiro, Brazil, 1991.

Mathur, I., and V. Subrahmanyam. 1991. An analysis of the Scandinavian stock indices, *Journal of International Financial Markets, Institutions and Money* 1(1):91–114.

Meric, I., and G. Meric. 1989. Potential gains from international portfolio diversification and inter-temporal stability and seasonality in international stock market relationships, *Journal of Banking and Finance* 13(4–5):627–640.

Östermark, R. 1989. Arbitrage pricing models for two Scandinavian stock exchanges, *OMEGA International Journal of Management Science* 17(5):437–447.

Philippatos, G. C., A. Christofi, and P. Christofi. 1989. The inter-temporal stability of international stock market relationships: Another view, *Financial Management*, 63–69.

Roll, R., and S. H. Ross. 1989. An empirical investigation of the arbitrage pricing theory, *Journal of Finance* 35(5):1073–1103.

Ross, S. H. 1976. The arbitrage pricing theory of capital asset pricing, *Journal of Economic Theory* 13(1):341–360.

Sharpe, W. F. 1964. Capital asset prices: A theory of market equilibrium under conditions of risk, *Journal of Finance* 19(5):425–442.

Solnik, B. 1977. Testing international asset pricing: Some pessimistic views, *Journal of Finance* 32:503–512.

Solnik, B. 1983. International arbitrage pricing theory, *Journal of Finance* 38(2):449–457.

Solnik, B. 1983. *International Investments*, Reading, MA: Addison-Wesley.

Virtanen, I., and P. Yli-Olli. 1987. Predicting stock returns in a thin security market, *OMEGA International Journal of Management Science* 15(2):145–155.

von Furstenberg, G. M., and B. N. Jeon. 1989. International stock price movements: Links and messages, *Brookings Papers on Economic Activity*, No. 1, 125–179.

Wheatley, S. 1988. Some tests of international equity market integration, *Journal of Financial Economics* 21:177–212.

Yli-Olli, P., I. Virtanen, and T. Martikainen. 1990. Common factors in the arbitrage pricing model in two Scandinavian countries, *OMEGA International Journal of Management Science* 18(6):615–624.

Chapter 11

Defeased Debt in International Capital Markets: Benefits and Problems

Emiel W. Owens and Ronald F. Singer

With the accelerated growth of organized securities markets, emerging nations must determine what rules will be implemented to assure well-functioning markets. One problem they face will be to develop standardized accounting rules so investors can interpret the statements of public corporations. In the United States this rule-making authority is the Financial Accounting Standards Board (FASB), which issues regulations on accounting conventions.

This chapter examines a specific rule, FASB 76, on the welfare of investors. It provides an investigation of defeasance and in-substances defeasance, including examples of in-substance defeasance transactions using corporate and government securities.[1] A model assessing market reaction to defeasance (Event Study) is also presented. It is hoped that the experience of this rule will effect the implementation of similar rules in emerging nations.

DEFINITIONS, SAMPLE, AND DATA SOURCE

Several official statements have been issued in recent years focusing on debt extinguishment. Statement 76 was issued in late 1983 by FASB.[2] Statement 76 allows, as alternatives to payment to the creditors, defeasance and in-substance defeasance. In the statement, defeasance is defined as the legal satisfaction of a debt, where by written agreement the debt is legally satisfied without necessar-

---

[1]Kay, R. 1984. Extinguishment of debt: Discussion of FASB '76, *Certified Public Accountant Journal* 54(4):62–65.

[2]McGoldrick, B., 1984. Why are CFOs so excited about defeasance? *Institutional Investor* 18(3):75–83.

ily being retired.[3] In-substance defeasance (called simply defeasance in this chapter) allows corporations to collateralize their outstanding low-coupon long-term debt by placing the debt obligation in an irrevocable trust, while simultaneously placing with the trustee sufficient cash or government securities to guarantee the cash flow needed to pay future interest and principal payments of the original bond issue when due.

The in-substance defeasance requirements further stipulate that the securities in the trust are risk-free (with respect to the amount, timing, and collection of interest and principal) and are limited to direct obligations of the United States government or securities backed by the United States government.[4] The matching of the cash flows thus requires the solution of an immunization problem and may necessitate the use of stripped bonds to properly satisfy the cash flow requirements.[5]

Table 1 shows data for matched pairs of corporate and government bonds and what happens when the firms defease a debt issue.[6] Notice that the bonds are matched as to coupon and maturity dates, so the cash flows from the government issue purchased would be just enough to make the debt service payments on the corporate issuer's bonds. Notice also, that on 14 Nov 1983, the

[3]Kay, R. 1984. Debt extinguishment, *Institutional Investor* 54(4):62–65.

[4]Sudner, S. 1973. Relationship between accounting changes and stock prices: Problems of measurement and some empirical evidence, *Empirical Research in Accounting: Selected Studies*, 1–45.

[5]Stripped bonds are bonds that have been separated into interest and principal components and sold separately. Names given to identify these bonds include CATs and TIGRs.

[6]Sudner, S. 1973. Relationships between accounting changes and stock prices, *Empirical Research in Accounting: Selected Studies*, 1–45.

Table 1

De Facto Defeasance Premiums and U.S. Government and Corporate Bonds Matched for Maturity Date and Coupon Rate (price on 11/16/83; percent of par)

Corporations (Treasury issued)	Corporate bond rating	Corporate bond (%)	Government bond (%)	Defease premium (%)
Columbia Gas (9 of 1994–1995)	A2	81.125	85.15	6.3
DuPont (8 of 1986)	Aa2	93.25	93.69	0.5
GE Credit (11½ of 1990)	Aa1	99.75	99.78	0.0
GMAC (9¼ of 1989)	Aa3	89.125	92.0	3.2
GMAC (14⅝ of 1989)	Aa2	108.0	112.125	3.8
Phila El (12¾ of 1982)	Baa3	104.0	110.625	6.4
PS of Indiana (14 of 1987)	A3	100.5	108.0	7.5
Rapid America (10¾ of 2003)		77.5	91.0	18.4
Tiger International (11½ of 1995)		67.875	99.0	45.9
Wheel. Frye (11¾ of 2005)	A1	90.0	99.41	10.5

Columbia Gas 9s of 1994 sold for 81.125% of par, while the United States government 9s of 1994 sold for 85.16% of par. The shareholders of Columbia Gas receive a gain of \$40.35 (\$1000 × (.8516 − .81125)) on each bond. If Columbia Gas were to repurchase one of its bonds, it would report a gain of \$198.75, assuming that the bond was originally issued at par. If it defeases its bond by purchasing the Treasury, it will report a gain of only \$149.50 (\$1000 − \$851.60). Restated, retirement by defeasance transfers about \$50, or 6%, of previously unrealized shareholder gain back to bondholders. Before the transaction, the bondholder would have claims only on the cash, earnings, and assets of Columbia Gas; but afterward they have an additional claim on the distinctly less risky cash flows provided by a United States government security.[7] Some corporations have set up an "instant arbitrage," using foreign securities for defeasance, but this procedure is presently under study.[8]

IMPACT AND MOTIVATION-DEFEASANCE

The motivations behind the defeasance transactions may be twofold: (1) reporting of earnings from the transactions, and (2) the alteration of capital structure through the extinguishment of debt. During a period of rising interest rates, the gain arising from a defeased transaction may substantially increase earnings and reduce the reported financial leverage ratios of the defeasing corporation. Because the responsibility for servicing the debt passes to the trustee, the company no longer deducts the interest expenses on the debt from its earnings. With yields on newer treasuries persistently higher than the coupon on much of the old corporate debt, companies may find they can discharge their debt at less than face value, thus giving them immediate capital gains.[9] While the company reports the gain as extraordinary income right away, it may not have to pay the tax on its gain until the matching securities mature, sometimes many years in the future.[10]

However, in assessing the attractiveness of using a trust arrangement to defease debt, there are a number of factors to consider in addition to the income and balance sheet effects. Let us again consider some financial consequences of a firm defeasing a debt issue by observing in Table 2 some effects a defeasance transaction has on the income statement of Riverside Corporation. Table 2 shows that the

---

[7]The FASB considers some debt issues ineligible for this treatment such as (1) debt with floating interest rates, (2) debt that is payable on demand, and (3) convertible debentures. Defeasance may also be available for some (1) capital leases, (2) leveraged lease financing, (3) cross-default provision debt issues, and (4) negative pledge covenants.

[8]Eurobond Defeasance (Arbitrage); Early 1984, three U.S. corporations namely, Pepsico, Baxter Traveno Laboratories, and Sterling Drugs, went to West Germany to issue Eurobonds (Wilson, 1984). What was unusual about this transaction was the eagerness of the corporations to turn defeasance into a prearbitrage ploy in the Deutsche mark market.

[9]A risk-free way to reduce company debt, *Business Week, Corporate Finance* (21 Nov 1983).

[10]In late 1983 the FASB argued that such arrangements did not actually relieve a company from its obligation to bondholders, and that the companies were underserving booking earnings from the transactions. This issue is being further evaluated (see *Business Week,* 2 Nov 1983).

Table 2
Income Statement for Riverside Corporation
for the Year Ended 31 December 19x9

Statement	Predefeasance	Postdefeasance
Sales	$1,100,000	$1,100,000
Cost of goods sold	600,000	600,000
Gross profit margin	500,000	500,000
Depreciation	100,000	100,000
Other operating expenses	166,300	166,300
Net operating income	233,700	233,700
Gain on defeasance transaction		81,347
Earnings before interest and taxes	233,700	315,047
Interest expense	118,000	118,000
Earnings before tax	115,700	197,047
Taxes	34,700	50,969
Net income	$81,000	$146,078
Available to stockholders	81,000	146,078
Primary earnings per share	.18	.32

defeasance transaction generated $.14 additional earnings per common share outstanding or a 78% increase over the original net income. In a recent article, Gombola and Ketz (1983) cautioned investors that when a defeasance transaction occurs, net income plus depreciation (a popularly used proxy for cash flows) will overstate cash flow behavior of financial leverage, profitability, interest coverage, and cash flow ratios, although the reported time-series improvement may not represent true financial ratios of the corporation's performance.[11]

Table 3 shows the values of selected financial ratios derived from the income statement in Table 2. After defeasance, historical credit analysis and risk assessment tools were found giving investors misleading investment signals. As illustrated in Table 3, after a defeasance transaction, the liquidity ratio of Riverside Corporation declined, which could be interpreted as the corporation becoming more risky. On the other hand, the declining leverage ratio could imply that the corporation is becoming less risky. Observe that negative liquidity ratios were offset by significant improvements in the leverage and profitability ratios. The assumption is made that the interest coverage ratio (earnings before interest and taxes divided by interest expense) will also improve in future years because interest payments associated with defeased debt will be deleted from the income statement.

[11]Phillips, A. L., and S. M. Moody. 1989. The effect of defeased debt and loan decision, *The Journal of Commercial Bank Lending*, 33.

In summary, there are both pros and cons to undertaking an in-substance defeasance transaction. However, it seems clear that given the potential wealth transfer associated with this transaction, the average stockholder will suffer as a result of this transaction. In addition, the negative impact on defeased corporations associated with the potential distortion of the true value of traditional financial performance ratios will have to be evaluated. In the next section statistics are presented that are suggestive of a reduction in stockholder wealth as a result of the announcement of in-substance defeasance.

AN EMPIRICAL TEST OF THE IMPACT OF DEFEASANCE ON SECURITY HOLDERS' WEALTH

This section presents an empirical investigation into the impact of in-substance defeasance on security holders' wealth. Using this "event study" methodology, it is possible to determine if the equity of a sample of firms that have announced the intention of defeasing some of this debt undergoes abnormal price movements. If it is determined that security returns are abnormally low around the time of an announcement, then this will be interpreted as evidence that in-substance defeasance has a negative impact on stockholders' wealth. On the other hand, if it is determined that returns are unusually high around the announcement date, then this can be interpreted as evidence that in-substance defeasance has, on average, a positive impact on stockholders' wealth.

DESCRIPTION OF DATA

Utilizing the services of Mead Data Central (Lexis and Nexis), O'Neal Data Base, Vols. 1 and 2 (1987), 35 firms were identified to have defeased at least a portion of their outstanding debt between 1982 and 1988. Since the announce-

Table 3
Selected Financial Ratios, Riverside Corporation

	Predefeasance	Postdefeasance
Liquidity		
Current ratio	2.14	1.86
Quick ratio	1.31	1.03
Leverage		
Total debt + total assets	46.3%	41.1%
Long-term debt + total assets	29.6%	23.2%
Total debt + total equity	81.2%	67.3%
Long-term debt + total equity	55.2%	39.6%
EBIT + interest expense	1.98%	2.67%
Profitability		
Net income + total assets	3.0%	5.7%
Net income + total equity	5.6%	9.5%
Net income + sales	7.4%	13.3%

ment of plans for defeasance is rarely reported in the press, it was necessary to obtain the dates of the first announcement of a defeasance directly from the financial officers of each firm. These announcements were generally reported in a press release that was not deemed sufficiently newsworthy to publish in *The Wall Street Journal, The New York Times,* or other readily available indexed sources. In fact, one of the firms in our sample first announced its defeasance in its quarterly report after the actual defeasance took place. Of the 35 firms in our sample, announcement dates were found for only 20.

The list of firms and the earliest announcement dates are given in Table 4. From each of these firms, daily closing prices, dividend payments, and dividend dates were collected for a period of 60 days before and after the announcement data. Daily returns and average daily returns for each firm were then calculated over this time and used as the basic data set for the analysis.

EQUITY METHODOLOGY AND ANALYSIS

If the announcement of in-substance defeasance has an important effect on stockholders' wealth then we would expect to observe unusual price movements around such an announcement. Essentially, investors will react to the announcement, thereby causing an unusual price change around the announcement date.

Table 4
Description of Sample

Firm	Announcement date
Gifford Hill Corp.	20 Jan 1981
Exxon Corp.	6 Jul 1982
Dekalb Agresearch	13 Dec 1982
Kellogg Corp.	29 Jun 1982
Teco. Inc.	30 Aug 1983
Equimark Corp.	30 Dec 1983
Florida Progressive Corp.	1 Dec 1983
Right Financial Corp.	31 Dec 1983
Union Carbide	31 Dec 1983
Duke Power Company	27 Jan 1984
Ual Inc.	29 Jun 1982
Kaiser Steel Corp.	28 Feb 1984
Morrison Inc.	22 May 1984
Houston Natural Gas	31 May 1984
Peoples Energy Corp.	30 Sep 1984
Burlington Industries	30 Sep 1984
General Mills	3 Oct 1984
Dupont Corp.	20 Dec 1984
Long Star Industries	29 Mar 1985
United States Steel Corp.	25 Mar 1985
Dekalb Engineering	24 Aug 1988

This of course assumes that (1) the announcement has important implications for the stockholders, (2) the "unusual price movements" are correctly defined, and (3) the stock market is reasonably efficient in the sense that prices rapidly and fully adjust when new information is made public.

In the typical event study, unusual price movements are defined in many ways. However, Brown and Warner (1980) find that the return deviation around the mean return over a given period does as good a job in detecting shifts in the probability distribution of return as do more sophisticated models. Thus, we use the following as our test of abnormal returns AR_t:

$$AR_t = \sum_{i=1}^{N_t} \frac{\tilde{R}_{it} - \bar{R}_i}{N_t}$$

where t = -60 to $+60$, the date in "event time"
N_t = the number of firms in the sample on each day t
i = 1 to 20, the index of each firm
$\tilde{R}_{it}$ = the return of stock i on date
$\bar{R}_i$ = average return of firm i over the entire sample period

Another statistic to be considered is the cumulative average residual, defined as CAR_t, where

$$CAR_t = \sum_{j=-60}^{t} AR_j$$

Thus, the cumulative average residual gives the average return that would be received if the entire sample of firms were purchased and held from the beginning of the test period to time t.

Now it is possible to test for abnormal price movements over the time period considered. Notice that the time t is defined with respect to days from or after the day of the announcement of the intent to defease a debt issue and is not representative of calendar time. Day 0 is the announcement date and is related to calendar time for each firm by the dates in Figure 1.

Figure 1 presents graphically the cumulative average residual for the entire sample for the 120-day time period. The variance of the residuals diminishes substantially in the 10-day period surrounding the announcement. This could indicate that the market has reached a consensus with respect to the effect of the announcement and, in particular, that the announcement is unfavorable to the stockholders' position.

INTERPRETATION OF THE STATISTICAL RESULTS

From the patterns presented in Figures 1 and 2 it is apparent that the announcement of an in-substance defeasance is indicative of a loss in stockholders'

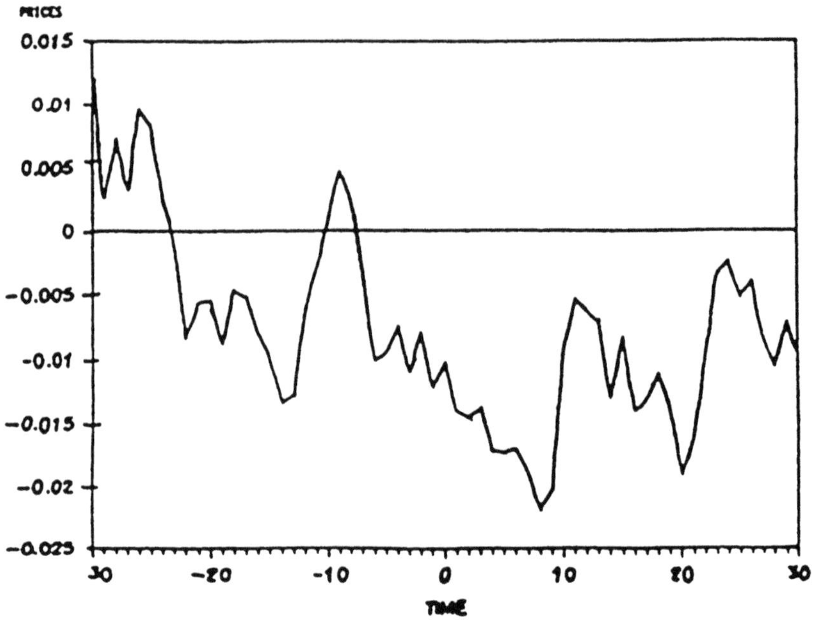

Figure 1 Cumulative average residuals.

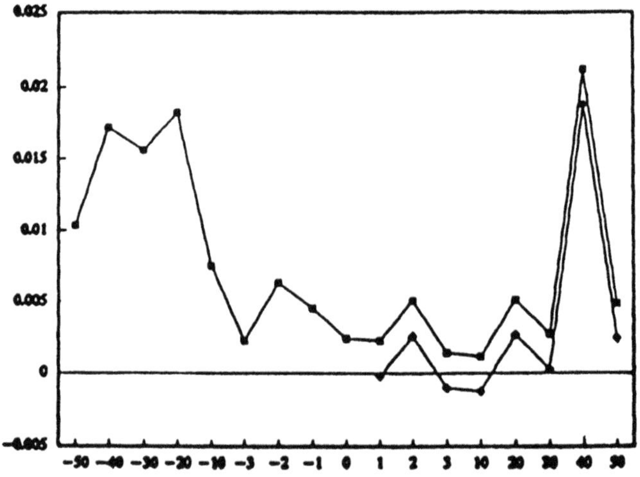

Figure 2 Cumulative excess returns derived from calculations.

wealth. In fact, the effect can be seen in the data as much as 10 days prior to the announcement and appears to continue for approximately 8 days after the announcement. The negative effect prior to the announcement can be explained by information with respect to the impending announcement leaking out to the public over the pre-announcement period. However, the continued decrease in the CAR after the announcement is difficult to interpret. In an efficient market, prices should fully reflect the information embodied in the announcement at that time. However, the statistical evidence indicates that unusually low returns persist for some time after the information is made public. One possible explanation is that the announcement date is only an approximation, obtained from the firm itself. Since these announcements are not carried by the press, there is no way to verify the exact announcement date.

BOND METHODOLOGY AND ANALYSIS

In this section the patterns of returns of the defeased debt are analyzed to determine the impact of defeasance on those issues. Theoretically, defeasance guarantees payments to the bondholders through the trust. Therefore, there should be a positive abnormal return on the date of the announcement of the defeasance. Thereafter, the return from these bonds should be equal to the return of treasury bonds of a similar maturity.

To test this hypothesis, bond data was collected from *The Wall Street Journal*, Moody's, and the Standard and Poor's Corporate Bond Index. The cumulative abnormal return was then calculated as the excess return over the average return of these bonds over the 121-day test period. Figure 2 shows the CAR over the period 60 days before the announcement date of the defeasance to 60 days after the defeasance announcement. Also shown is the CAR for the defeased bonds from the date of the announcement of the defeasance.

The null hypothesis (H_0), which implies no cumulative excess returns during the time period of the study (t), is tested using the t statistic as given by

$$t = \frac{\bar{x} - u}{s/\sqrt{N}}$$

where s = standard deviation
$\bar{x}$ = sample mean
u = population mean

$$s = \left[\frac{1}{N - 1}\Sigma(\tilde{X} - \bar{X})^2\right]^{1/2}$$

where $\bar{x}$ = average of daily returns
Notice that the CAR declines substantially over the 20-day period prior to the announcement date. There appears to be anticipation of the defeasance causing

an increase in price prior to this 20-day period and a subsequent decrease in yields as predicted by the wealth transfer hypothesis. Furthermore the CARs subsequent to the announcement date do not appear to manifest a discernable pattern, indicating that the defeased bonds experience a permanent decrease in yields as a result of the defeasance.

In general, these results support the wealth transfer arguments. In-substance defeasance appears to penalize the existing stockholders while benefiting the bondholders of the defeased debt.

SUMMARY AND CONCLUSIONS

Statistical evidence in this study shows that when earning trend analysis or financial ratio analysis is used in predicting the financial stress that a corporation may encounter, there exists a potential for making inaccurate decisions. This is due to the distortion of key performance ratios after defeasance transactions. The statistical results indicate that security prices react to economic rather than cosmetic efforts of changes in accounting numbers. This is consistent with the results found in previous empirical studies on the effect of accounting changes on stockholders' wealth. For example, Weil (1983) shows that in a defeasance transaction, bondholders trade risky corporate bonds for "riskless" government bonds with exactly the same cash throw-offs, and the shareholders pay the premium to reduce the bondholders' risk.

The experience of Rule 76 can provide a general message to countries considering implementing similar rules. This rule is an example of a conflict between accounting versus finance. The result is that stock prices (and investors' welfare) appear to react to the financial realities rather than mere accounting numbers. It is hoped that the governments of other countries will consider this lesson before implementing similar regulations or conventions.

REFERENCES

Aksudelo, J., and J. Harmon. 1984. Debt defeasance: Its impact on corporate financial reporting, *Ohio Certified Public Accountant Journal* 43(2):61–65.

Brown, S. J., and J. B. Warner. 1980. Measuring security price performance, *Journal of Financial Economics* 8(2):205–258.

Calvert, R. B. 1985. The application and effects of in-substance defeasance, *Journal of Commercial Bank Lending* 67(5).

Fama, E. F., L. Fisher, M. Jensen, and R. Roll. 1969. The adjustment of stock prices to new information, *International Economic Review* 10(1):1–21.

Financial Accounting Standards Board (FASB). 1983. *Statement of Financial Accounting Standards No. 76: Extinguishment of Debt: An Amendment of APB Opinion No. 26,* Stanford, CT: FASB.

Friar, J. W. 1984. Deals: Clouds over morning-to-midnight defeasance, *Institutional Investor* 18(6):37–40.

Gombola, M. J., and J. E. Ketz. 1983. A caveat on measuring cash flow and solvency, *Financial Analysis Journal* 39(5):66–72.

Gray, D., and M. A. Seville. 1985. In-substance defeasance: Altering the shape of debt management, *Journal of Accountancy* 159(1):100–107.

Green, R. 1984. The missing number, *Forbes* 133(14):123.

Gup, B. E. 1984. Defeasance: What is its effect on your firm? *Financial Executive,* 31–47.

Hong, H., R. S. Kaplan, and G. Mandelker. 1978. Pooling vs. purchase: The effects of accounting for mergers on stock prices, *The Accounting Review* 53(1):31–47.

Jensen, M. C., and W. M. Meckling. 1976. Theory of the firm: Managerial behavior, agency cost and ownership structure, *Journal of Financial Economics,* 305–360.

Klein, R. 1984. Eliminating debt by defeasance, *Business* 34(4):23–28.

Mielke, D. E., and J. Siefert. 1987. A survey on the effects of defeasing debt, *Journal of Accounting, Auditing & Finance* 2(1):65–78.

Weil, R. L. 1983. De- or misfeasance? A look at the new FASB ruling, *Barron's* 63(49):50.

Wilson, C. O. 1984. Deutsche mark in-substance defeasance, *International Financial Law Review* 3(3):26–27.

Chapter 12

Deregulation of Financial Institutions: Lessons from the North American Experience with Savings and Loan Associations

William A. Dowling and George C. Philippatos

The 1980s were traumatic for the U.S. savings and loan industry. During the early part of the decade, the industry was subjected to deregulation in the form of the Depository Institutions Deregulation and Monetary Control Act of 1980 (DIDMCA) and the Garn–St.Germain Act in 1982. A torrent of mergers occurred in anticipation of and as a result of deregulation. These and other events have resulted in a federally assisted industry bailout that it expected to cost over 300 billion U.S. dollars. As a result, there has been a focusing of scholarly and regulatory attention on both the operating characteristics and the efficiency of the savings and loan industry. Additionally, competition has forced S&Ls to strive for increased operational efficiency as exemplified by cost reduction per unit of output in order to survive.

The large number of mergers among S&Ls in the United States and the encouragement of the regulatory authority to merge is prima facia evidence of an attempt on the part of the S&Ls and the Federal Home Loan Bank Board (FHLBB) to restructure the industry and to take advantage of perceived economies of scale in order to reduce costs per unit of output. Therefore, the main question addressed in this research is whether the cost functions for the U.S. S&L industry allow for reductions in cost through economies of scale. In this spirit, we propose to test the hypothesis that S&Ls may benefit from cost reductions per unit of output through output expansion.

The search for the existence of scale economies has been a popular theme both in the U.S. S&L industry and in the area of financial institutions in general. Past results of the investigations in this area are inconsistent, due in part to (1) the use of limited samples, in terms of either numbers of institutions exam-

---

This paper is a revision of a work originally included in the *Proceedings of the International Trade and Finance Association* in Marseille in May 1991. The authors are grateful for those comments provided that contributed to this revision.

ined or time periods tested, and (2) the bias of results through the inclusion of data on institutions that more nearly resemble commercial banks than S&Ls. Hence, we propose to use the entire population of S&L institutions: those that were insured by the Federal Savings and Loan Insurance Corporation; those that were required to file regular financial reports with the (FHLBB) during the 1973–1987 time period and those that had a minimum of 60% of total assets invested in mortgages. Given this data base, a variant of the Translog cost function is employed to estimate cost elasticities. Additionally, a version of the Frontier Frame methodology is used to determine if scale economies were present in the industry.

PREVIOUS RESEARCH

Brigham (1964) and Brigham and Pettit (1970) were able to confirm the existence of significant scale economies for the smaller institutions whose size was proxied by the value of total assets. Verbrugge, Shick, and Thygerson (1976) and Atkinson (1977, 1979) reported similar results. McNulty (1981, 1982), using data from a sample of Florida thrifts, found significant economies of scale for asset levels of approximately $500 million. In a 1982 study, McNulty employed a Translog cost function and concluded that limiting the number of branches relative to asset size was as effective a method of controlling costs as unconstrained growth in total assets.

In a 1983 merger-focused study, Dowling, Philippatos, and Choi reported the existence of significant economies of scale for associations with assets less than a billion dollars, using a version of the Translog function identical to that used by McNulty. However, in another U.S. savings and loan merger-related study, Choi, Philippatos, and Dowling (1986) found that when the cost function was approximated by a simplified form of the Translog function, where the primary explanatory variable was total assets, previous studies had overestimated significantly the degree of cost reductions available.

In 1990, Dowling and Philippatos, in an attempt to resolve the question of scale economies, tested several variants of the Translog cost function to estimate cost elasticities and a Frontier Frame methodology to determine whether scale economies were present in the thrift industry during the 1973–1983 time period. Both approaches yielded similar results and suggested that cost reductions through asset expansion were possible for firms in the U.S. S&L industry for the time period tested. A significant change in operating costs and in the estimated augmented elasticity measure was observed during the entire period, but especially when making a pre- and post-DIDMCA comparison. However, the study was limited by both the specification of the Translog model used and the lack of a sufficient number of observations following DIDMCA.

A review of the literature suggests that both the existence and significance of scale economies in the S&L industry and a proper determination of the significance of pre- and post-DIDMCA cost differences are as yet unresolved. Therefore, the following questions are addressed in this chapter: (1) Are there scale economies in the U.S. savings and loan industry? (2) If economies of scale exist, what is the range of asset sizes in which they are economically significant? (3) Has there been a significant change in the structure of the U.S. savings and loan industry as a result of DIDMCA?

DATA AND METHODOLOGY

Data Base

The data base used is derived from the financial reports that all federally insured S&Ls are required to file with the FHLBB. The FHLBB supplied the raw financial information in tape format and it was necessary to annualize the data for the purposes of this research.

An analysis of the data reveals that during the 15-year period covered by this study, the average total assets increased from 65 million dollars to 324 million dollars, an annual compound rate of growth of approximately 12.2%. When these data are broken down into a pre- and post-DIDMCA comparison, we find that from 1973 to 1979 (the year preceding the implementation of DIDMCA), the average increase in assets was 13.6%, whereas the growth rate in assets from 1980 through 1987 was 11%.

While assets were growing, so too were the number of branches per association. In 1973 the average number of branches per association was 2.6, for a total of over 10,000 for the population. By the end of 1979, the average had increased to 4.7 branches per S&L, for a total of 18,500 total branches. From 1980 through 1985 the average number of branches increased from 5.1 in 1980 to 6.8 by the end of 1985.[1] The number of branches increased 8.3% per year from 1973 through 1985, while the total number of S&Ls declined at a rate of 2% per year. The largest reduction in the number of associations came as the result of the wave of mergers that took place from 1979 to 1983, giving further credence to the assertion that U.S. S&Ls were attempting to expand their asset base to lower the cost of production per unit.

Deregulation encouraged some thrift institutions to diversify from the traditional line of commerce (mortgage lending) to other areas of commercial banking. Therefore, this analysis was restricted to those institutions that had at least 60% of their assets in mortgages, in order to ensure consistency and comparability of results. Additionally, it should be noted, the mean value of the mortgage as a percentage of total assets variable declined during the entire period studied. Thus, while the 60% figure is somewhat below the threshold demanded

[1]Here, it is appropriate to note that beginning in 1986 the FHLBB supplied a range of branches owned rather than the actual number of branches controlled by each association. To ensure consistency with earlier studies, it was decided to employ a branch estimation technique for the years 1986 and 1987.

by the Internal Revenue Service for tax purposes (although it still allows for some asset diversification), it facilitates the proper delineation between the traditional business of mortgage lending and the recent forays into commercial banking. This stratification is important for another reason: It gives a consistent data set, in that the primary activities of the institutions studied in the late 1980s are the same as those studied in the early to mid 1970s.[2]

Total mortgage loans and contracts grew at an average annual rate of 10.6% over the entire period, but from 1973 to 1979 the rate of growth was 13.7% versus 8.4% for the 1980 to 1987 time frame. Mortgages declined as a proportion of assets from over 87% in 1973 to approximately 80% in 1983 to less than 75% by 1987.

While fixed asset portfolios were undergoing realignment, liquidity, as measured by cash and investment securities as a percentage of assets, remained at a constant 10% of total assets. Additionally, nonmortgage loans grew from 2% of assets in 1973 to 5% of assets by 1983 (an annual rate of over 20%). Among the institutions included for study, this figure remained at 5% through 1987. This indicates that S&Ls were diversifying their fixed asset portfolio and the process appears to have been complete by the end of 1983.

The composition of the liabilities necessary to support the assets changed during the time period studied. Whereas S&Ls have previously had a stable deposit base on which to depend, inflation, disintermediation, and deregulation-induced competition drastically altered the mix and cost of funds. In fact, S&Ls saw the cost of funds exceed the return earned on the assets supported by these funds during the late 1970s and early 1980s.

The end of controlled interest rate ceilings (the termination of Regulation Q) forced the industry to compete for deposits at the existing market rate. The industry reacted by seeking alternative sources of funds, and as a result borrowed money increased at an average annual rate of over 20%. Not unexpectedly, total dividend and interest charges as a percentage of total assets grew from 8.5 to 13.7% by 1983 (subsequently it declined to 10.1% by 1987).

Concurrent with the increase in expenses associated with the cost of money, noninterest operating expenses increased for the entire period. The operating expense ratio (operating expenses divided by total assets) increased from 1.24% in 1973 to 1.43% by 1979, an annual rate of change of 2.4%. In contrast, the rate of change in operating expenses as a percentage of assets during the 1981 through 1987 period was approximately 6.5%.

Methodology and Models Tested

The testing methodology used consisted of (1) estimating the long-run average cost curve (LRAC) and a branching equation, and (2) deriving from them

[2]The authors are presently engaged in a study that bifurcates the population into those with more than 60% of total assets invested in mortgages and those with less than 60% of assets in mortgages.

measures of elasticity for the population of U.S. savings and loan associations for each year studied. The cost curves and elasticity measures used here are estimated using a form of the Translog model, which was initially applied to the financial institutions sector by Benston, Hanweck, and Humphrey (1982).

The general form of the model employed in this research is

$$\ln C = a_i + \sum_{i=1}^{n} \ln(X_i) + D_i + u \tag{1}$$

where C = expenses
X_i = factors thought to determine expenses
D_i = dummy variables
u = disturbance term.

Given the nature of the deregulated environment in which firms found themselves operating and the changing nature of the asset mix during the 1980s, it was decided to examine the following primary explanatory variables:

($Y1$) total mortgage loans
($Y2$) total other loans
($Y3$) total cash and investment securities
(B) number of branches.

In addition to the independent variables listed above, the following relative measures of cost were included as independent variables:

($P1$) the ratio of the sum of director's fees, office and employee compensation, pension plan costs, other employee benefits, directors, officer and employee expenses and management and consulting fees as a percentage of total deposit and savings accounts balances.

($P2$) the ratio of the sum of interest charges on savings accounts earnings, accruals for bonus accounts, advances from FHLBB, subordinated debentures, mortgage-backed bonds and other borrowed money as a percentage of fixed assets (office buildings + leasehold improvements + fixed asset appraisal increment less depreciation).

($P3$) the ratio of the sum of dividend and interest charges on savings account earnings, accruals for bonus accounts, advances from FHLBB, subordinated debentures, mortgage-backed bonds, and other borrowed money as a percentage of the sum of total deposits and savings accounts and total borrowed money.[3]

---

[3]This chapter contains the final results of a project (whose preliminary results were published elsewhere) for the period 1973–1983. Initially five versions of the Translog model were used and the Wilson Frontier Frame was used as a check for the entire 1973–1987 time period. However, after reviewing the preliminary results it was decided to focus on only one of the Translog models and the Wilson methodology. Thus, this chapter is an exposition of the specifications of the Translog and Wilson models and a discussion of the results and their implications.

Specifically, the Translog model tested here was

$$\begin{aligned}\ln C = {} & \ln P1 + \ln P2 + \ln P3 + \ln Y1 + \ln Y2 + \ln Y3 \\ & + \ln(Y1)^2/2 + \ln(Y1\,Y2) + \ln(Y1\,Y3) + \ln(Y2)^2/2 \\ & + \ln(Y2\,Y3) + \ln(Y3)^2/2 + \ln(P1)^2/2 + \ln(P1P2) \\ & + \ln(P1P3) + \ln(P2)^2/2 + \ln(P2P3) + \ln(P3)^2/2 \\ & + \ln(P1\,Y1) + \ln(P1\,Y2) + \ln(P1\,Y3) + \ln(P2\,Y1) \\ & + \ln(P2\,Y2) + \ln(P2\,Y3) + \ln(P3\,Y1) + \ln(P3\,Y2) \\ & + \ln(P3\,Y3) + \ln B + \ln(B)^2/2 + \ln(B\,Y1) \\ & + \ln(B\,Y2) + \ln(B\,Y3) + D1 \end{aligned} \tag{2}$$

with the following restrictions:
Restrict

(1) $\ln P1 + \ln P2 + \ln P3 = 1$

(2) $\ln(P1\,Y1) + \ln(P1\,Y2) + \ln(P1\,Y3) + \ln(P2\,Y1) + \ln(P2\,Y2) + \ln(P2\,Y3) + \ln(P3\,Y1) + \ln(P3\,Y2) + \ln(P3\,Y3) = 0$

(3) $2(\ln P1^2) + \ln(P1P2) + \ln(P1P3) = 0$

(4) $2(\ln P2^2) + \ln(P1P2) + \ln(P2P3) = 0$

(5) $2(\ln P3^2) + \ln(P2P3) + \ln(P1P3) = 0.$

The traditional measure of elasticity employed is found by taking the partial differential of the cost equation with respect to output:

$$\tau = \frac{\delta \ln(\text{Expenses})}{\delta \ln(\text{Output})}$$

The magnitude of τ determines the size of the cost savings available. A value of $\tau < 1$ signifies economies of scale, whereas $\tau > 1$ indicates diseconomies of scale. However, this measure of cost elasticity assumes that output can be increased without an increase in the number of branches. This does not reflect the reality of the situation in the industry. Many associations expanded primarily by establishing additional branch offices either de novo or through merger, as was evidenced in the data analysis section. To reflect this practice the modified elasticity measure τ^* is employed.[4] The measure is defined as follows:

$$\tau^* = \tau + \left[\frac{\delta \ln(\text{Expenses})}{\delta \ln(\text{Number of branches})}\right]\left[\frac{\delta \ln(\text{Number of branches})}{\delta \ln(\text{Output})}\right]$$

$$\text{where } \frac{\delta \ln(\text{Expenses})}{\delta \ln(\text{Number of branches})}$$

is the cost elasticity of the number of offices, which measures office economies, and

$$\frac{\delta \ln(\text{Number of branches})}{\delta \ln(\text{Output})}$$

is a ratio of the percentage change in the number of offices with respect to an increase in output as defined earlier. Thus, it was necessary to regress the number of branches against output, and the general form of the branching model employed was as follows:

$$\ln N = b_i + \sum_{i=1}^{n} \ln X_i + u \qquad (3)$$

In this research it was posited that output was primarily mortgages, other loans, and cash and investments. Thus, for consistency, the number of branches was held to be a function of the same determinants of output and the specific form used was

$$\ln B = \ln Y1 + \ln Y2 + \ln Y3 \qquad (4)$$

The other methodological approach used in this research was the Frontier Frame (FF) methodology, developed and employed by Wilson (1981). The FF is a locus of points depicting the actual minimum average cost attained by associations producing at various levels of output and is constructed in such a manner that all observations fall in the space defined by average operating expenses as a percentage of total assets. However, this frontier may be composed of outliers (since the cost levels predicted are so unlike those predicted by ordinary least squares), and it was decided to restrict the analysis to the mean operating expense ratio, which is given as

$$\text{OPER} = \frac{\text{Total operating expenses}}{\text{Total assets}}$$

[4] Benston, Hanweck, and Humphrey (1982) were the first to apply the augmented scale economy measure to the financial institutional sector, and Philippatos, Choi, and Dowling (1985) were the first to utilize the measure on the S&L industry.

for the various asset categories.

RESULTS AND DISCUSSION

The results from the model for several of the years between 1973 and 1987 are presented in Table 1.[5] The estimated augmented elasticities suggest that the LRAC shifted during the 1973–1980 time period. Specifically, there was a change in both the intercept and the slope of the estimated LRAC. In fact, by 1980, the minimum efficient scale of operations had increased markedly from between 25 and 50 million dollars of assets to an amount in excess of 250 million. From a post-DIDMCA standpoint, by 1985 the minimum efficient scale had increased to a level in excess of 500 million, and further by the end of 1987. This model indicates that asset expansion is attractive throughout the range and during all time periods tested with few exceptions.[6] It is interesting to note that during the 1980–1987 period, the greater than 10 billion dollars category had the least value of cost elasticity, implying that the most efficient and thus the optimal size S&L is one that creates output in excess of 10 billion dollars. Another interpretation is that larger institutions are able to take advantage of the possible existence of scope economies. A further analysis of the 1985–1987 results reveals that by 1987 the minimum efficient scale of operation was in the 250–500 million dollar category. When this is compared to the 1973 minimum scale size of 25 million dollars, it is clear that the cost structure of the industry changed significantly. When the evidence presented here is considered in toto, it supports the thesis that the primary force driving the changes in cost structure in the industry has been competition, and the root cause of competition during the 1980s was the deregulation of the industry that was accomplished through DIDMCA and the Garn–St. Germain Act.

---

[5]Only selected results are presented here. A copy of the complete results is available from the authors.

[6]These results are in contrast to those obtained and published by Dowling and Philippatos in *Applied Economics* (1990), where it was found that "the estimated elasticities indicate that the LRAC slopes upward with only a minor downturn at the $2000–$2500 million dollar level." However, it must be noted that the disparity of the results is due to the differences in (1) definition of the dependent variable (the earlier paper used operating expenses only), and (2) the formulation of the Translog model used here, which is substantially different from the one used to obtain the results published earlier. Specifically, the differences in model specification involve the selection of the independent explanatory variables. The earlier paper used only total assets and the number of branches as explanatory variables in contrast to the specification used here.

Further, it should be noted that the results for 1984 are not consistent with the rest of the time period tested. At this time, the authors are unable to explain this anomaly, but since the same regression model and variable definitions were used to estimate this year as were used to estimate both prior and succeeding years, and the means of the variables used were all within expectations, it appears that changes in the data base, entry classifications, reporting periods, and data format initiated in 1984 may explain the distortions. This explanation appears to be more acceptable when the 1984 results are considered in light of those of the 1985–1987 time period. The results of the latter are internally consistent as well as being consistent with expectations and the findings from previous researchers.

Table 1
Cost Elasticities (τ^*) Based on the Translog Model

Assets in millions	1973	1975	1977	1979	1980	1981	1983	1985	1987
0–25	1.0004	1.0124	1.0095	1.0195	1.0224	1.0333	1.0172	1.0161	1.0440
25–50	0.9876	1.0008	1.0019	1.0093	1.0132	1.0170	0.9999	1.0119	1.0347
50–100	0.9823	0.9978	0.9966	1.0025	1.0067	1.0078	0.9937	1.0066	1.0220
100–250	0.9785	0.9941	0.9919	0.9959	1.0001	0.9989	0.9902	1.0000	1.0100
250–500	0.9734	0.9867	0.9879	0.9894	0.9940	0.9888	0.9904	0.9930	0.9937
500–1000	0.9722	0.9859	0.9839	0.9851	0.9894	0.9798	0.9888	0.9870	0.9795
1000–1500	0.9620	0.9820	0.9810	0.9810	0.9850	0.9720	0.9900	0.9820	0.9706
1500–2000	0.9640	0.9660	0.9810	0.9800	0.9820	0.9690	0.9820	0.9790	0.9669
2000–2500	0.9630	0.9610	0.9750	0.9700	0.9780	0.9630	0.9890	0.9800	0.9582
2500–5000	0.9590	0.9710	0.9770	0.9730	0.9790	0.9620	0.9890	0.9740	0.9578
5000–7500[a]	0.9590	0.9550	N/A	0.9670	0.9730	0.9460	0.9850	0.9720	0.9302
7500–10,000[a]	N/A	N/A	0.9700	0.9680	0.9720	0.9500	0.9940	0.9660	N/A
>10,000[a]	N/A	N/A	N/A	0.9680	0.9710	0.9450	0.9670	0.9640	N/A
Population	0.9929	1.0032	1.0002	1.0053	1.0085	1.0097	0.9968	1.0024	1.0148

Note. The reported augmented elasticities are group averages of individual elasticities that are computed based on the coefficient estimates of the Translog model.
[a]The augmented elasticity value in these asset classes in earlier years should be treated with caution because there is only one observation present for a particular asset classification.

Table 2 presents the results from the Frontier Frame methodology. The results presented clearly indicate that, according to this technique, the LRAC shifted upward during the 1973–1987 period. Additionally, the LRAC was downward sloping throughout the range and thus economies of scale were achievable through asset expansion for the entire time period studied. With respect to scope economies, further evidence can be found by considering the low OPER contained in the 1987 results for firms with asset levels in excess of 10 billion dollars (relative to other asset categories). These low values of the OPER variable are consistent with the existence of scope economies.

The results presented here are consistent with those from earlier studies and the existence of economies of scale is confirmed. The results reveal that operating expenses have increased within each asset category over all time periods examined. It is notable that the FF indicates the existence of significant scale economies, and the results of the model were largely consistent with those of the Translog model. What is surprising is that given the simplicity of this model, it appears to be measuring the same changes in operating environment reflected in the results of the previously discussed Translog model. To wit, with respect to the pre- and post-DIDMCA comparison, this model indicates that the LRAC was less steeply sloped after DIDMCA than it was prior to the event, which is consistent with the results obtained from the Translog testing methodology. When the LRACs generated by the Translog and the FF are examined around the DIDMCA date, it is seen that both continue to shift upward and maintain their negative slope. This implies that DIDMCA might have forced associations to seek cost reductions through scale expansion (perhaps through increased costs due to competition for funds, which is observable through the continued increases in the mean operating expense ratio).

SUMMARY AND CONCLUSIONS

In this chapter we attempted to provide definitive answers to the following questions: (1) Are there scale economies in the U.S. savings and loan industry? (2) If economies of scale exist, what is the range of asset sizes in which they are economically significant? (3) Has there been a significant change in the structure of the U.S. savings and loan industry as a result of DIDMCA?

Based on the evidence presented here, it is apparent that the cost structure of the savings and loan industry has changed significantly over the time period examined and that the increases in costs continue to increase at an increasing rate. Thus, for S&Ls that chose not to pursue a strategy of growth, it would have been difficult to earn the same levels of net revenue while suffering increases in costs.

It is logical to assume, according to evidence presented here, that cost reductions were available through asset expansion and, for most of the period examined, cost reductions were available throughout the range of asset categories. Thus, the pursuit of scale economies as a motivation for the increased number

Table 2
Operating Expense Ratios

Assets in millions	1973	1975	1977	1979	1980	1981	1983	1985	1987
0–25	0.01295	0.01429	0.01494	0.01647	0.01750	0.01825	0.01943	0.02312	0.02679
25–50	0.01195	0.01265	0.01268	0.01388	0.01391	0.01476	0.01597	0.02030	0.02443
50–100	0.01210	0.01252	0.01262	0.01354	0.01382	0.01415	0.01522	0.01930	0.02307
100–250	0.01160	0.01250	0.01270	0.01340	0.01370	0.01430	0.01540	0.01920	0.02182
250–500	0.01120	0.01200	0.01230	0.01340	0.01390	0.01410	0.01540	0.01900	0.02106
500–1000	0.01050	0.01180	0.01280	0.01310	0.01340	0.01380	0.01600	0.02000	0.02055
1000–1500	0.01100	0.01100	0.01200	0.01300	0.01300	0.01500	0.01600	0.01800	0.01964
1500–2000	0.01100	0.01100	0.01200	0.01200	0.01200	0.01300	0.01500	0.02000	0.01811
2000–2500	0.00700	0.00900	0.01100	0.01200	0.01400	0.01200	0.01600	0.01700	0.01921
2500–5000	0.00700	0.01100	0.01200	0.01100	0.01000	0.01200	0.01600	0.01800	0.01746
5000–7500[a]	0.00070	0.00800	N/A	0.01100	0.01100	0.01100	0.01700	0.01700	0.01992
7500–10,000[a]	N/A	N/A	0.00700	0.00700	0.00600	0.00900	0.01300	0.01600	N/A
>10,000[a]	N/A	N/A	N/A	0.00800	0.00800	0.00900	0.01200	0.01500	0.01697
Population	0.01238	0.01322	0.01340	0.01430	0.01470	0.01520	0.01620	0.01980	0.02279

[a]The augmented elasticity value in these asset classes in earlier years should be treated with caution because there is only one observation present for a particular asset classification.

of mergers following DIDMCA was a legitimate strategic option for S&Ls. This research implies that the attempts to encourage mergers among small healthy institutions, among failing S&Ls, and between failing and healthy S&Ls based on the premise of achieving scale economies through output expansion was largely correct and was a fundamentally sound policy.

This result raises several interesting questions. Among them, if the achievement of cost reductions was possible through scale expansion, why have so many institutions that experienced substantial growth during the period studied subsequently failed? We suspect that the answer to the question might well lie in a study of those institutions excluded from this study. That is, those institutions whose mortgage to total asset ratio was less than 60%, indicating that these institutions strayed from the traditional role of the savings and loan association, which was providing mortgages. Concomitant with the above observations, the regulatory authorities should consider the asset mix of combining institutions, since the results presented here indicate that cost reductions are available for those savings and loan associations that have a minimum of 60% of mortgage with respect to assets. Last, it should be noted that when the entire population is considered, a significantly different picture with respect to scale expansion may well appear.

REFERENCES

Atkinson, J. F. 1977. The structure of cost in the savings and loan industry during 1974, *Federal Home Loan Bank Board, Research Working Paper No. 67.*

Atkinson, J. F. 1979. Firm size in the savings and loan industry, *Federal Home Loan Bank Board, Research Working Paper No. 29.*

Benston, G. J., G. A. Hanweck, and D. B. Humphrey. 1982. Scale economies in banking: A restructuring and reassessment, *Journal of Money, Credit, and Banking* 14:435–456.

Brigham, E. F. 1964. Economies of scale in the savings and loan industry, *Western Economics Journal* 3:7–20.

Brigham, E. F., and R. R. Pettit. 1970. Effects of structure on performance in the savings and loan industry, *Federal Home Loan Bank Board, Study in Savings and Loan Industry,* 971–1290.

Choi, D., G. C. Philippatos, and W. A. Dowling. 1986. Operational economies in the thrift industry: Assessment of potential benefits from mergers, *College of Business Working Paper Series, No. 217,* Knoxville: University of Tennessee.

Dowling, W. A., and G. C. Philippatos. 1990. Economies of scale in the savings and loan industry, 1973–1983, *Applied Economics* 22:237–248.

Dowling, W. A., G. C. Philippatos, and D. Choi. 1983. Economies of scale through mergers in the S & L industry, Proceedings of a Conference on Bank Structure and Competition, Chicago, IL: Federal Reserve Bank of Chicago, pp. 480–497.

McNulty, J. E. 1981. Economies of scale in the S & L industry: New evidence and implications for profitability, *Federal Home Loan Bank Board Journal* 14:2–7.

McNulty, J. E. 1982. Economies of scale: A case study of the Florida savings and loan industry, *Federal Reserve Bank of Atlanta Economic Review* 67:22–31.

Philippatos, G. C., D. Choi, and W. A. Dowling. 1985. Effects of mergers on operational efficiency: A study of the S & L industry in transition, *Northeast Journal of Business and Economics*, 1–14.

Verbrugge, J. A., R. A. Shick, and K. J. Thygerson. 1976. An analysis of savings and loan profit performance, *Journal of Finance* 31:1427–1442.

Wilson, J. H. 1981. A note on scale economies in the savings and loan industry, *Business Economics* 16:45–49.

Chapter 13

The "Round-Tripping" Effect of Debt–Equity Swaps

M. T. Vaziri and Hossein Shalchi

Given the difficulties in defining and estimating capital flight and the channels to which it moves, the large-scale exodus of private capital is often cited as one of the prime contributing factors to the external debt crisis of debtor nations (Glynn and Koening, 1984; Dooley, 1986; Decoodt, 1986; Khan and ul Haque, 1987; Guddington, 1986). A reversal of more than U.S. $100 billion of Latin American assets that have fled to industrial countries would make it possible to pay off most of the external debt of troubled debtor nations, since much of the debt was incurred to finance the outflow of private capital in the first place (Dornbush, 1987). According to some estimates, overall the debtor nations added $381.5 billion to the external foreign debt for the years 1978–1983. But approximately $103.1 billion of that amount flowed back out as flight capital or unidentified outflows, sapping local economies, draining central bank reserves, and forcing nations to default on their loans (Glynn and Koening, 1984).

Debt swaps have been used as a mechanism to reduce the debt burden of troubled debtor nations. When swaps include the equity (debt–equity swaps), the foreign investor can exchange the less developed country (LDC) external debt at a deep discount for debtor countries' equity. The swaps enable the investors in the debtor nations to purchase the foreign debt at a discount and then convert it into domestic currency (commonly known as debt–peso swaps). Purchase of the equity through debt swaps will be at face value, and conversion of the debt to domestic currency will be at a special discount rate that is much cheaper than the official exchange rate (Ramon and Moreno, 1987).

Any debt–equity swap transaction offers some implicit subsidy to the investor in the form of a preferential exchange rate, a differential between average price of debt and its marginal value, or a differential between the secondary market discount of debt–equity swap transactions and the central bank commission. However, such subsidy could be very expensive and quite large for the debtor nations in terms of fiscal cost and the operational deficit of the public sector.

For example, the total subsidy in Chile, the country with the most successful debt-swaps operation, reached $357 million during 1985–1987 on Chapter XIX and DI 600 operations, and over $600 on all debt swaps. In 1987 alone, the true debt-swaps subsidy was $265 million, which amounted to 1.5% of the gross domestic product, 142% of the budget deficit, and 26% of the country's money supply (Chile Economic Report, 1988).

The subsidy, in terms of an implicit preferential exchange rate, is also astonishing. Since most of the LDC debts are deeply discounted in the debt–equity swaps secondary market, and since the central bank of the debtor nation titles the same debt at close to the face value, the investor is effectively receiving an exchange rate totally subsidized by the debtor nations (Data Resources, 1988).

Many speculators and residents have misused the debt-swaps operation and have received subsidy for the repatriation of their capital. Such reversal pattern of capital is known as the "round-tripping" effect (Data Resources, 1988, pp. 20–21).

The outrush of capital and the round-tripping effect of debt–equity swaps have done more damage to the economies of the debtor nations than their external debt. According to recent estimates made by Morgan Guaranty, $109 million left Mexico, Venezuela, and Argentina during the last decade. During the same period, more than $200 billion flew out of 18 debtor nations, increasing their international debt by 50% collectively.

Financing the round-tripping effect of capital flight can distort the effectiveness of the debt–equity swaps process as follows:

(1) If the round-tripping is stimulated by debt currency swaps, the increase in the money supply will provoke a rapid increase in inflation.
(2) If the central bank of the debtor nation issues a domestic debt title to repurchase the existing foreign debt, then the subsidy will be financed through government deficits. However, if the new debt causes the interest rate of the debtor nation to increase, the subsidy will be financed by local investors and a crowding effect will occur in the interest rate market.
(3) If debt–equity swap transactions occur between foreign investors and local debtors without the presence of a central bank, the local debtors will bear the burden of the subsidy as they transfer its assets to foreign investors at deeply discounted prices.

Given the advance effects of financing the round-tripping of debt–equity swaps, the objective of this chapter is to analyze round-trip capital flight and its responses to changes in interest rates, inflation rates, government deficit, and exchange rates, as well as the investment structure of the debtor nations.

REASONS FOR CAPITAL FLIGHT

The exodus of short-term speculative capital outflows is often associated with a variety of related controllable and uncontrollable factors. Some of these factors, such as domestic political and financial crises, heavier taxes, prospective tightening of capital control, major devaluation of the domestic currency, and actual hyperinflation, are well documented throughout the literature (Guddington, 1986). Other things being equal, an expected depreciation of the domestic currency would likely cause domestic residents to alter their domestic assets to foreign ones (Ramirez-Royas, 1986).

Financial sector constraints, such as interest rate control, often result in lower nominal interest rates than comparative foreign financial instruments, as well as in negative real rate adjusted for inflation. Such financial constraints, along with the lack of domestic investment opportunities, encourage domestic residents to invest in foreign assets and further promote capital flight.

Erosion of the value of domestic assets due to fluctuating monetary policies and growing fiscal deficits are other reasons for the purchase of foreign assets. The safer haven theory of capital movement (where industrial nations have been perceived as safer investment opportunities by risk-avertor domestic investors, elimination of the withholding tax on nonresident asset holding in the United States, and secrecy about bank accounts) not only makes it possible for foreigners to use the United States and other industrial countries' financial systems as a tax haven but facilitates illegal transactions and tax evasions (Khan and ul Haque, 1987).

METHODS OF ESTIMATING CAPITAL FLIGHT

Although there is no generally accepted definition or method of measuring capital flight, some researchers (e.g., Bhagwati, Krueger, and Wibulswasdi, 1974) have attempted to estimate capital flight by calculating the underinvoicing of exports and overinvoicing of imports using a partner-country trade data comparison. Based on this method of measurement, the definition of capital flight should be limited to illegal capital outflows.

Other estimates with a large margin of error have been made as an indirect calculation of capital flight from eight heavily indebted developing countries for the period of 1974–1982 (Khan and ul Haque, 1987). These methods define capital flight as gross private short-term capital flows plus net errors and omissions in the countries' balance of payments accounts. Some other estimates include the errors and omissions category in the measurement of capital flight based on the concept that omissions largely reflect unrecorded short-term capital flows. These estimates also include certain subcategories of line items, such as other short-term capital (Guddington, 1986).

Some of these estimates (Khan and ul Haque, 1987) conclude that based on short-term capital flow and net errors and omissions, the ratio of accumulated capital flight to external debt in 1987 for all eight heavily indebted nations was averaged around 30%, implying that for every U.S. dollar loaned to these countries as a group, some 30% came out.

METHODOLOGY OF STUDY

To distinguish between capital outflows motivated by normal portfolio decisions and the propensity for foreign asset substitution motivated by the perceived risk of nonresident investors, this study estimates the aggregate stock of private and official claims on nonresident assets using Dooley's method of estimate of capital flight (Dooley, 1986). The observed information has been obtained from balance-of-payment data of Brazil, Chile, Argentina, Mexico, and Venezuela (five troubled debtor nations with mixed debt–equity swaps mechanism) between 1980 and 1989. The aggregate stock of errors and omissions also has been calculated as an estimate of unrecorded capital outflows. The aggregate cumulative capital outflow was tabulated by adding the errors and omissions and claims of nonresidents other than those resulting from direct investment.

To correct the problem of underestimation of the stock of external claims (since balance of payments data seems to underestimate the aggregate accumulated external debt), the unrecorded stock of external claims has been calculated using the differences between the debt recorded by the World Bank and balance of payments data. Table 1 summarizes the calculations of total stock of external claims on the countries under study.

Since we are using Dooley's method of estimation of capital flight, it is appropriate to calculate the stock of claims implied by investment income receipts and market interest rate. The differences between this estimate and total stock of external claims (calculated in Table 1) is the aggregate calculated capital flight or its best approximation. Such stock of aggregate flight of capital accounted for more than 45% of the total stock of the external debt of Argentina (a country with a high volume of debt–equity swap transactions), 28% of the external accumulated debt of Brazil (a country with a low volume of debt–equity swap transactions), and 21% of external debt of Mexico and Venezuela.

EXPLANATION OF CAPITAL FLIGHT

Avoidance of inflation tax by nonresident investors and attempts by foreign asset holders to arbitrage both the yield differentials and exchange rate differential (in case of debt to currency swap transaction) are incentives for capital flight and the round-trip outflow of assets from troubled debtor nations. Although round-trip capital flows have their limitations due either to specific government actions such as tax on financial positions or, in the case of Chile, Chapter 18 regulations and restriction on capital repatriations as well as the

Table 1
Summary of the Calculations of Total Stock of External Claims on the Countries Under Study Between 1980 and 1989 (in billions of U.S. dollars)

Year	Aggregate stock of private and official claims of nonresident asset (cumulated) BOP (1)	Aggregate stock of errors and omissions (cumulated)[a] BOP (2)	Aggregate cumulative capital outflows (2) + (1) (3)	Unrecorded stock of external claims[b] (4)	Cumulative stock of external claims (3) + (4) (5)
1980	59.2	2.9	62.1	49.6	111.7
1981	62.6	11.5	74.1	50.1	124.2
1982	61.2	19.7	80.9	58.3	139.7
1983	66.9	21.8	88.7	62.1	150.8
1984	75.3	20.1	95.4	68.9	164.3
1985	79.1	22.8	101.9	75.5	177.4
1986	84.6	24.6	109.2	78.1	187.4
1987	89.2	29.1	118.3	82.3	200.6
1988	90.1	31.4	121.5	87.6	209.1
1989	95.3	30.1	125.4	91.2	216.6

[a]Aggregate stock of errors and omission has been calculated as an estimate of unrecorded capital outflows.

[b]Unrecorded stock of external claims has been calculated using the differences between the debt recorded by the World Bank and balance of payments (BOP) data.

perceived risk faced by nonresident creditors, consequences of large gross capital flight remain a threatening factor to the economies of debtor nations.

Identification of the possible determinants of capital flight is essential in explaining round-trip capital flows and formulating possible public policy. As discussed earlier, capital flight is a phenomenon that responds to a variety of variables, such as major devaluation of domestic currency, actual or incipient hyperinflation, heavier taxes, interest rates, and growing fiscal deficits. The relatively large perceived risk associated with investment in debtor nations as well as many incentives in the recipient industrial countries, such as almost risk-free bearer bonds, deposit insurance, and absence of withholding taxes on certain types of nonresident claims, are other factors that stimulate the outflow of financial assets.

In this study the relationship between round-trip capital flight and its several possible determinants is tested empirically using a pooled regression for the annual individual observations for Brazil, Chile, Mexico, Venezuela, and Argentina for the 1980–1989 time period.

The independent variables used to explain the variation of round-trip capital flight for the countries under study are change in annual exchange rate, domestic inflation rate (DIN), ratio of fiscal deficit to GNP, accumulated changes in gross external debt, and domestic interest rate. Annual observations for five countries under study (Argentina, Brazil, Chile, Mexico, and Venezuela) during 1980–1989 have been gathered. Simultaneity biases have been reduced by using an instrument variable estimation technique and ordinary least squares estimates. All other variables with *t* statistics less than unity were dropped.

REGRESSION RESULTS

The results of a pooled regression for annual observations of the five troubled debtor nations under study during the 1980–1989 time period are shown in Table 2. The positive coefficient for the domestic inflation rate indicates that the perceived domestic inflation motivates domestic residents to convert major portions of their domestic financial assets to foreign assets. The positive relationship between domestic currency depreciation and round-trip capital flight also suggests that resident investors and speculators acquire foreign financial assets to hedge against the exchange rate risk and to channel the outflow of the capital.

Financial restraint and domestic interest rate control also play a role in the channeling of round-trip capital flight. The negative coefficient on the

Table 2

Results of a Pooled Regression for Annual Observations for Five Troubled Debtor Nations Under Study Between 1980 and 1989

$$CF = \underset{(3.86)}{14.20\Delta ER} + \underset{(4.25)}{18.90DIF} - \underset{(-1.22)}{2.64RD/GNP} + \underset{(2.62)}{6.50DIR}$$

$R^2 = .72$

Variable/Instrument	Definition
CF (capital flight)	Derived by subtracting the aggregate stock of external claims (calculated on Table 1) from the stock of claims implied by investment income receipts and market interest rates
ΔER (change in annual exchange rate)	Annual observation international financial statistics (IFS) line ac various issues
DIF (domestic inflation rate)	IFS, line 64, 1980/89
FD/CNP (fiscal deficit/gross national product)	Fiscal deficit: IFS line 802F; GNP: IFS line 99a
DIR (domestic interest rate)	Domestic time deposit interest rate, individual country interest rate statistics
ΔED (accumulated changes in gross external debt)	World Debt Tables, World Bank 1980/89

Note. Numbers inside parentheses are *t* statistics and R^2 is the coefficient of determination.

government deficit, however, indicates the expected negative impact on the outflow of financial assets. Growing financial constraints and government deficits have tended to limit the magnitude of round-trip capital flight transactions.

SUMMARY AND CONCLUSION

The accumulation of external debt of the debtor nations under study is the result of the complex interaction of many exogenous and indigenous factors and causes. It is very difficult to assign appropriate weights to the various explanatory factors and ignore the chain of causality. It is also difficult to analyze the debt problems of the debtor nation in isolation and recommend specific financial solutions. Inducement of debt–equity swaps as a panacea for debt crisis in many troubled debtor nations has a serious shortcoming. The large budgetary impact of debt–equity swaps not only adds to existing inflationary pressures through potential monetization, but provides excessive crowding effects on the loanable funds markets (in the cases of Brazil and Mexico). Since debt–equity swaps generally are an exchange of the country's external debt to internal debt, they adversely affect the fiscal cost and fiscal deficit of debtor nations.

The round-tripping effect of debt–equity swaps has also helped to deprive debtor nations of one of their scarcest resources—investment capital. The exodus of huge amounts of capital outflow generated $50 billion of external debt for Argentina instead of $1 billion, and $31 billion of foreign debt for Venezuela rather than a surplus of $12 billion, according to a recent estimate by Morgan Guaranty. A host of long- and short-term measures have been suggested by international organizations, such as removing foreign investment barriers, avoiding currency overvaluation, exchange control, and tight monetary policies. However, very few debtor nation policymakers have the tenacity either to initiate the policies or to stay with them long enough to stem the tide of capital flight.

Comparative analysis of existing research suggests that the comprehensive and more elaborate representation of debt structure and debt servicing capabilities of debtor nations would be more useful than analysis of a simple financial position such as interest or debt service payments to evaluate the external debt crisis of the debtor nations. The complex interaction of many factors such as changes in annual exchange rates, domestic inflation rate, proportion of fiscal deficit out of GNP, accumulated changes in gross external debt, and domestic interest rate has been analyzed to explain the round-tripping effect of debt–equity swaps and capital flight for the countries under study.

Historical evaluation of debt structure of the debtor nations and results of the statistical analysis for the countries under study suggest that the complex interaction of many financial incentives within these countries appears to be an important determination of their aggregate external claims and capital outflow.

Although the explanatory factors of capital outflow are several and interlinked, designing a methodology to assign appropriate weights is not useful in determining the aggregate external claims of the countries under study. However, length of historical data and transferability of these factors from one country to others can play an important role in understanding the debt structure of these troubled debtor nations.

REFERENCES

Bhagwati, J. A. O. Krueger, and C. Wibulswasdi. 1974. Capital flight from LDC: A statistical analysis, in *Illegal Transactions in International Trade*, Amsterdam: North-Holland, Vol. I.

Chile Economic Report. 1988. *Debt-for-Equity Deals Play Integral Role in the Economy,* New York, Vol. I.

Data Resources. 1988. Debt equity swaps in Latin America: An overview, Working paper.

Decoodt, P. 1986. The debt crisis of the third world: Some aspects of causes and solutions, *Columbia Journal of World Business* 21(3).

Dooley, M. 1986. *Capital Flight, a Response of Differences in Financial Risk,* Washington: Department Memorandum DM/27/17.

Dornbush, R. 1987. International debt and economic instability, *Economic Review.*

Glynn, L., and P. Koening. 1984. The capital flight crisis, *Institutional Investor.*

Guddington, J. T. 1986. *Capital Flight Estimates, Issues, and Explanations,* New York: Princeton University, Vol. 58.

Khan, M. S., and N. ul Haque. 1987. Capital flight from developing countries, *Finance and Development* 24.

Ramirez-Royas, C. L. 1986. Monetary substitution in developing countries, *Finance and Development* 23.

Ramon J. T., and Moreno, L. 1987. L.D.C. debt swaps, *Federal Reserve Bank of San Francisco Weekly Letter.*

Chapter 14

Emerging Capital Markets and Economic Development

Edgar Ortiz

In response to the debt crisis and the increased globalization of real and financial markets, developing countries are promoting important structural changes in their economies. Inward-oriented development models are rapidly being replaced by ambitious outward-oriented growth models. Decades of excessive government intervention in the economy and excessive regulation and protectionism are also ending through the implementation of significant plans for free trade and economic integration, privatization of state enterprises, strengthening of local market activity, and less bureaucratism. Thus, local markets and institutions are undergoing important modernization changes. Underlying these changes are two basic facts needed to promote economic development in the aftermath of the debt crisis: the need to become competitive at the international level in order to participate in and benefit from expected global changes in trade and finance, and the need for increasing local savings and finding alternative ways to foreign debt financing to mobilize greater local and international resources for investments.

These processes of modernization have led policymakers and financial economists to reassess the role of the financial sector and its markets and institutions. For this reason, appraising the contribution of capital markets to economic development is receiving increased attention. However, financial intermediation models still limit their analysis to debt securities and emphasize money demand and interest rate determination. Risk is also ignored in the savings investment process. This chapter presents a synthetic model that overcomes those limitations.

RESOURCE ALLOCATION AND BUSINESS FINANCE IN IMPERFECT MARKETS

Financial Intermediation and Development

The importance of financial intermediation in economic development has been stressed in many studies. Early economic development studies assigned financial institutions a rather passive "demand-following" role in economic activity. This view changed with the pioneering works of Goldsmith (1969), Gurley and Shaw (1960), McKinnon (1973), Patrick (1966), and Shaw (1973). Based on empirical studies dealing with the experiences of both developed and developing countries, their basic ideas supported and modeled the creation of innovative "supply-leading" financial institutions, whereby financial innovation can promote economic growth. Financial innovation includes the creation of modern financial institutions, new and diversified financial assets, and new and improved services. Policies oriented in this way promote "financial deepening," i.e., an increase of financial assets in relation to output. In turn, this means increased savings, increased corporate indirect financing, through financial instruments issued by financial intermediaries, lower costs of capital for corporations, and a more efficient allocation of resources to the most profitable investments. In sum, corporations are able to invest beyond their own resources and at lower costs; therefore, employment and output increase. Moreover, risk of investment activities are bundled and borne by a larger spectrum of the society.

These situations are depicted in Figures 1 and 2. In Figure 1, financial intermediation induces growth by lowering interest rates and improving monetary policy. Liquidity is an important characteristic of indirect securities created by financial intermediaries, to the extent that they become substitutes for money. This increased liquidity of indirect securities causes the demand curve for money D to become more elastic and to shift leftward, D'. If money supply remains constant, say at M^sA, then interest rates decline from i_3 to i_2. Similarly, if monetary authorities decrease interest rates to i_1, they must increase real money supply by open market purchases of securities by less than would be otherwise necessary in the case of an elastic demand curve for money D_E', assuming the absence of financial intermediaries and indirect debt. Figure 2 depicts the alternative contributions of financial intermediation to increased investments. Financial intermediation shifts downward the marginal cost of capital curve, from *MCOC* to *MCOC'*. Corporate cost of capital decreases from *COC* to *COC'*. Investments become cheaper and the range of feasible investments increases from *OA* to *OA*.* Rigorous credit allocation should lead to sound resource allocation to projects with marginal returns above marginal cost of capital. At the aggregate level, output and employment increase, leading to greater economic growth and welfare.

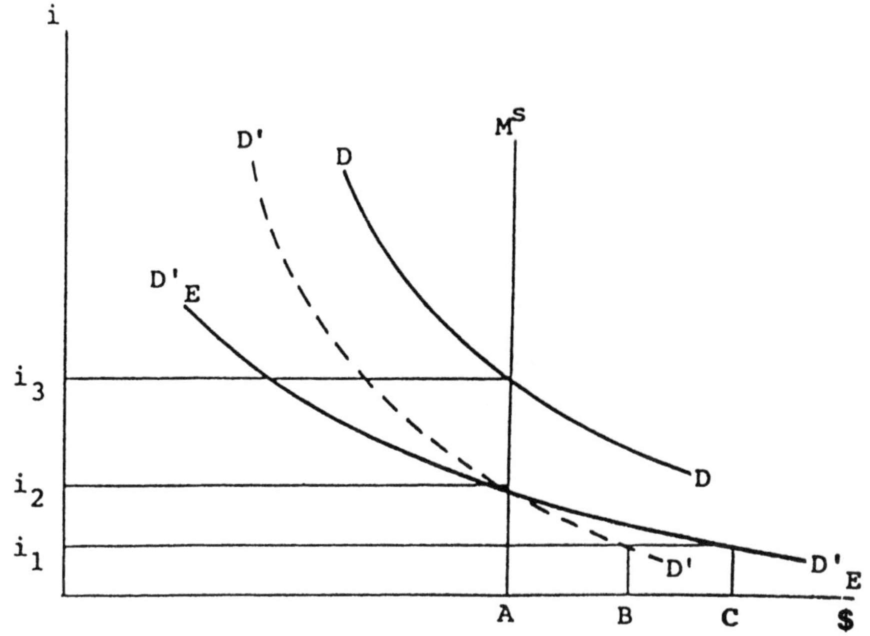

Figure 1 Impact of financial intermediation on interest rates and demand for money.

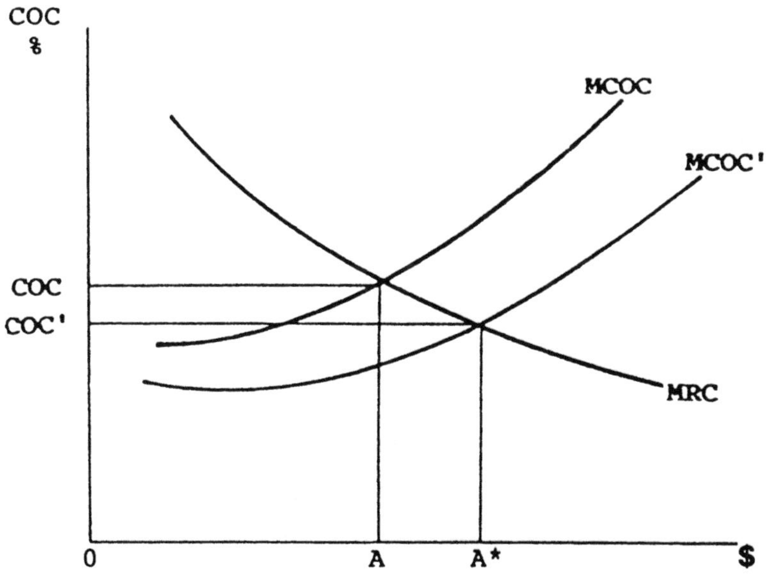

Figure 2 Impact of financial intermediation on corporate cost of capital and investments.

Capital Markets and Economic Development

Capital market activity is an important part of the financial intermediation processes outlined above. However, although the importance of these markets has been widely recognized, their contributions to economic growth have not been fully determined. Most studies dealing with the relationship between the financial sector and financial intermediation with economic growth have concentrated in the relationship between money and growth, and in the role of monetary intermediaries, i.e., banking institutions. Models usually include three financial markets—money demand and supply, indirect securities, and primary securities—as part of a general equilibrium model. However, analytical representations of capital markets are often limited to debt securities, subsumed in a context of either money demand or interest rate determination (Bennet, 1965; Fry, 1988, 1989; Galbis, 1977; Gupta, 1984; Hosek and Zahn, 1977; Patinkin, 1965; Sargent, 1965; Sijben, 1977; Skull, 1985; Smith, 1978; Spellman, 1976; Townsend, 1983). Empirical studies have concentrated on money, inflation, financial repression, and the role of banking institutions (Basant, 1986; Bencivenga and Smith, 1989; Buffie, 1984; Courakis, 1984; Diaz Alejandro, 1985; Dornbusch and Reynoso, 1989; Taylor, 1983). Consequently, policy suggestions have concentrated on monetary policy, suggesting primarily financial liberalization and/or a strengthening of the banking system, including, particularly in earlier models, the creation of development financing banks.

Paradoxically, capital market theory has made important strides during the last few decades. Its building blocks are centered around market efficiency and asset pricing. Its important principles have led to partial equilibrium models based on risk and returns (Lintner, 1965; Markowitz, 1959; Mossin, 1977; Ross, 1976; Sharpe, 1970).[1] An integration of these contributions to general equilibrium models and development financing has not taken place, albeit this situation has changed. Factors leading economists to reconsider the role of capital markets on economic activity are the globalization of financial markets, the remarkable growth of capital markets in some Southeast Asian countries, and the negative impacts on the debt crisis on the mobilization of international resources to the developing countries. Finally, limited availability of local savings and international resources for development financing have focused on capital markets as an alternative to the banking system to promote local savings and induce favorable international capital movements to promote private business in the developing nations.

The increased importance of the financial sector in some Southeast Asian countries has led economists and policymakers to assess which conditions diminish its growth, and which have been contributors to economic growth in those nations. A number of studies have stressed financial liberalization and its

[1]Capital markets theory has led to significant modeling and empirical research in the last three decades. Important advances are reported in Bamberg and Spremann (1986), Duffie (1988), Guimaraes et al. (1988), Krouse (1986), and Levy (1979–1990).

impact on local capital markets and economic development (Cheng, 1980; Cho, 1986; Dailami, 1986, 1990; Darrat and Muharjee, 1986; Dawson, 1984; Kapur and Ravaillon, 1988; Joong-Wong, 1988; Khambata and Khambata, 1989; Laurence, 1981; Sharma, 1983; Toida, 1990; Ziemba et al., 1991). In the Latin American case, some pioneering works have dealt with capital markets (Aspe, 1981; de la Calle, 1991; de Tarso Medeiros, 1981; Errunza, 1979; Errunza and Losq, 1985; Errunza and Rosenberg, 1982; Fischer et al., 1991; Geyikdaki and Geyikdaki, 1989; Gonzalez Fraga, 1982; Haugen et al., 1985; Kitchen, 1987; Lessard, 1975; Ortiz, 1979, 1980, in press; Ramos, 1988; Sarmiento, 1988).

Those studies can be summed up in four points: (1) Economic activity is determined by real and financial variables; general equilibrium involves clearing of all markets. Disturbances in any market are transmitted to others through their links in common real or financial variables. (2) Capital markets contribute decisively to economic growth, increasing savings and linking them directly with long-term economic activity and financial innovation with lower costs of capital and/or increased investment opportunities, and a better composition in the debt-equity mix. (3) Efficient capital markets provide an important framework of reference for portfolio choices and corporate financial decisions. (4) Efficient local capital markets integrate smoothly to the international capital markets and promote the mobilization of direct and indirect investments to the developing countries.

The role of capital markets on steady growth can be conceptualized by desegregating financial markets in a simple general market equilibrium model. A fully developed economy is divided in four sectors[2]: households, business, government, and the financial intermediation sector. Households are a surplus sector, i.e., their income is greater than their expenditures. Government and business are deficit sectors, to which savings from households are transferred for investments through financial intermediaries. The economy is composed of three types of markets: labor, commodities, and financial markets. In turn, financial markets are subdivided in money markets and capital markets. Money markets comprise demand and supply for money; demand and supply for indirect securities, i.e., short-term securities created by the monetary intermediaries; and a market for short-term securities issued and traded in exchange markets.[3] Bonds and equity are traded in the capital markets. In all these mar-

[2]To stress the importance of capital markets on development, the model first assumes perfect markets and leaves the role of the government implicit. These assumptions are relaxed by analyzing quantitative and qualitative implications of capital markets on development, and by extending the model to include the government both as regulator and a participant in the capital markets.

[3]This representation recognizes the fact that not all short-term securities are "inside money" i.e., liabilities of the banking system. This subdivision is also consistent with current conceptualizations of money as *M*1, *M*2, and *M*3. Indirect securities are separated from short-term securities traded in exchange markets to stress the different nature of their markets, their issuers, and their regulation. Near money instruments characteristic of *M*3 (and *M*4 in some countries) can also be included in this market. Thus, capital markets would be mainly represented by bonds and stocks issued by private or parastatal corporations.

kets, demand and supply are determined by real and financial variables, as well as by technological or institutional innovations. General equilibrium conditions can be represented as follows[4]:

$$N^d(R, F, T) - N^s(R, F, T) = 0 \text{ Labor market} \tag{1}$$

$$C(R, F, T) - Y(R, F, T) = 0 \text{ Commodities market} \tag{2}$$

$$L(R, F, T) - \frac{M}{P}(R, F, T) = 0 \text{ Money demand–supply market} \tag{3}$$

$$b^d(R, F, T) - b^s(R, F, T) = 0 \text{ Indirect securities market} \tag{4}$$

$$m^d(R, F, T) - m^s(R, F, T) = 0 \text{ Liquid exchange assets} \tag{5}$$

$$B^d(R, F, T) - B^s(R, F, T) = 0 \text{ Bonds market} \tag{6}$$

$$E^d(R, F, T) - E^s(R, F, T) = 0 \text{ Equity market} \tag{7}$$

where the superscripts d and s represent demand and supply, N is labor, C is demand for goods and services, Y is national output, L is demand for money, M/P is money supply adjusted by the price index P, b is indirect securities issued by monetary intermediaries, m is short-term securities traded in exchange markets, B is bonds, and E is equity, R and F refer to relevant real and financial variables, respectively, and T refers to innovations in science and technology, education, management, or in local institutions.[5]

General equilibrium requires clearing of all markets. Thus, disequilibria in the capital markets lead to disequilibria on other real and financial markets. For instance, disregarding momentarily risk, demand for bonds and stocks is determined by their real rates of return r_B and r_E. These parameters are also two determinants of the demand for commodities. Consequently, a disequilibrium in either the bonds or equity markets can disrupt equilibrium in the commodities market. Similarly, an excess supply of bonds can affect the equilibrium in other financial markets and in the commodities market. The labor market also would be affected, even though those variables are not direct determinants of its demand. The demand for labor depends partly on real money balances held by corporations, while labor supply depends on real wages. However, excesses in the financial markets cannot be cleared through changes in the price level alone. Thus, disequilibrium in the financial markets affects labor supply and demand.

---

[4]This representation is akin to the models developed by Gurley and Shaw (1960), and Patinkin (1965), which have influenced financial intermediation modeling to the present. However, here, in addition to money demand and supply (which depend on exogenous monetary policy), financial intermediation is represented by four different markets. Capital markets have been desegregated in their conventional components, bonds and equity markets.

[5]Innovations, represented by the variable T, are also included in the case of the labor markets to take into account training, health care, family planning, social security, etc.

This synthetic representation also implies that economies lacking capital markets or with "incomplete" capital markets have a restricted spectrum to mobilize savings and investments. It also highlights the importance of emerging capital markets and the need for promoting capital markets development. Finally, the model makes clear that financial innovation promotes economic growth. These assertions become clearer when an extended production function is introduced, representing aggregate supply, along with more extended representations for savings, and demand and supply for the bonds and equity as follows, incorporating risk and returns as basic parameters for the valuation of financial assets, according to modern financial theory[6]:

$$Y = f\left(W, \frac{S}{P}, K, L, V, Z\right) \tag{8}$$

$$S = f\left(W, Y, \frac{M}{P}, r_f, \frac{r_b}{\pi_b}\pi_k, \frac{r_m}{\pi_m}\pi_k, \frac{r_B}{\pi_B}\pi_k, \frac{r_E}{\pi_E}\pi_k, Z\right) \tag{9}$$

$$\begin{aligned} B^d &= f\left(Y, W, \frac{M}{P}, r_f, \frac{r_b}{\pi_b}\pi_k, \frac{r_m}{\pi_m}\pi_k, \frac{r_B}{\pi_B}\pi_k, \frac{r_E}{\pi_E}\pi_k\right) \\ &= B^s = f\left(Y, W, \frac{M}{P}, r_f, \frac{r_b}{\pi_b}\pi_k, \frac{r_m}{\pi_m}\pi_k, \frac{r_B}{\pi_B}\pi_k, \frac{r_E}{\pi_E}\pi_E, Z_B\right) \end{aligned} \tag{10}$$

$$\begin{aligned} E_s &= f\left(Y, W, \frac{M}{P}, r_f, \frac{r_b}{\pi_b}\pi_k, \frac{r_m}{\pi_m}\pi_k, \frac{r_B}{\pi_B}\pi_k, \frac{r_E}{\pi_E}\pi_k\right) \\ &= E^s = f\left(Y, W, \frac{M}{P}, r_f, \frac{r_b}{\pi_b}\pi_k, \frac{r_m}{\pi_m}\pi_k, \frac{r_B}{\pi_B}\pi_k, \frac{r_E}{\pi_E}\pi_k, Z_E\right) \end{aligned} \tag{11}$$

where W = wealth
S = savings
r = real interest, interest rates, i adjusted by P = i/P = real required rates of return: risk free asset f, indirect securities b, liquid exchange assets m, bonds B, equity E
π = standard deviation of indirect securities
π_k = standard deviations of total market returns
V = innovations in science and technology
Z = supply-led financial innovation in financial institutions and services.

---

[6]Here, the extension to conventional financial intermediation models includes the four financial markets, presented in the macroeconomic financial intermediation model, and integrates risk and returns as the parameters determining the valuation of financial assets. Real rates of return required by investors, adjusted by risk and their correlation with market risk, replace conventional real interest rates as key financial variables in an economy.

By extending conventional models, Eq. (8) pinpoints the fact that national output is a function of wealth, real savings, capital, labor, innovations in science and technology, and innovations in financial intermediation.[7] Savings, Eq. (9), is a function of wealth, income, real money supply,[8] a real risk-free rate of return (commonly associated with Treasury bills), real interest rates for financial assets offered in the economy, and innovations in financial institutions and financial services. However, rates of return are also adjusted by their corresponding standard deviation and their correlation with total market portfolio risk π_k, i.e., systematic risk. The opportunity costs of holding cash balances are the real rates of return, risk adjusted, offered by financial assets. Equations (10) and (11) show that demand and supply for bonds and equity in an economy are a function of real output, wealth, and the real rates of return available in four financial markets, adjusted by their corresponding standard deviations, as well as their correlation with total market portfolio risk π_k. Supply in the capital markets is also a function of innovative financial intermediation Z, for which there are ample opportunities for developing in the emerging capital markets.

Several important propositions can be derived from the above equations, in relation to the role of capital markets in steady growth. First, the rate of growth g of an economy can be associated with changes in real savings, capital, labor, innovations in science and technology, and innovations in financial intermediation. Taking a given year as a point of reference, wealth (which includes land) remains fixed. Thus, economic growth can be represented as follows:

$$\frac{\delta Y}{Y} = g = \frac{\alpha S/P}{Y}\frac{\delta S/P}{Y} + \frac{\beta K}{Y}\frac{\delta K}{Y} + \frac{\gamma N}{Y}\frac{\delta N}{Y} + \frac{\delta V}{Y} + \frac{\delta Z}{Y} \tag{12}$$

where, $(\delta S/P)/Y$, $\delta K/Y$, $\delta N/Y$, $\delta V/Y$, and $\delta Z/Y$ represent rates of increase in savings, capital, labor, technological progress, and financial innovation, respectively; $(\alpha S/P)/Y$, $\beta K/Y$, and $\gamma N/Y$ represent the elasticities of output with respect to savings, capital, and labor. The role of financial intermediation and hence capital markets is present in two aspects: mobilization of savings and supply-led financial innovations. The latter are considered separately from savings levels in the same sense that technological progress is considered a separate factor of capital stock.

Second, savings are determined by wealth, income, and the returns (risk-adjusted) offered by a portfolio of alternative investments in a risk-free asset, near money assets, and long-term assets offered in the capital markets. Additionally, supply-led advances in financial intermediation create a variety of as-

[7]Strictly, this is an extension of Meade's (1962) modification of the neoclassical approach containing flexible factor proportions and factor prices modeled by Solow (1956). In turn, by using a Cobb–Douglas production function Solow attempted to overcome the rigidities of the Harrod–Domar model, which related the rate of growth to the marginal propensity to save divided by the capital-output ratio s/k. See Harrod (1951) and Domar (1948, 1957).

[8]Money supply needed for transactions or precautionary or speculative motives. The latter refer to the allocation of money in earning interest financial assets.

sets tailored to meet the liquidity, returns, maturity, and risk-aversion needs of individual investors.

Third, supply and demand functions for bonds and equity are complex functions that share with savings the same variables. Since total capital market activity is the sum of the bonds and stock markets, this fact underlines its importance on equilibrium and growth. It also underlines its complexity and the importance of partial equilibrium in the bonds and stock markets, which has been a matter of extensive concern in modern financial thought. The multiplicity of rates of return that intervene in the savings-investment process stresses the fact that risk and arbitrage are an important to the allocation of savings in portfolio holdings. Furthermore, arbitrage between bonds and equity takes place in the capital markets. Finally, financial innovations are an important part of the supply for bonds and stocks. Creative securitization and financial services can promote greater demand for bonds and equity, that is, greater savings and investments.

Fourth, the model highlights the fact that financial markets respond to fundamental factors in the economy. This is reflected in the market as a whole, which can be identified with systematic risk. Risk of individual assets is determined by the uncertainty of their own cash flows (nonsystematic risk) and overall market risk. Thus, a risky asset *i* must offer a risk premium over a riskless investment, commonly associated with Treasury bills; a premium λ must be associated with each of *n* fundamental factors to which the market is sensitive. These premiums depend on the sensitivity *b* of each asset to market fundamentals. These can be represented by the arbitrage price model[9]:

$$E(r_i) = r_f + \lambda_i b_{i1} + \cdots + \lambda_n b_{in} \qquad (13)$$

Many factors affect the savings–investment process. Rational investors seek to minimize risk and maximize returns. Thus, savings levels depend, to a great extent, on the degree that financial markets offer portfolio diversification alternatives. The allocation of resources to each alternative depends on their rate of return, their risk level, and the correlation with other investment alternatives. In this respect, capital markets play an important role in the mobilization of savings, offering ample asset choices to portfolio investors, as well as a dynamic setup to make portfolio adjustments. In addition, innovative financial intermediation creates alternatives to cushion risk. In this respect, it is worth mentioning the experience of India, where capital markets development in the 1980s increased savings and changed their structure, and capital markets assets

[9]This is a representation of the arbitrage pricing model (APM) developed by Ross (1976). Here, *n* factors impact the behavior of securities and the market. A simplified, but earlier version, on this relationship between risk and returns is the capital asset pricing model (CAPM) (Lintner, 1965; Mossin, 1977; Sharpe, 1970), wherein the returns of an asset are sensitive to only one factor: overall market performance.

held by households increased in relation to total savings or gross domestic product (Hanson, 1989).

Fifth, savings are mobilized for investments. Money and near money instruments support working capital needs of corporations, which are needed to carry out outstanding investments and to start up new ones. The direct link between savings and investments constitute the capital markets. Purchases of new bonds and stock issues (long run in nature) finance corporate investments. The conventional equilibrium identity for savings and investments can be pictured with increases in bond and equity holdings as their main component:

$$S = \Delta B^d + \Delta E^d + \Delta O^d + \Delta Q^d = \Delta B^s + \Delta E^s + \Delta O^s + \Delta Q^s = I \quad (14)$$

Savings are equal to new holdings in bonds and equity (ΔB^d and ΔE^d), which in equilibrium must be equal to the new issues of bonds and stocks (ΔB^s and ΔE^s) offered by corporations and the government to initiate investments.[10] ΔO's represent new holdings/issues in "other" financial assets, which support starting up activities of new investments. ΔQ's represents all other direct and indirect short-term securities, which support working capital necessary for past investments, i.e., current operations. Demand for investment-related securities is matched by securities issued by deficit spending, investing, units, government and the business sector. Funds are used to carry out real investments I. In this respect, it is important to note that the bonds, equity, and financial assets that support working capital needs of new projects can be identified with gross fixed capital formation. This relationship needs to be carefully examined.

Due to arbitrage, the costs of financing investments should be independent of either bonds or equity. However, taxes can make bonds more attractive than stocks, or vice versa. But segmentation of the equity markets due to regulations concerning ownership would hinder arbitrage and bias portfolio holdings toward debt securities priced at higher (than unregulated) required rates of return, i.e., higher cost of capital. Similarly, tax considerations can make issuing long-term debt in lieu of equity more attractive to corporations, as put forth by Modigliani and Miller (1963).[11] Corporate governance interests, i.e., maintaining ownership and/or control, might also lead to the same situation, and hence excessive leverage.

---

[10] Equation (14) can be further desegregated to identify private and government supply and demand for funds.

[11] Modigliani and Miller (1958), disregarding taxes, originally suggested that the debt–equity ratio does not affect the cost of capital, and that changes in the debt–equity mix do not change the value of the firm. In the revised version of their work Modigliani and Miller did not consider personal taxes paid by stockholders. Later, Miller dealt with the issue (1977). His model shows that personal taxes lower the benefits from corporate debt financing. At equilibrium, the personal tax rate on income from debt T_d would equal the product of corporate tax rate T_c times the personal tax rate on income from stocks T_s. (Formally: $(1 - T_d) = (1 - T_c)(1 - T_s)$). Thus, the tax advantage of debt to the firm would be exactly offset by personal taxation, and capital structure would have no

Sixth, capital market activity (and overall savings), and hence investments, also depend on systematic risk. This tends to be high in unstable economics, as well as in economics with a high degree of regulation and state intervention in the economy. Intervention and excessive regulation increase "political risk" and hence market systematic risk (Fischer et al., 1991). In addition, returns, represented by interest rate policies, would be below premiums expected by investors. Foreign debt would have a similar impact, increasing systematic risk. Thus, investors would seek alternative investments in real estate, overconsumption, and investing in foreign markets (capital flights), which would depress local savings and investments.

Seventh, as a corollary to the previous point, the mobilization of international resources to local capital markets also depends on systematic risk. Indeed, low or negative correlations among capital markets offer the opportunity to diversify systematic risk. However, thin and unstable capital markets offer limited opportunities for risk diversification to the international portfolio investor. A risk premium must be offered over an international risk-free asset, and in the numeraire of the foreign investor. Thus, even if the correlation of returns is low, risk premia offered in the less developed markets might be below the returns required by international portfolio investors, in relation to the risk perceived as undertaken. Moreover, those returns are usually undercut by tax laws and lagging exchange rate adjustments. This situation is well depicted in Eq. (15), which shows the random nature of the returns[12] of an asset measured in a foreign currency:

$$\tilde{r}_i^j = r_i - \tilde{D}_j - r_i\tilde{D}_j + \tilde{\pi}_j^2 \tag{15}$$

where $\tilde{r}$ = random return on asset i measured in foreign currency
r_i = return of asset i measured in its domestic currency
$\tilde{D}_j$ = random variation in D, the exchange rate of currency j expressed as units of the domestic currency
r_iD_j = covariance between r_i and $\tilde{D}_j$
$\tilde{\pi}_j^2$ = variance of D_j

Hence, the potential to mobilize international resources to developing financial markets is limited, unless their efficiency and growth is promoted through innovative policy making, effective control of inflation, adequate exchange rate adjustments, sound regulation, and innovative financial intermediation.

effects on a firm's value and cost of capital. Extensions and tests of this model have led to different conclusions (Bhattacharya, 1988; Durand, 1989; Gordon, 1989; Gordon and Gould, 1978; Ross, 1988; Stiglitz, 1988; Weston, 1989; see also Miller, 1988; Modigliani, 1988). It appears that $(1 - T_c)(1 - T_s) < (1 - T_d)$, so that in practice there is an advantage to the use of corporate debt.

[12] Returns are a linear function of n fundamental factors, as expressed in Eq. (13). Hyperinflation is undoubtedly one of those fundamental factors. Lagged adjustments in exchange rates leads to losses in purchasing power (lower returns), which makes unattractive financial assets affected by that type of events. For a fine survey on the issues concerning purchasing power parity and international portfolio choice see Adler and Dumas (1983).

Finally, equilibrium and growth are possible without full capital market development, but would be restricted in scope. That would be the case of economies with thin or nonexistent capital markets. Savings and investments would be limited. The mobilization of international resources for investments would also be limited. Equilibrium could be achieved in a simpler macroeconomic context, but growth would be limited and high unemployment and inequities would be present. A similar situation would also result from financial repression to the capital markets. Hence, innovative, supply-leading financial intermediation, properly supported with government policies, can aid in promoting higher rates of economic growth.

Financial Decisions and Capital Markets

The importance of capital markets is not limited to capital formation. Two other important contributions are provision of a framework of reference for efficient decision making, and provision of a dynamic alternative for expanded corporate growth through socialized corporate governance. In developed economies, corporate valuation is made in the capital markets. Financial intermediation creates a variety of primary securities, which bundle subsets of total cash flows generated by corporate activity. Investors price those securities based on the risk-return trade-off of the cash flows. Thus, the availability and cost of resources for future investment is ultimately established in the market. That is, valuation in the capital markets determines optimum investment choices and competitive performance (Fischer et al., 1991; Thomadikis, 1988).

Capital markets also determine the goal of the firm, which is to maximize the stockholders' wealth.[13] In that context, corporate decision making must be responsive to asset pricing in the capital markets. This means that efficient markets are an important condition to promote efficient corporate decision making (Ortiz, in press). In efficient capital markets information is widely spread and easily accessible to all investors. These markets can also be characterized by dynamic trade, wide corporate participation, and a large pool of investors mobilizing their savings and meeting their liquidity needs by continually restructuring their portfolios.

[13]This translates into maximizing the price of the firm's common stock. Firms have other goals, too, but modern financial theory identifies shareholders' wealth maximization as the most important one. This approach recognizes that shareholders buy stock because they seek to gain financially. It also recognizes that managers are hired by stockholders and must act in their best interests, although agency problems might arise. It also acknowledges that stockholders have the final claim to and responsibility for the corporation; the corporation might have other stakeholders, but their claims are of different nature. Finally, this goal acknowledges the fact that the ultimate measure of performance is not what the corporation earns (profits), but how those earnings are valued by the investor. For alternative views on corporate goals and objectives see Cornell and Shapiro (1987), Seitz (1982), and Treynor (1981). Rappaport (1986) reconciles corporate long-run strategies and value creation.

Thus, all relevant information about corporate performance and capital market price behavior is quickly incorporated into the price of financial assets. This process enables investors to change their portfolio selections as they see fit for their liquidity, risk, and return requirements. It also enables corporations to count with a fair valuation and estimate of the required rate of return sought by investors of their securities—indeed indicative of corporate performance and investment opportunities—and a market for investment financing. Market indicators are, therefore, a key framework of reference for efficient corporate financial decisions. The market, as a leading indicator of economic activity, gives the financial manager an unbiased perspective for selecting and timing decisions. Thus, efficient capital markets promote an efficient mobilization of savings and investments and efficient resource acquisition and allocation.

Inefficient markets hinder sound financial decision making. In the absence of fair valuation indicators, corporate decisions might be rational, but they are bound by market imperfections. Consequently, resource allocation and investment decisions are at best a second choice. Moreover, since savings mobilization is limited and market activity unstable, equilibrium and growth also would be limited and unstable.

Capital market activity also provides a dynamic alternative for corporate growth and social decision making. Additional financing allows corporations to expand and take advantage of economies of scale. As the firm grows, obtaining funds in the securities markets leads to separation of control and ownership. From an initial venture, tightly owned by its creators, corporations become publicly owned. This is a key issue for economic development. By socializing the ownership and financing of the firm, risk and corporate decisions are also socialized. Specialized, well-trained managers are in charge of the corporation. However, their decision-making processes cannot be arbitrary. They are made in relation to what investors express in the market, i.e., the valuation of the firm's financial assets in the capital markets.

In developing nations, capital markets are thin and highly concentrated and information is often scarce. Thus, in the absence of arms-length capital markets, savings mobilization, resource allocation, and corporate decision making are sharply limited. Well-planned reforms and innovative financial intermediation are necessary to exploit their potential. Indeed, the success of current development policies undertaken by the debtor countries depends, to a large extent, on their ability to mobilize local and international savings. Although debt renegotiations has tended to diminish the impact of foreign debt obligations, financial pressures will continue. Development needs are many, international resources will remain limited, and domestic debt is high. Thus, in the aftermath of the debt crisis, it is imperative to promote development in the capital markets of these nations as an alternative to mobilizing local and international resources.

GOVERNMENT AND CAPITAL MARKETS

Financial Markets and the New Role of the State on Economic Development

The limitations of past inward development models have led developing countries to correct their approaches to promote economic activity. Excessive state intervention in the economy is one problem that is now being solved by privatization, liberalization, and deregulation programs. Before the 1980s the state dominated the economy; now the private sector is the engine for growth. This change in approaches means that governments have a new role to play in the promotion of economic development: providing real and institutional conditions to support economic growth within the context of market oriented economic activity. It also means that the market should serve the state as a tool to respond to social needs, which previously were dealt with in different ways.

In the past, efforts to promote economic development by controlling interest rates, directing credit by preestablished shares to different sectors, and participating directly in the financial sector with an excessive array of institutions and programs led to financial repression, which distorted the financial system, prevented its development, and inhibited its participation in economic growth. Similarly, the state secured inexpensive funding, but by promoting monetary and fiscal laxness, which in turn led to inflation and instability. As a result, economic growth often presented severe setbacks. In relation to the mobilization of savings and investments, this means that to promote economic growth governments should now (1) foster the development of a solid, market-determined financial system, which can effectively contribute to economic development, and (2) provide a framework of macroeconomic stability, for example, by financing its operations in a healthy way. Enhancing the financial system includes improving the legal, accounting, taxing, and regulatory systems. It also includes promoting the development of innovative finance and upgrading information channels and disclosure rules. Sound monetary and fiscal policy making also include deregulation, but above all mean fiscal and monetary discipline, and financing through market operations.

Capital markets play a critical role in this scheme. The form in which capital information is provided impacts the behavior of its beneficiaries. In this respect, similar to the case of entrepreneurs, capital markets furnish policy makers from the public sector with a broad view of the economy and its perspectives, capital markets indicators, some directly related to government issues, and provide them with a framework for monitoring economic activity and evaluating their own past decisions. In relation to financing, capital markets provide public decision makers with the alternative to properly weight different alternatives to support concrete key development projects, taking into account costs and risks in an ongoing and multiperiod basis, so that projects are carried out properly and the state budget does not show unwanted unbalances. As in the case of the corporations, this should be reflected in socially oriented decisions. This point should be stressed, for current transformations of the state do not mean that the state should ignore its social responsibilities. In fact, capital markets should enhance the ability of the state to respond to social needs. Replacing outdated practices, innovative policy making, and development financing should contribute to identify, for instance, concrete development projects in infrastructure, education, health, and housing that can be totally or partially supported through government issues in the capital markets. In short, capital markets can provide the government with the opportunity to specialize in development promotion and socially oriented actions. In turn, government can intervene to improve the quality of the financial markets, which show many imperfections in the developing countries.

Capital Markets and Government Participation

The importance of government participation in the capital markets can be shown by presenting the components of total demand and supply for securities and by extending the model previously presented by incorporating the government sector in the demand and supply functions from capital markets. For simplicity, only extensions of Eqs. (8)–(11) are presented.

$$B_g^d + B_p^d + B_{fi}^d + E_g^d + E_p^d + E_{fi}^d = B_g^s + B_p^p + B_{fi}^s + E_g^s + E_p^s + E_{fi}^s \tag{16}$$

$$Y = f\left(W, \frac{S}{P}, K, N, V, Z, G, H\right) \tag{17}$$

$$S = f\left(W, Y, \frac{M}{P}, r_f, \frac{r_b}{\pi_b}\pi_k, \frac{r_m}{\pi_m}\pi_k, \frac{r_B}{\pi_B}\pi_k, \frac{r_E}{\pi_E}\pi_k, Z, G, H\right) \tag{18}$$

$$B^d = f\left(Y, W, \frac{M}{P}, r_f, \frac{r_b}{\pi_b}\pi_k, \frac{r_m}{\pi_m}\pi_k, \frac{r_B}{\pi_B}\pi_k, \frac{r_E}{\pi_E}\pi_k, J\right)$$

$$= B^s = f\left(Y, W, \frac{M}{P}, r_f, \frac{r_b}{\pi_b}\pi_k, \frac{r_m}{\pi_m}\pi_k, \frac{r_B}{\pi_B}\pi_k, \frac{r_E}{\pi_E}\pi_E, Z_B, G, H_B\right) \tag{19}$$

$$E_s = f\left(Y, W, \frac{M}{P}, r_f, \frac{r_b}{\pi_b}\pi_k, \frac{r_m}{\pi_m}\pi_k, \frac{r_B}{\pi_B}\pi_k, \frac{r_E}{\pi_E}\pi_k, J\right)$$

$$= E^s = f\left(Y, W, \frac{M}{P}, r_f, \frac{r_b}{\pi_b}\pi_k, \frac{r_m}{\pi_m}\pi_k, \frac{r_B}{\pi_B}\pi_k, \frac{r_E}{\pi_E}\pi_k, Z_E, G, H_E\right) \tag{20}$$

where G represents the government and its policies, H specifies financial innovation fostered by the government, and Z is the financial innovation from the private sector. The subscripts g, p, and fi refer to the government, business, and financial intermediation sectors, respectively. The superscripts d and s mean demand and supply.

Equation (16) simply says that total demand for securities in the capital markets is composed of demand for government bonds, private bonds, and financial intermediation bonds, plus equity issues from the government, the private sector, and financial intermediaries. Similarly, on the supply side, total supply of long-term securities is composed of bond and equity offerings made by the government, private, and financial intermediation sectors. In the markets, demand for government securities is made by households, financial intermediaries, and the business sector. It is worth noting that financial intermediaries also issue bonds, creating in the economy indirect debt.

Equation (17) highlights the role of the state as another factor of production, for the way a society is organized and administered impacts aggregate output. Moreover, the variables that stress government policy making and financial innovation, and financial innovations from the private sector pinpoint the fact that, contrary to earlier views on development, capital accumulation is not enough.[14] Indeed, by integrating Eq. (17) into the model previously presented, it can be asserted (as an extension of Eq. (12)) that economic development depends on the quality of economic policies carried out by the government as well as by state-led financial innovations, which include proper regulation, promotion of financial institutions development, and promotion of balanced and innovative government financing.

Equation (18) shows the role of the state in the savings process. It is a determinant not only in some key variables, such as money supply and the riskless free rate, but also in the set of other policies derived from macroeconomic policy making and financial innovation included in G and H. The nature of the savings function would be reflected in real investments carried out by the private and government sectors. Indeed, as an active participant in the development of infrastructure and social projects, the state must participate in the financial markets to find additional resources to those derived from taxation.

Equations (19) and (20) present the state as a participant in the capital markets. They reveal the impact that government policy making can have in strengthening or weakening emerging capital markets, that is, the importance of having sound macroeconomic and financial policies and well-balanced government regulation, intervention, and innovative financing. As pointed out earlier, excesses in monetary management or artificial controls on credit and interest rates can lead to overall instability and financial market disequilibria. Similarly, markets will not clear and disequilibrium will take place if government promotes excess supply or demand for bonds or stocks, either by participating directly or by excessive regulation. In other words, abuses in public financing,

[14]This idea is in accord with current developments on development finance, albeit here is extended to include the public sector. For a brief presentation on this issue see Stiglitz (1990).

implemented through regulation and distorted offerings, unbalance capital markets and hinder their growth.

Equations (19) and (20) also show that the state can participate directly in stock markets with the securities of its public enterprises. This should help to improve the efficiency of all those firms that cannot be privatized. But the participation of the government in that market would usually be limited due to the nature of its activities. However, its participation in stock markets is very important, particularly concerning regulation. Appropriate regulation promotes savings and investment through share purchases and sales. It also provides the contractual framework that investors in the capital markets and firms need to carry out separate but complementary decisions in savings and production, which ultimately is reflected in higher national output and welfare.

Similarly, free from excessive regulation, and strengthened by government policies, bond markets can offer the government "unbiased" opportunities for financing. The government should be able to expand its financing opportunities beyond current tax revenues. However, this deficit spending would not go beyond its capacity, for it would be socially validated by the market. In short, "forced" borrowing by the government is possible only through financial repression. However, as previously suggested, this does not mean that a total free market solution, proposed by some economists, is the solution to promote development through the capital markets and balanced financing for the government. It means that economic decisions are taken by both the private and the government sector.

Thus, the government, as an agent of all citizens, must promote capital market development to achieve optimum pareto solutions for society. The limit to its intervention possibilities is the private market. There is a specific space for intervention and participation, but to improve general welfare. Intervention per se does not solve market inefficiencies that might be present in the case of emerging markets.[15] Optimum pareto solutions must be promoted, albeit a second best might be socially acceptable when market indicators are insufficient, but taken within the context of ongoing capital markets development policies. Moreover, socially oriented projects can be funded with socially raised funds, namely taxes, but evaluating them thoroughly in terms of national welfare, including social equity and stability. Key infrastructure projects that require significant financing can be financed through the capital markets, which would assign resources to all efficient projects, from a social point of view, without a need for public subsidies. As a complementary alternative, key development projects can be "concessioned" to the business sector, which in turn would finance those projects through the capital markets. In brief, properly developed

[15]This assertion stresses the importance of adequate regulation (which, considering past trends in interventionism, means deregulation and liberalization), and balanced intervention and the promotion of market solutions (which can be identified with capital markets development). Nonmarket solutions and institutions do not always eliminate market failures. Considerations along these lines are found in Arnott and Stiglitz (1988).

and regulated securities markets increase the efficiency and ability of the state to promote development and respond to social needs.

CONCLUSIONS

Capital markets can play a leading role in the economic recovery of highly indebted countries. Innovative financial intermediation promotes economic growth. Financial assets tailored to meet liquidity, returns, and risk-aversion requirements of investors induce greater savings. In turn, this induces growth by improving monetary policy, lowering costs of capital, and increasing the set of feasible investments in an economy. Capital markets activity is an important part of these processes. Securities markets strengthen the financial system and make an economy more stable and richer in alternatives for savings and corporate financing. Moreover, capital formation in the capital markets is directly linked with gross fixed capital formation in an economy. Similarly, efficient capital markets provide an important frame of reference for portfolio choices, efficient resource allocation in an economy, and sound corporate decisions. In addition, widely held corporate ownership socializes risk, returns, and corporate decision making. Efficient capital markets also promote the mobilization of international resources. Capital markets enhance government efficiency and development policies. They provide the government with key indicators for decision making and for monitoring the economy. Capital markets provide governments with alternatives for sound financing and the formulation of socially validated development projects. In turn, through regulation, proper macroeconomic and financial policy making, and a balanced participation in the capital markets, governments can play a key role in the development of capital markets, which are often inefficient in developing countries. Thus, in the aftermath of the debt crisis it is imperative to promote capital market development as a way to increase local savings and induce favorable international capital movements to promote private business activity, as well as a more efficient, balanced, and socially valid participation of the government in economic growth in developing countries. Considering the credit and foreign direct investment crunch precipitated by the debt crisis and current changes in Eastern Europe, the key for economic recovery of the developing countries lies in the ability of these countries to increase local savings and induce favorable international capital movement to increase needed investments.

REFERENCES

Adler, M., and B. Dumas. 1983. International portfolio choice and corporation finance: A synthesis, *Journal of Finance* 38(3):985–989.

Arnott, R. and J. E. Stiglitz. 1988. Dysfunctional non-market institutions and the market, *NBER Working Paper No. 2666.*

Aspe, P. 1981. El Desarrollo del Mercado de Valores en el Periodo Post-Devaluatorio

Mexicano, in B. Paul (Ed.), *El Desarrollo Financiero de America Latina*, Caracas: Instituto Interamericano de Mercados de Capital.
Bamberg, G., and K. Spremann. 1986. *Capital Market Equilibria*, Berlin: Springer.
Basant, K. K. 1986. *Studies on Inflationary Dynamics: Financial Repression and Financial Liberalization in Less Developed Countries*, Singapore: Singapore University Press.
Bencivenga, V. R., and B. D. Smith. 1989. Financial intermediation and endogenous growth, mimeo, Cornell University.
Bennet, R. L. 1965. *The Financial Sector and Economic Development: The Mexican Case*, Baltimore: The Johns Hopkins Press.
Bhattacharya, S. 1988. Corporate finance and the legacy of Miller and Modigliani, *Journal of Economic Perspectives* 2(4):135–147.
Buffie, E. F. 1984. Financial repression, the new structuralist, and stabilization policy in semiindustralized economies, *Journal of Development Studies (Netherlands)* 10(14):305–322.
Cheng, H. 1980. Financial deepening in the Pacific Basin countries, *Economic Review*, Federal Reserve Bank of San Francisco, pp. 43–56.
Cho, Y. J. 1986. The effects of financial liberalization on the development of the financial market and the allocation of credit to corporate sectors: The Korean case, *Discussion Paper, Development Research Department, No. 166, The World Bank.*
Cornell, B., and A. Shapiro. 1987. Corporate stakeholders and corporate finance, *Financial Management* 16(1):5–14.
Courakis, A. S. 1984. Constraints on bank choices and financial repression in less developed countries, *Oxford Bulletin of Economics and Statistics* 46(4):341–370.
Dailami, M. 1986. Optimal corporate debt financing and real investment decisions under controlled banking systems, *Working Papers/PREA, The World Bank.*
Dailami, M. 1990. Financial policy and corporate investment in imperfect capital markets: The case of Korea, *Working Paper/PREA, The World Bank.*
Darrat, A. F., and T. K. Muharjee. 1986. Behavior of the stock market of a developing economy, *Economics Letters* 22(2)273–278.
Dawson, S. M. 1984. The trend toward efficiency for less developed stock exchanges: Hong Kong, *Journal of Business Finance and Accounting* 11(2):151–161.
de la Calle, L. F. 1991. Diversification of macroeconomic risk and international integration of capital markets: The case of Mexico, *The World Bank Economic Review* 5:415–436.
de Tarso Medeiros, P. 1981. El Desarrollo del Sistema Financiero y los Mercados de Valores: El Caso de Brazil, in B. Paul (Ed.), *El Desarrollo Financiero de America Latina y el Caribe*, Caracas: Instituto Interamericano de Mercados de Capital.
Diaz Alejandro, C. 1985. Goodbye financial repression, hello financial crash, *Journal of Development Economics* 18:1–24.
Domar, E. D. 1948. The problem of capital accumulation, *American Economic Review* 38:34–55.
Domar, E. D. 1957. *Essays in the Theory of Economic Growth*, New York: Oxford University Press.
Dornbusch, R., and A. Reynoso. 1989. Financial factors in economic development. *Working Paper Series, Working Paper 2889, National Bureau of Economic Research.*
Duffie, D. 1988. *Security Markets: Stochastic Models*, New York: Academic.

Durand, D. 1989. Afterthoughts on a controversy with MM, plus new thoughts on growth and the cost of capital, *Financial Management* 18:12–17.

Errunza, V. R. 1979. Efficiency and the programs to develop capital markets: The Brazilian experience, *Journal of Banking and Finance* 3(4):355–382.

Errunza, V. R., and E. Losq. 1985. International asset pricing under mild segmentation: Theory and tests. *Journal of Finance* 40(1):105–124.

Errunza, V. R., and B. Rosenberg. 1982. Investment in developed and less developed countries, *Journal of Financial and Quantitative Analysis* 17(5):741–762.

Fischer, K., E. Ortiz, and A. Palasvirta. 1991. The industrial group and risk management in imperfect markets, in D. Dimon (Ed.), *Business Association of Latin American Studies, Proceedings*, San Diego: University of San Diego.

Fry, M. 1988. *Money, Interest and Banking in Economic Development*, Baltimore: Johns Hopkins University Press.

Fry. M. 1989. Financial development: Theories and recent experience, *Oxford Review of Economic Policy* 5(4):13–28.

Galbis, V. 1977. Financial intermediation and economic growth in less-developed countries: A theoretical approach, in P. C. I. Arye (Ed.), *Finance in Developing Countries*, London: Frank Cass.

Geyikdaki, Y. M., and N. V. Geyikdaki. 1989. International diversification in Latin America and the developing countries, *Management International Review* 29(3):62–71.

Goldsmith, R. W. 1969. *Financial Structure and Development*, New Haven, CT: Yale University Press.

Gonzalez Fraga, J. 1982. The impact of inflation on securities markets, in N. Bruck (Ed.), *Capital Markets Under Inflation*, Buenos Aires: Buenos Aires Stock Exchange.

Gordon, M. J. 1989. Corporate finance under the MM theorems, *Financial Management* 18:19–28.

Gordon, M. J., and L. I. Gould. 1978. The cost of equity capital with personal income taxes and flotation costs, *Journal of Finance* 33(4):1201–1212.

Guimaraes, R. M. C., B. C. Kingsman, and S. Taylor. 1988. *A Reappraisal of the Efficiency of Financial Markets*, Berlin: Springer.

Gupta, K. 1984. *Finance and Growth in Developing Countries*, London: Croom Helm.

Gurley, J. G., and E. S. Shaw. 1960. *Money in a Theory of Finance*, Washington, DC: Brookings Institution.

Hanson, J. 1989. Profile of financial sector in India, mimeo, The World Bank.

Harrod, R. F. 1951. *Toward a Dynamic Economics*, London: MacMillan.

Haugen, R. A., E. Ortiz, and E. Arjona. 1985. Market efficiency: Mexico versus the U.S., *Journal of Portfolio Management* 12(1):28–32.

Hosek, W. R., and F. Zahn. 1977. *Monetary Theory, Policy, & Financial Markets*, New York: McGraw-Hill.

Joong-Wong, K. 1988. Economic development and financial liberalization in the Republic of Korea: Policy reforms and future prospects, in M. Urrutia (Ed.), *Financial Liberalization and the Internal Structure of Capital Markets in Asia and Latin America*, Tokyo: The United Nations University.

Kapur, D., and M. Ravaillon. 1988. Rational expectations and long-run equilibria: Tests for Indian securities, *Economics Letters* 26(4):363–367.

Khambata, F., and D. Khambata. 1989. Emerging capital markets: A case study of equity markets in India, *The Journal of Developing Areas* 23:125–138.

Khan, M. S. 1985. Analytical approach to interest rate determination in developing countries, *Pakistan Development Review* 24:481–495.

Kitchen, R. 1987. The role of the Jamaica Stock Exchange in the capital market: An historical analysis, *Savings and Development* 11(3):249–274.

Krouse, C. G. 1986. *Capital Markets and Prices,* Amsterdam: North Holland.

Laurence, M. M. 1981. Some efficiency characteristics of the Kusla-Lampur and Singapore stock markets, *Working Paper, University of Singapore.*

Lessard, D. 1975. The structure of returns and gains from international diversification: A multivariate analysis, in E. J. Elton and M. J. Gruber (Eds.), *International Capital Markets,* Amsterdam: North Holland.

Levy, H. 1990. *Research in Finance. A Research Annual,* New York: JAI (Vol. 1, 1979–Vol. 8, 1990).

Lintner, J. 1965. The valuation of risk assets and the selection of risky investments in stock portfolios and capital budgets, *Review of Economics and Statistics* 47:13–37.

Markowitz, H. M. 1959. *Portfolio Selection,* New York: Wiley.

McKinnon, R. I. 1973. *Money and Capital in Economic Development,* Washington, DC: Brookings Institution.

Meade, J. 1962. *A Neo-Classical Theory of Economic Growth,* London: Unwin.

Miller, M. H. 1977. Debt and taxes, *Journal of Finance* 32(2):261–275.

Miller, M. H. 1988. The Modigliani–Miller propositions after thirty years, *The Journal of Economic Perspectives* 2(4):19–120.

Modigliani, F. 1988. MM: Past, present, future, *Journal of Economic Perspectives* 2(4):149–158.

Modigliani, F., and M. H. Miller. 1958. The cost of capital, corporation finance and the theory of investment, *American Economic Review* 48:261–297.

Modigliani, F., and M. H. Miller. 1963. Corporate income taxes and the cost of capital: A correction, *American Economic Review* 53:433–443.

Mossin, J. 1977. *The Economic Efficiency of Financial Markets,* Lexington, MA: Lexington Books.

Ortiz, E. 1979. Inflacion y Estructura Financiera de las Empresas Registradas en la Bolsa Mexicana de Valores, *Seminario Sobre la Prospectiva de la Administracion en Mexico Hacia 1990: Antologia,* Mexico, DF DEP/FCA/UNAM.

Ortiz, E. 1980. Caminata al Azar en Mexico: Importancia y Efficiencia de la Bolsa Mexicana de Valores, *Contaduria/Administracion,* 112.

Ortiz, E. Business finance and goal programming in imperfect capital markets, in K. P. Fischer and G. Pappaioannou (Eds.), *Business Finance in Less Developed Capital Markets,* New York: Greenwood (in press).

Patinkin, D. 1965. *Money, Interest, and Prices,* New York: Harper & Row.

Patrick, H. T. 1966. Financial development and economic growth in underdeveloped countries, *Economic Development and Cultural Change* 14(2):177–197.

Ramos, J. 1988. The rise and fall of capital markets in the southern cone, in M. Urrutia (Ed.), *Financial Liberalization and the Internal Structure of Capital Markets in Asia and Latin America,* Tokyo: United Nations University.

Rappaport, A. 1986. *Creating Shareholder Value: The New Standard for Business Performance,* New York: Free Press.

Ross, S. A. 1976. The arbitrage theory of capital asset pricing, *Journal of Economic Theory* 13:341–360.

Ross, S. A. 1988. Comment on the Modigliani–Miller propositions, *Journal of Economic Perspectives* 2(4):127–133.

Sargent, T. J. 1965. *Macroeconomic Theory*, New York: Academic.

Sarmiento, E. 1988. The failures of capital markets: A Latin American view, in M. Urrutia (Ed.), *Financial Liberalization and the Internal Structure of Capital Markets in Asia and Latin America*, Tokyo: United Nations University.

Seitz, N. 1982. Shareholder goals, firm goals, and firm financing decisions, *Financial Management* 11(3):20–26.

Sharma, J. L. 1983. Efficient capital markets and random character of stock price behavior in a developing economy, *Indian Economic Journal* 31:53–68.

Sharpe, W. F. 1970. *Portfolio Theory and Capital Markets*, New York: McGraw-Hill.

Shaw, E. S. 1973. *Financial Deepening in Economic Development*, New York: Oxford University Press.

Sijben, J. J. 1977. *Money and Economic Growth*, Leiden: Martinus Nihoff.

Skull, M. T. 1985. *Financial Institutions and Markets in the Southwest Pacific*. London: MacMillan.

Smith, P. F. 1978. *Money and Financial Intermediation*, Englewood Cliffs, NJ: Prentice–Hall.

Solow, R. 1956. A contribution to the theory of economic growth, *Quarterly Journal of Economics* 70(1):65–94.

Spellman, L. J. 1976. Economic growth and financial intermediation, in R. I. McKinnon (Ed.), *Money and Finance in Economic Growth and Development*, New York: Dekker.

Stiglitz, J. E. 1988. Why financial structure matters, *Journal of Economic Perspectives* 2(4):121–126.

Stiglitz, J. E. 1990. Financial markets and development, *Oxford Review of Economic Policy* 5(4):55–68.

Taylor, L. 1983. *Structuralist Macroeconomics: Applicable Models for the Third World*, New York: Basic Books.

Thomadikis, S. 1988. Enterprise governance and growth: Notes on the theory of the firm in less-developed countries, Paper, Business Finance in Less Developed Capital Markets, International Symposium, Hofstra University.

Toida, J. 1990. More than a passing trend: Emerging Asian stock markets, *Tokyo Business Today* (August):12–15.

Townsend, R. 1983. Financial structure and economic activity, *American Economic Review* 73:895–911.

Treynor, J. L. 1981. The financial objective of a widely held corporation, *Financial Analyst Journal* 37(2):68–71.

Weston, J. F. 1989. What MM have brought, *Financial Management* 18:29–38.

Ziemba, W. T., W. Bailey, and Y. Hamas. 1991. *Japanese Financial Market Research*, Amsterdam: North-Holland.

Part Three

International Financial Management

Chapters 15–18 examine the international evidence of conditional heteroskedasticity in stock returns, the effects of monetary gains and losses on the univariate time series characteristics of CDA earnings, the survival of business failures, and stockholder objectives and government incentives in Eastern European joint ventures.

In Chapter 15, Albert Corhay and Alireza Rad investigate the presence of nonlinear dependence in daily stock returns on several stock exchanges of different countries. In Chapter 16, Hossein Shalchi and M. T. Vaziri examine empirically the statistical properties of nondeflated and deflated constant dollar accounting earnings signals. In Chapter 17, Rafael Solis presents a simplified version of the survival analysis theory and its application to the analysis of business mortality. In Chapter 18, David Bangert examines the desirability of joint ventures in Eastern European countries from the perspective of the major stakeholders and the potential incentives that host governments may use to encourage joint ventures while securing minimum aspiration levels for the various stockholders.

Chapter 15

Conditional Heteroskedasticity in Stock Returns: International Evidence

Albert Corhay and Alireza Tourani Rad

Knowledge of the distribution of security returns is important for both theoretical and empirical studies in finance. For instance, the distributional characteristics of stock returns have important implications for mean-variance portfolio theory, theoretical models of capital asset pricing, and valuation of contingent claims. Moreover, empirical tests of asset pricing models and the efficient market hypothesis make statistical inferences based on distributional assumptions of stock returns, and estimation of the variance is crucial for the pricing of derivative securities.

The most convenient assumption underlying the distribution of security returns is that of a multivariate normality with stationary parameters over time. Since the normal distribution is stable under addition, any portfolio of stocks will also be normally distributed. If it is also assumed that investors are risk averse, mean-variance portfolio theory can be derived. Moreover, the assumptions of normality and parameter stability are implied by most of the statistical methods usually employed in empirical financial studies.

Tests of the normality hypothesis were first reported by Osborne (1964). He investigated returns of stock indices over several time periods and concluded that they approximately follow normal processes. Other studies questioned the normality assumption and showed that distributions of returns have fatter tails and are more peaked than the normal distribution. Mandelbrot (1963) and Fama (1965) observed that the family of stable Paretian distributions whose members exhibit heavy tails conforms better to the distribution of stock returns.

These studies and many more recent ones in both U.S. and non-U.S. markets have shown that time series of daily stock returns exhibit a certain level of autocorrelation for short differencing intervals. However, it is generally accepted that changes in returns are uncorrelated over time for two reasons: First, because of the transaction costs, the pattern of the autocorrelations cannot be used in a profitable trading rule. Second, the significance of the sample coefficients is likely to be overstated because the empirical distributions of daily returns are different from Gaussian distributions.

A common and misleading assumption derived from the lack of serial correlation in stock returns is statistical independence. The lack of serial correlation leads to statistical independence only when stock prices follow a Gaussian stochastic process. This important fact is often neglected, and many models of stock price behavior simply assume independence. Because the empirical distributions of stock returns generally depart significantly from Gaussain distributions, the assumption of independence is incorrect. Another common and inade quate assumption concerning stock price behavior is the linearity of the return-generating process with parameters that are independent of the past realizations. There is, indeed, no reason to believe that series of stock returns are generated by a linear process. The choice of such an assumption relies only on the easiness of statistical analysis. Hinich and Patterson (1985) proved, for example, that stock return series are not made of a process of independent increments.

These two assumptions, independence and linearity, can be particularly questioned in speculative markets. Neftçi (1984) proved that there is no theoretical reason supporting these assumptions, and results of several empirical studies showed that linearity and intertemporal independence cannot be expected (Perry, 1982; Pindyck, 1984; Poterba and Summers, 1986; Akgiray, 1989).

There is yet no unanimity regarding the best stochastic return-generating model. The general conclusion, however, seems to be that stock returns are approximately uncorrelated, but not independent, and described by distributions with fatter tails. One of the most recently proposed classes of return-generating processes in the literature that can capture the temporal dependence of stock return series is the class of autoregressive conditional heteroskedastic processes introduced by Engle (1982) and its generalized version by Bollerslev (1986). These models allow for volatility clustering; that is, large changes are followed by large changes, and small by small, which has long been recognized as an important feature of stock returns behavior. Empirical studies showed, indeed, that such processes are successful in modeling various time series (French et al., 1987; Baillie and Bollerslev, 1989; Hsieh, 1989; Baillie and De Gennaro, 1990).

This class of models has been mainly applied to American stock markets. This chapter shows whether such models can adequately describe stock price behavior of capital markets that are much smaller and thinner than the American markets. To that end, nine countries throughout the world have been selected. The study of stock price behavior in these markets is interesting, for it can provide further evidence in favor of or against the use of this type of model for describing stock price behavior.

THE DATA

For this study, we have selected the indices of nine major stock markets representing three geographical areas: North America, Europe, and the Far East.

The daily market indices were collected from DATASTREAM for the period 1 Jan 1980 to 30 Sep 1990. These indices are for the United States (Standard & Poor's Composite), Canada (Toronto Composite), the United Kingdom (FT All-shares), France (CAC General), Italy (Milan Banca), Japan (Nikkei Dow Jones), Australia (All Ordinary Shares), Singapore (Straits-Times), and South Korea (Composite). The daily returns of these market indices are continuously compounded returns. They are calculated as the difference in natural logarithm of the index value for two consecutive days, $R_t = \log P_t - \log P_{t-1}$.

STATISTICAL ANALYSIS

This section contains analysis of the distributional and time series properties of the stock market indices returns in the sample. A range of descriptive statistics are presented in Table 1. The results confirm the well-known fact that daily stock returns are not normally distributed, but are leptokurtic and skewed, whatever the country concerned. All distributions are negatively highly skewed, indicating that they are nonsymmetric, and they all exhibit high levels of kurtosis, meaning that they are more peaked and have fatter tails than normal distributions.

To test the hypothesis of whether returns are strict white noise, that is, random walk, the Box–Pierce test statistics up to lag 25 are calculated and presented in the table. This is a joint test that the first k autocorrelation coefficients are zero. Under the null hypothesis that the sample autocorrelations are not asymptotically correlated, the Box–Pierce statistic, $Q = n \sum_{i=1}^{k} \rho(i)^2$, has chi-square distribution with k degrees of freedom, where $\rho(i)$ is the ith autocorrelation. All values of Q are significant at the 5% level except that of the United States. This implies that the null hypothesis of strict white noise is rejected for eight countries, reflecting a rather long range of dependency in the returns series. However, it can be questioned whether this test accounts for the full probability distribution of the returns series, since heteroskedasticity can lead to the underestimation of the standard error, $\sqrt{1/n}$ of each sample, and therefore to the overestimation of the t and chi-square statistics. Diebold (1987) provides a heteroskedasticity-consistent estimate of the standard error for the ith sample autocorrelation coefficient:

$$S(i) = \sqrt{1/n(1 + \gamma_R^2(i)/\sigma^4} \tag{1}$$

where $\gamma_R^2(i)$ is the ith sample autocovariance of the square data and σ is the sample standard deviation of the data.

Using these adjusted standard errors, Diebold proposes an adjusted Box–Pierce statistic:

Table 1
Sample Statistics on Daily Returns Series

	Australia	Canada	France	Italy	Japan	Korea	Singapore	United Kingdom	United States
Mean ($\times 10^3$)	0.360	0.198	0.470	0.682	0.414	0.576	0.330	0.511	0.372
t (mean = 0)	1.674	1.198	2.399	2.526	2.274	2.476	1.337	2.991	1.815
Variance ($\times 10^3$)	0.130	0.077	0.107	0.204	0.093	0.151	0.171	0.082	0.118
Skewness	−6.11	−0.98	−1.51	−0.99	−1.69	−0.96	−3.19	−1.69	−3.52
Kurtosis	150.46	22.28	16.94	11.74	36.69	18.36	50.61	19.66	75.08
Autocorrelation	0.119	0.169	0.146	0.137	0.060	0.069	0.208	0.137	0.033
$Q(25)$	191.43	130.89	154.23	139.58	102.09	41.40	171.41	111.2	29.95
$Q^*(25)$	36.32	27.43	65.66	52.64	30.56	27.96	28.83	26.30	09.95

Note. Underlined numbers indicate 5% significance level.

$$Q^* = \sum_{i=1}^{k} \frac{\rho(i)}{S(i)^2} \tag{2}$$

which is asymptotically chi-square distributed with k degrees of freedom, under the null hypothesis of no serial correlation in the data. The values of Q^* in Table 1 are much lower than the nonadjusted ones. They are significant at the 5% level for France and Italy only. So, even after adjusting for heteroskedasticity, some significant autocorrelation remains in the series of returns for these two countries.

A comparison between the values of Q and Q^* suggests that the rejection of serial independence using Q, which is based on the standard testing procedure, is due to the presence of heteroskedasticity in the returns series. The presence of significant values of Q^* in the French and Italian returns indices, however, indicates that these returns series are not strict white noise processes. Furthermore, the fact that the first-order autocorrelation is significant for seven countries implies the rejection of white noise, that is, an uncorrelated process. Therefore, we must eliminate the serial correlation in the return series before searching for appropriate models that could account for heteroskedasticity in the returns. One way to do this is to apply Autoregressive Moving Average (ARMA) models.

ARMA MODELS

The class of univariate ARMA models might adequately represent the behavior of the stock returns. Therefore, several ARMA models were applied to the returns series. An AR(1) model appears to fit returns series best:

$$R_t = \Phi_0 + \Phi_1 R_{t-1} + \epsilon_t \tag{3}$$

The estimates of the above regression model for each country are presented in Table 2. To observe whether the residuals ϵ_t obtained from Eq. (3) are uncorrelated, we applied the same tests for normality and serial correlation as for the returns series. As before, the values of the first-order autocorrelation coefficients are presented in Table 2. The first-order autocorrelation coefficient for all countries is not significantly different from zero. Thus, the results indicate that the AR(1) provides an uncorrelated series of residuals.

The estimate of Φ_1 is statistically significant, except for the United States. The Dickey–Fuller test for unit roots indicates that Φ_1 is significantly less than one. The series of returns appear to follow a stationary random walk. The assumption of normality of the residuals can be rejected. The residual series appear to be leptokurtic and skewed. A comparison between values of Q and Q^* indicates that the residuals series still exhibit heteroskedasticity.

The presence of heteroskedasticity in stock prices and in the market model has already been documented (Morgan, 1976). But while previous studies fo-

Table 2
The Autoregressive Model

	Australia	Canada	France	Italy	Japan	Korea	Singapore	United Kingdom	United States
ϕ_0	0.003	0.002	$\underline{0.004}$	$\underline{0.006}$	$\underline{0.004}$	$\underline{0.005}$	0.003	$\underline{0.004}$	0.004
ϕ_1	$\underline{0.120}$	$\underline{0.170}$	$\underline{0.146}$	$\underline{0.137}$	$\underline{0.060}$	$\underline{0.069}$	$\underline{0.208}$	$\underline{0.137}$	0.033
Fuller's test	2469.5	2329.1	2813.1	2781.8	2634.8	2610.6	2219.5	2815.5	2709.3
Residuals statistics									
Mean ($\times 10^3$)	0.000	0.000	0.000	0.000	0.000	0.000	0.000	0.000	0.000
Variance ($\times 10^3$)	0.128	0.750	0.105	0.201	0.093	0.015	0.016	0.080	0.117
Skewness	$\underline{-5.87}$	$\underline{-0.39}$	$\underline{-1.42}$	$\underline{-0.83}$	$\underline{-1.50}$	$\underline{-0.93}$	$\underline{-2.68}$	$\underline{-1.31}$	$\underline{-3.44}$
Kurtosis	$\underline{146.46}$	$\underline{25.49}$	$\underline{17.36}$	$\underline{12.14}$	$\underline{36.87}$	$\underline{18.66}$	$\underline{42.09}$	$\underline{16.84}$	$\underline{73.19}$
Autocorrelation	0.005	0.001	0.004	0.008	0.006	0.000	0.010	−0.005	0.001
$Q(25)$	$\underline{139.84}$	$\underline{48.91}$	$\underline{76.32}$	$\underline{92.09}$	$\underline{92.14}$	$\underline{23.67}$	$\underline{44.59}$	$\underline{43.95}$	26.80
$Q^*(25)$	27.84	21.86	34.54	$\underline{38.34}$	29.22	19.27	17.17	17.67	9.32

Note. Underlined numbers indicate 5% significance level.

cused on unconditional heteroskedasticity, in this chapter, we use Engle's Autoregressive Conditional Heteroskedastic (ARCH) model, which focuses on conditional volatility movements. It is interesting to note that, according to Diebold et al. (1988), the presence of the ARCH effect appears to be generally independent of unconditional heteroskedasticity. Excess kurtosis observed in both returns and residuals series can be related to conditional heteroskedasticity; that is, its presence can be due to a time varying pattern of the volatility.

CONDITIONAL HETEROSKEDASTIC MODELS

The ARCH process imposes an autoregressive structure on the conditional variance, which permits volatility shocks to persist over time. In this process, the conditional error distribution is normal, with a conditional variance that is a linear function of past squared innovations. The model, denoted by ARCH(p), is as follows:

$$\epsilon_t \mid \Psi_{t-1} \sim N(0, h_t)$$
$$h_t = \alpha_0 + \sum_{i=1}^{p} \alpha_i \epsilon_{t-1}^2 \tag{4}$$

with $p > 0$, $\alpha_i > 0$, $i = 0, \ldots, p$, and where Ψ_t is the information set of all information through time t.

An important extension of the ARCH model is the Generalized Autoregressive Conditional Heteroskedasticity (GARCH) process of Bollerslev (1986), denoted by GARCH (p, q). In this model, the linear function of the conditional variance includes lagged conditional variances as well. Equation (4) in the case of a GARCH model becomes

$$h_t = \alpha_0 + \sum_{i=1}^{p} \alpha_i \epsilon_{t-i}^2 + \sum_{i=1}^{q} \beta_j h_{t-j} \tag{5}$$

where $q \geq 0$ and $\beta_j \geq 0$, $j = 1, \ldots, q$. The parameters of a (G)ARCH model are obtained through a maximum likelihood estimation. Given the return series and initial values of ϵ_1 and h_1, for $1 = 0, \ldots, r$ and with $r = \max(p, q)$, the following log-likelihood function must be maximized for a normal distribution:

$$L(\phi \mid p, q) = -\frac{1}{2} T \ln(2\pi) + \sum_{t=r}^{T} \ln \frac{1}{\sqrt{h_t}} \exp \frac{-\epsilon_t^2}{2h_t} \tag{6}$$

where T is the number of observations; h_t is the conditional variance, defined by Eqs. (4) and (5) for the ARCH and GARCH models, respectively; and ϵ_t^2 are the residuals obtained from the appropriate linear regression model according to the country in consideration.

Because the values of p and q have to be prespecified in the model, we tested several combinations of p and q. The values of the maximized likelihood functions for all pairs of p and q are presented in Table 3. We also calculated the generalized likelihood ratio LR $= -2\{L(\phi_n) - (\phi_a)\}$ of the maximized likelihood functions under the null hypothesis, that is, the normal distribution, and the various alternative hypotheses. Under the null hypothesis, LR is chi-squared distributed with degrees of freedom equal to the difference in the number of parameters under the two hypotheses. Table 3 gives the values of the LR test for each model. It can be observed that the value of the LR test for all (G)ARCH models is statistically significant at the 1% level, which means that all of these models fit the data more likely than does the normal distribution.

To distinguish between an improvement in the likelihood function due to a better fit and an improvement due to an increase in the number of parameters, we also calculated Schwarz's order selection criterion, SIC $= -2L(\phi) + (\ln T)K$, where K is the number of parameters in the model. According to this criterion, the model with the lowest SIC value fits the data best. The SIC values are reported in Table 3. The GARCH (1, 1) model has the lowest SIC values for all countries except France. For France no GARCH model converged and ARCH(3) is the best. Table 4 contains the results of the best model fitting the series of returns for each country.

The sum of $\Sigma_{i=1}^{p} \alpha_i + \Sigma_{j=1}^{q} \beta_j$ in the conditional variance equations measures the persistence of the volatility. Engle and Bollerslev (1982, 1986) have shown that if this sum is equal to one, the GARCH process becomes an Integrated GARCH (IGARCH) process. Such an integrated model implies the persistence of a forecast of the conditional variance over all future horizons and an infinite variance of the unconditional distribution of ϵ_t. The sums of the parameters $\Sigma_{i=1}^{p} \alpha_i + \Sigma_{j=1}^{q} \beta_j$ for the appropriate (G)ARCH models were calculated. They are all less than unity, though rather close to one for some, which indicates a long persistence of shocks in volatility. This means that the process is second-order stationary and that the second moment exists. The unconditional variances of residuals, shown in Table 4, are, respectively, $\sigma_\epsilon^2 = \alpha_0/(1 - \Sigma_{i=1}^{3} \alpha_i)$ for France and $\sigma_\epsilon^2 = \alpha_0/(1 - \alpha_1\beta_i)$ for the other countries. The unconditional variance of returns are $\sigma_R^2 = \sigma_\epsilon^2/(1 - \Phi_1^2)$; they are reported in Table 4 as well.

CONCLUSIONS AND IMPLICATIONS

This chapter provides empirical support for the hypothesis that stock market indices of nine different countries exhibit nonlinear dependency that cannot be accounted for by the random walk model. Descriptive statistics and normality tests reveal that the distribution of returns is not normal, whatever the country concerned. It has further been shown that the residuals obtained after applying an AR(1) model, which accounts for the presence of serial correlation in the

Table 3
Maximum Log Likelihood for (G)ARCH Models

Model	p, q	Log likelihood	LR	SIC
		Australia		
Normal	—	11 142.20		
ARCH	(1, 0)	11 747.09	1 209.78	−23 486.24
ARCH	(2, 0)	11 791.97	1 299.54	−23 568.06
ARCH	(3, 0)	11 799.43	1 314.46	−23 575.04
GARCH	(1, 1)	11 815.91	1 347.42	−23 615.94
GARCH	(2, 1)	. . .		
GARCH	(1, 2)	11 815.75	1 347.10	−23 607.68
GARCH	(2, 2)	. . .		
		Canada		
Normal	—	11 896.45		
ARCH	(1, 0)	12 220.90	24 441.80	−24 433.86
ARCH	(2, 0)	12 320.07	24 640.14	−24 624.26
ARCH	(3, 0)	12 360.68	24 721.36	−24 697.54
GARCH	(1, 1)	12 429.54	24 859.08	−24 843.20
GARCH	(2, 1)	12 431.64	24 863.28	−24 839.46
GARCH	(1, 2)	. . .		
GARCH	(2, 2)	12 424.74	24 849.48	−24 817.73
		France		
Normal	—	11 406.50		
ARCH	(1, 0)	11 560.95	308.90	−23 113.96
ARCH	(2, 0)	11 664.35	515.70	−23 312.82
ARCH	(3, 0)	11 677.31	541.62	−23 330.80
GARCH	(1, 1)	. . .		
GARCH	(2, 1)	. . .		
GARCH	(1, 2)	. . .		
GARCH	(2, 2)	. . .		
		Italy		
Normal	—	10 506.12		
ARCH	(1, 0)	10 653.91	295.58	−21 299.88
ARCH	(2, 0)	10 757.64	503.04	−21 499.40
ARCH	(3, 0)	10 886.73	761.22	−21 749.64
GARCH	(1, 1)	10 992.68	973.12	−21 969.48
GARCH	(2, 1)	. . .		
GARCH	(1, 2)	. . .		
GARCH	(2, 2)	10 998.15	984.06	−21 964.55
		Japan		
Normal	—	11 608.42		
ARCH	(1, 0)	12 004.09	791.34	−24 000.24
ARCH	(2, 0)	12 175.28	1 133.72	−24 334.68

(*Table continues on next page*)

Table 3
Maximum Log Likelihood for (G)ARCH Models (*Continued*)

Model	p, q	Log likelihood	LR	SIC
		Japan (*continued*)		
ARCH	(3, 0)	12 209.14	1 201.44	−24 394.46
GARCH	(1, 1)	12 276.02	1 335.20	−24 536.16
GARCH	(2, 1)	12 273.66	1 330.48	−24 523.50
GARCH	(1, 2)	· · ·		
GARCH	(2, 2)	· · ·		
		Korea		
Normal	—	10 924.09		
ARCH	(1, 0)	11 006.52	164.86	−22 005.10
ARCH	(2, 0)	11 197.96	547.74	−22 380.04
ARCH	(3, 0)	11 204.59	561.00	−22 385.36
GARCH	(1, 1)	11 226.24	604.30	−22 436.60
GARCH	(2, 1)	11 228.10	608.02	−22 432.38
GARCH	(1, 2)	11 228.82	609.46	−22 433.82
GARCH	(2, 2)	· · ·		
		Singapore		
Normal	—	10 754.82		
ARCH	(1, 0)	11 220.27	1 428.30	−22 432.60
ARCH	(2, 0)	11 250.69	1 489.14	−22 485.50
ARCH	(3, 0)	11 263.74	1 515.24	−22 503.66
GARCH	(1, 1)	11 310.22	1 608.20	−22 604.56
GARCH	(2, 1)	· · ·		
GARCH	(1, 2)	11 309.73	1 607.22	−22 595.64
		United Kingdom		
Normal	—	11 789.03		
ARCH	(1, 0)	11 991.12	404.18	−23 974.30
ARCH	(2, 0)	12 046.90	515.74	−24 077.92
GARCH	(1, 1)	12 097.46	616.86	−24 179.04
GARCH	(2, 1)	12 091.50	604.94	−24 159.18
GARCH	(1, 2)	· · ·		
GARCH	(2, 2)	· · ·		
		United States		
Normal	—	11 280.33		
ARCH	(1, 0)	11 518.75	476.84	−23 029.56
ARCH	(2, 0)	11 550.89	541.12	−23 085.90
ARCH	(3, 0)	11 579.58	598.50	−23 135.34
GARCH	(1, 1)	11 628.24	695.82	−23 240.60
GARCH	(2, 1)	11 609.84	659.02	−23 195.86
GARCH	(1, 2)	11 623.64	686.62	−23 223.46
GARCH	(2, 2)	· · ·		

Note. · · · indicates where the optimization routine failed.

Table 4
GARCH Model Estimation

	Australia	Canada	France	Italy	Japan	Korea	Singapore	United Kingdom	United States
ϕ_0	0.464	0.203	0.688	0.806	0.750	0.535	0.707	0.678	0.566
ϕ_1	0.278	0.240	0.203	0.191	0.112	0.078	0.023	0.152	0.036
α_0	0.015	0.004	0.058	0.006	0.003	0.015	0.013	0.005	0.006
α_1	0.358	0.166	0.174	0.140	0.252	0.141	0.162	0.113	0.093
α_2			0.161						
α_3			0.098						
β_1	0.536	0.778	—	0.837	0.746	0.755	0.754	0.815	0.855
$\alpha_1 + \beta_1$	0.894	0.944	0.433[a]	0.976	0.997	0.896	0.916	0.928	0.948
$\sigma^2\ (\times 10^3)$	0.144	0.072	0.103	0.268	0.214	0.141	0.155	0.074	0.109
$\sigma_R^2\ (\times 10^3)$	0.156	0.076	0.107	0.278	0.230	0.141	0.156	0.076	0.110

Note. Underlined numbers indicate 5% significance level.
[a]$(\alpha_1 + \alpha_2 + \alpha_3)$ are parameters of the ARCH model.

returns, exhibit nonlinear dependence and non-normality. We tested various models belonging to the class of autoregressive conditional heteroskedasticity models. The results reveal that this class of models supersedes the random walk model. And among the different models the GARCH (1, 1) fits the data best for all countries except France, for which ARCH (3) fits better.

Conditional heteroskedasticity implies that the variance of the returns depends on information about recent returns. This can have important implications for research in finance. For example, GARCH models may be used to analyze the relationships between volatility and expected returns. In the Capital Asset Pricing Model, the expected return or risk premium can be influenced by the conditional second moment of returns. Volatility estimation is also an important feature for pricing derivative securities. GARCH models can indeed lead to better forecasts of volatility than alternative estimation methods.

REFERENCES

Akgiray, V. 1989. Conditional heteroskedasticity in time series of stock returns: Evidence and forecasts, *Journal of Business* 62:55–80.

Baillie, R. T., and T. Bollerslev. 1989. The message in daily exchange rates: A conditional-variance tale, *Journal of Business & Economic Statistics* 7:297–305.

Baillie, R. T., and R. P. De Gennaro. 1990. Stock returns and volatility, *Journal of Financial and Quantitative Analysis* 25:203–214.

Bollerslev, T. 1986. Generalized autoregressive conditional heteroskedasticity, *Journal of Econometrics* 31:307–327.

Diebold, F. X. 1987. Testing for serial correlation in the presence of ARCH, *Proceedings of the American Statistic Association*, Business and Economic Statistics Section, pp. 323–328.

Diebold, F. X., I. Jong, and C. Jevons Lee. 1988. *Conditional Heteroskedasticity in the Market, Finance and Economics Discussion Series*, Vol. 42, Washington, DC: Division of Research and Statistics, Federal Reserve Board.

Engle, R. F. 1982. Autoregressive conditional heteroskedasticity with estimates of the variance of UK inflation, *Econometrica* 50:987–1008.

Fama, E. F. 1965. The behavior of stock market prices, *Journal of Business* 38:34–105.

French, K. R., W. G. Schwert, and R. F. Stambaugh. 1987. Expected stock returns and volatility, *Journal of Financial Economics* 19:3–29.

Hsieh, D. A. 1989. Modelling heteroskedasticity in daily foreign-exchange rates, *Journal of Business & Economic Statistics* 7:307–317.

Hinich, M. J. and D. M. Patterson. 1985. Evidence of nonlinearity in daily stock returns, *Journal of Business & Economic Statistics* 3:69–77.

Mandelbrot, B. 1963. The variation of certain speculative prices, *Journal of Business* 36:394–419.

Merton, R. 1982. On the mathematics and economics assumptions of continuous-time models, in W. Sharpe and C. Cootner (Eds.), *Financial Economics,* Englewood Cliffs, NJ: Prentice-Hall.

Morgan, I. 1967. Stock prices and heteroskedasticity, *Journal of Business* 49:496–508.

Neftçi, S. N. 1984. Are economic time series asymmetric over the business cycle? *Journal of Political Economy* 92:307–328.

Osborne, M. F. 1964. Brownian motion in the stock market, in P. H. Cootner (Ed.), *The Random Character of Stock Market Prices*, Cambridge, MA: MIT Press.

Perry, P. R. 1982. The time-variance relationship of security returns: Implications for the return-generating stochastic process, *Journal of Finance* 37:857–870.

Pindyck, R. S. 1984. Risk, inflation and the stock market, *American Economic Review* 74:335–351.

Poterba, J. M., and L. H. Summers. 1986. The persistence of volatility and stock market fluctuations, *American Economic Review* 76:1142–1151.

Schwarz, G. 1978. Estimating the dimension of a model, *The Annals of Statistics* 6:461–464.

Chapter 16

Effects of Monetary Gains and Losses on the Univariate Time-Series Characteristics of CDA Earnings

Hossein Shalchi and M. T. Vaziri

Recent years have witnessed an increasing interest in the time-series properties of historical cost (HC) accounting data (e.g., Foster, 1977; Brown and Rozeff, 1978; Hopwood and McKeown, 1981; Fries, 1985), but research on the statistical characteristics of accounting signals generated by inflation adjusted income measures have been lacking (e.g., Hillison et al., 1983; Shalchi and Smith, 1985). Indeed, virtually nothing is known about the degree to which actual accounting time-series differ under various alternatives, presumably due to the unavailability of such data. This void has usually been filled by making a priori assumptions about the processes generating such data. For instance, studies by Beaver et al. (1982) and Beaver and Landsman (1983) on the information content of constant dollar accounting (CDA) earnings make implicit assumptions, with no prior empirical evidence, about the earnings-expectation models appropriate for such data.[1] Given the fact that the results of such studies are earnings-expectation dependent, possible misspecification of the earnings-expectation models is likely to induce erroneous inferences on their findings. The present study provides explicit empirical evidence regarding the time-series characteristics of various deflated and nondeflated annual CDA-based income measures and the effects of monetary gains or losses on such series.

PRIOR RESEARCH

A number of accounting studies have investigated the descriptive properties of accounting earnings. The reason for this emphasis is that examination of time-series behavior of accounting earnings is not an end in itself; rather it is merely a means of modeling and developing reliable earnings-expectation models re-

---

[1]Throughout this chapter, the term constant dollar accounting is used instead of general purchasing power accounting or general price level accounting, in keeping with the term used in FAS 33.

quired for addressing various accounting and finance research issues. More specifically, construction and specification of reliable earnings-expectation models is a prerequisite of studies dealing with the information content of accounting data (e.g., Beaver and Landsman, 1983; Bublitz et al., 1985) and security valuation models (Modigliani and Miller, 1966; Givoly, 1985).

An examination of the accounting literature on the time-series properties of accounting signals indicates that the focus of such studies has been on the HC accounting numbers. Consequently, various parsimonious models have been identified as the process generating annual HC earnings (e.g., Albrecht et al., 1977; Hopwood and McKeown, 1981) and quarterly HC earnings date (e.g., Brown and Rozeff, 1978; Foster, 1977; Fries, 1985). In general, the extant empirical evidence suggests that HC earnings series exhibit time-series characteristics similar to a random walk model and that a random walk (moving average or mean reverting process) is a reasonable description of deflated earnings (for a detailed discussion see Griffin, 1982, pp. 65–97).

While the preceding discussion demonstrates the critical importance of understanding the time-series characteristics of accounting earnings generated by various inflation-adjusted accounting models, almost no research investigates this issue empirically. As was noted earlier, the major reason for this lack of interest is probably the unavailability of publicly disclosed information required for such investigation. Hillison et al. (1983) extended the time-series research to the CDA quarterly data by exploring the predictive value and time-series properties of CDA adjusted quarterly earnings for a sample of 24 firms in the airlines industry for the 1962–1978 period. CDA adjusted earnings were estimated using a restatement model. Firm-specific autoregressive integrated moving average models (ARIMAs) were developed for both CDA and HC data. Hillison et al. found that when the structure of the CDA models was similar to that of the HC models, the parameter values varied significantly. With respect to predictive content, the empirical results suggested the superiority of the HC predictions over the CDA predictions.

The logical next step is to examine the time-series characteristics of CDA annual earnings. This chapter explicitly deals with the CDA annual data. As such, it extends the recent trend toward modeling and eventually understanding the time-series characteristics of inflation-adjusted income measures. Other distinctive features of this empirical investigation include the following. First, it is one of the first studies to investigate the time-series properties of both deflated and nondeflated CDA annual earnings data. Second, unlike the Hillison et al. study, which is based on a small sample in a single regulated industry, the current research is based on a sample of firms from different industries. Third, the time-period covered in this study is the 1951–1981 period compared to the 1962–1978 period used in the Hillison et al. study. Finally, this study investigates the effects of CDA gains or losses on the time-series properties and predictive value of CDA annual earnings.

SAMPLE SELECTION AND RESEARCH METHODOLOGY

Sample Selection

The overriding sample constraint for all studies such as this is the need for substantial detailed HC annual financial data over a long period of time, owing to the CDA estimation model and the Box–Jenkins methodology data requirements, which result in both cross-sectional and time-series constraints. The results presented in the current study are based on a sample selected from the Compustat Annual Industrial tapes. The sample consists of all calendar year firms that met the following data requirements during the 1947–1984 period:

(1) Availability of the complete set of financial reports needed for the CDA estimation model.[2] In cases where the required financial data was missing on the Compustat tapes, other sources of information such as Moody's Industrial Manuals and 10-K reports were used.
(2) One inventory valuation method in each given year. This criterion was imposed to avoid extreme computational difficulties involved in the CDA estimations for companies using various inventory valuation methods for different segments.

All the firms that met the data requirements were included in the analysis. The resulting sample consisted of 47 firms. The names of these firms are listed in Table 1. It should be noted that since meeting the detailed data requirements was the main factor in selecting the firms, a necessary condition in the absence of actual data, the sample is not a random sample in the probabilistic sense. However, a breakdown of the sample by SIC two-digit industry codes revealed that 17 industries are represented in the final sample, indicating that the sample covers a broad cross section of the publicly traded firms.

Estimation of CDA Financial Statements

In the absence of any accounting pronouncement requiring the disclosure of CDA data prior to Statement of Financial Accounting Standards No. 33 (FAS 33) (FASB, 1979), this information must be estimated. Accordingly, a computer-based CDA estimation model in accordance with the CDA restatement procedures required under the FAS 33 was developed and used in this study. Given the use of the CDA estimation algorithm to generate CDA data, the accuracy of the restatement model employed becomes essential to the valid-

[2]The CDA restatement procedures used in this study require the availability of the following data for each year: cash and marketable securities, accounts and notes receivable, beginning and ending inventory, inventory valuation methods, current liabilities, long-term debt, preferred stock, common equity, beginning and ending retained earnings, gross plants, depreciation methods, depreciation and amortization expenses, accumulated depreciation, net sales, operating income, preferred dividends, common dividends, deferred taxes and investment credits, and cost of goods sold.

Table 1
Sample of Firms

Company name	Four-digit industry code
American Bakeries Co.	2050
American Home Products Corp.	2830
American Hospital Supply	3841
Baxter Tranvenol Laboratories	3841
Belding Heminway	2200
Bell and Howell Co.	3861
Braniff International Corp.	4511
Callahan Mining Corp.	3494
Caterpillar Tractor Co.	3531
Certain Teed Corp.	2950
Conrac Corp.	3662
Crane Co.	3310
Di Giorgio Corp.	5140
Eastern Airlines	4511
Evans Products Co.	5211
Freeport Minerals Co.	1499
General Hospital Corp.	2010
Johns-Manville Corp.	3290
Kraft Inc.	2020
Kroehler Manufacturing Co.	2510
Macmillan Inc.	2731
Minnesota Mining and Mfg. Co.	3861
Morrison-Knudson	1600
Motorola Inc.	3662
Nabisco Inc.	2000
National Steel Co.	3310
Northwest Airlines Inc.	4511
Pabst Brewing Co.	2082
Pan American World Airways	4511
Robertshaw Controls	3820
Ronson Corp.	3630
Seaboard World Airlines	4511
Searle (G. D.) and Co.	2830
Standard Brands Inc.	2000
Sterling Drug Inc.	2800
Stewart-Warner Corp.	3560
Sundstrand Corp.	3540
Tecumseh Products Co.	3580
Texasgulf Inc.	1499
Tootsie Roll Industries Inc.	2065
Trans World Corp.	4511
UAL Inc.	4511
Union Oil Co. of California	2911
U.S. Steel Corp.	3310
Western Airlines Inc.	4511
Xerox Corp.	3570

ity of the results reported herein. The accuracy of the restatement procedure was tested by comparing the CDA estimates obtained against the actual CDA data reported by sample companies that disclosed CDA information for 1980 and 1981. The absolute estimation error was between .006 and .05, with an average estimation error of less than 3%, indicating an acceptable level of accuracy for the restatement procedure employed.

Earnings Variables

The restatement algorithm was used to estimate CDA financial statements for the sample firms for each year from 1951 through 1984.[3] As noted by Foster (1978, p. 102) there is no reason that the nondeflated and deflated earnings series should follow the same time-series process. Thus, it is of considerable importance to examine the time-series properties of CDA earnings data on both deflated and nondeflated bases. Accordingly, three earnings variables were initially defined: (1) return on equity, defined as net income before extraordinary items deflated by common equity; (2) return on assets, defined as net income before extraordinary items deflated by total assets; and (3) net income before extraordinary items. Moreover, given the controversy over the inclusion of the CDA net monetary gains/losses in the calculation of CDA earnings, it was decided to examine the time-series properties of the three CDA earnings variables both with and without inclusion of CDA net monetary gains or losses (hereafter, the CDAIM and CDAEM methods, respectively).

The next stage of the research methodology was to develop univariate Box–Jenkins (1970) models for each of the six earnings series using the following general model:

$$\phi_p(B)\, \nabla^d X_t = \theta_0 + \theta_q(B)\epsilon_t$$

where ϵ_t is a white noise, X_t is earnings, and ∇ is a (backward) difference operator, which can be expressed in terms of the backshift operator B as $\nabla^d = (1 - B)^d$. This general ARIMA (p, d, q), represents the dth difference of the original series as a process containing p autoregressive and q moving average parameters and is capable of characterizing a wide class of parsimonious models. Parameter estimates for the identified models were examined for statistical significance and compliance with stationary–invertibility conditions. Moreover, various diagnostic tests, including the Box–Pierce Q statistic, were performed on each parsimoniously structured model to assure the adequacy of the fitted models.

---

[3]To estimate the CDA financial statements for any given year, the CDA estimation model required a minimum of five years of HC financial statements. Therefore, 1951 is the first year for which CDA financial statements could be estimated.

ANALYSIS OF THE RESULTS

Using the CDA earnings data over the 1951–1982 period (32 annual observations), six univariate B-J models were developed for each firm in the sample, three for the CDAEM earnings series and three for the CDAIM earnings measures. Therefore, the total number of the ARIMA models identified and estimated was 282. The results of the firm-specific ARIMA models developed for various time-series models for deflated and nondeflated earnings across the two alternative CDA accounting systems models led to the following tentative conclusion. The most commonly identified process for both CDAIM and CDAEM rate of return on equity series is a pure autoregressive process (71 models out of the total 94 series). Moreover, for all but two cases, the identified models were stationary and thus no differencing was necessary to become stationary. Further analysis of the empirical results reveals that there are 10 series for each of the CDAIM and CDAEM earnings series that can be described as white noise processes and only three models display both AR and MA parameters. Thus, the results suggest that the return on equity series may be either a stationary first-order autoregressive or white noise process.

The empirical results also show that all of the firm-specific models identified for the return on assets series were stationary and required no differencing of the original series. For the CDAIM series, 35 models had only AR parameters, two models displayed both AR and MA parameters, and nine series exhibited characteristics of a white noise process. Furthermore, the time-series models identified for the CDAEM return on assets series generally had parameters and statistical properties similar to those of the corresponding CDAIM series. The results also indicated that the most commonly identified model for both CDAIM and CDAEM earnings series are autoregressive processes. Indeed, the evidence provided indicates that 35 and 34 models of the CDAIM and CDAEM series, respectively, are purely autoregressive models. Here again, in all but six cases, the firm-specific models for the CDAIM and CDAEM series are stationary. A consistent finding of the time-series analysis of all series is that most of the identified models are stationary (only nine of the 282 models are nonstationary).

The statistical evidence of the stationary characteristic of the CDA series provided in this study is intuitively appealing and theoretically expected because adoption of the constant dollar accounting systems would result in earnings series that are more likely to be stationary. As expected, the stationary characteristic is even more evident for the rate of return earnings series than for the total earnings series. The main reason for this observation might be that during an inflationary period companies' net earnings generally grow faster than the rate of inflation.

A detailed analysis of the fitted models on the CDAIM and CDAEM series revealed that many models are identified as AR models that could be approximated by a random walk model. That is, when the coefficient of a first-order autoregressive (stationary) model is small, within one standard error of one, the underlying time series could be described as a random walk process as well. In view of this potential problem and because of the empirical support for the random walk behavior of the HC-based earnings in the literature (e.g., Beaver et al., 1980; Albrecht et al., 1977; Watts and Leftwich, 1977), the predictive ability of the firm-specific univariate Box–Jenkins (UBJ) models is compared with those generated by both a random walk (RW) model and a random walk with drift pattern (RWD) model:

Random walk model: $E(X_t) = X_{t-1}$

Random walk with drift model: $E(X_t) = X_{t-1} + \delta_t$

where X_t is earnings in period t, and δ_t is a drift term estimated as the average change in earnings over the base period. For each of the deflated and nondeflated earnings series, the three forecasting models were utilized to make predictions for two different forecast horizons (one year ahead and two years ahead). The accuracy of the prediction models were assessed using two different error measures: (1) mean absolute relative error (MARE) and (2) mean squared relative error (MSRE). MARE assigns equal weight to all forecast errors and is consistent with a linear log function. MSRE assigns proportionately greater weight to large forecast errors and is consistent with a quadratic loss function.

The statistical methodology employed in the present study to test the null hypothesis of no difference in the predictive ability of the forecast models is the Friedman two-way analysis of variance on rank (Siegel, 1971). The nonparametric Friedman test has power and flexibility comparable to the parametric ANOVA technique. In addition, and most importantly, it does not make assumptions about the form of the population distribution such as the normality assumption required in the ordinary ANOVA. For pairwise tests on the predictive value of the alternative forecast models, a proper test is the widely used Wilcoxon Matched-Pairs Signed-Ranks test. This test also has the advantage of avoiding the error measures being dominated by a few large outliers, as well as the problems of distributional assumptions required for the parametric tests.

Table 2 contains accuracy results of the three forecasting models for each of the three CDAIM income measures. Table 3 presents summary results of the CDAEM series. Each of these tables contain ranking of the predictive accuracy of the forecasts, Friedman test statistics (for tests of the three forecasting models as a group), and Wilcoxon rank test statistics (for paired comparisons) for each of the three income measures.

From Table 2 it can be observed that for the CDAIM return on assets series, RWD models yield smaller errors than the other time series models. Moreover, the Friedman test statistics are highly significant when the three forecast models are tested as a group; the null hypothesis of identically distributed distributions is rejected for both error measures. The pairwise Wilcoxon test statistics show

Table 2

Friedman and Wilcoxon Rank Tests of Error Measures Across the Alternative Forecasting Models for CDAIM Series

CDAIM return on assets series						
	MARE			MSRE		
Friedman statistics	$\chi^2 = 14.170$ Significant level = .001			$\chi^2 = 11.532$ Significant level = .003		
Wilcoxon statistics[a]						
Forecasting model	UBJ	RW	RWD	UBJ	RW	RWD
(Mean ranks)	(2.45)	(1.81)	(1.74)	(2.40)	(1.79)	(1.81)
RW	2.731[c]	—	—	3.093[c]	—	—
RWD	3.396[c]	0.544	—	2.509[c]	0.505	—
CDAIM return on equity series						
	MARE			MSRE		
Friedman statistics	$\chi^2 = 4.436$ Significant level = .109			$\chi^2 = 3.957$ Significant level = .138		
Wilcoxon statistics[a]						
Forecasting model	UBJ	RW	RWD	UBJ	RW	RWD
(Mean ranks)	(2.24)	(1.93)	(1.83)	(2.23)	(1.91)	(1.85)
RW	1.587[a]	—	—	1.447[a]	—	—
RWD	2.106[b]	0.556	—	1.882[b]	0.781	—

CDAIM net income series						
	MARE			MSRE		
Friedman statistics	$\chi^2 = 10.511$ Significant level = .005			$\chi^2 = 9.904$ Significant level = .007		
Wilcoxon statistics[a]						
Forecasting model	UBJ	RW	RWD	UBJ	RW	RWD
(Mean ranks)	(2.38)	(1.85)	(1.77)	(2.36)	(1.90)	(1.73)
RW	2.346[c]	—	—	1.797[b]	—	—
RWD	2.497[c]	0.544	—	1.832[b]	0.862	—

[a]Significant at the .10 level, one-tailed test.
[b]Significant at the .05 level, one-tailed test.
[c]Significant at the .01 level, one-tailed test.
[d]Each Wilcoxon test statistic results from comparing model at the top with model on the side.

Table 3

Friedman and Wilcoxon Rank Tests of Error Measures Across the Alternative Forecasting Models for CDAEM Series

	CDAEM return on assets series					
	MARE			MSRE		
Friedman statistics	$\chi^2 = 7.989$ Significant level = .018			$\chi^2 = 6.777$ Significant level = .034		
Wilcoxon statistics[a] Forecasting model	UBJ	RW	RWD	UBJ	RW	RWD
(Mean ranks)	(2.22)	(1.67)	(2.11)	(2.24)	(1.71)	(2.04)
RW	2.754[c]	—	—	2.532[c]	—	—
RWD	0.593	2.274[b]	—	0.265	1.902[b]	—
	CDAEM return on equity series					
	MARE			MSRE		
Friedman statistics	$\chi^2 = 5.436$ Significant level = .066			$\chi^2 = 3.840$ Significant level = .147		
Wilcoxon statistics[a] Forecasting model	UBJ	RW	RWD	UBJ	RW	RWD
(Mean ranks)	(2.20)	(1.73)	(2.06)	(2.20)	(1.80)	(2.00)
RW	2.194[b]	—	—	2.147[b]	—	—
RWD	0.367	2.173[b]	—	0.141	1.823[b]	—

CDAEM net income series						
	MARE			MSRE		
Friedman statistics	χ^2 = 3.734 Significant level = .115			χ^2 = 2.117 Significant level = .347		
Wilcoxon statistics[a]						
Forecasting model	UBJ	RW	RWD	UBJ	RW	RWD
(Mean ranks)	(2.16)	(1.78)	(2.06)	(2.14)	(1.84)	(2.02)
RW	2.195[b]	—	—	1.435[a]	—	—
RWD	0.570	1.891[b]	—	0.638	1.417[a]	—

[a]Significant at the 0.10 level, one-tailed test.
[b]Significant at the .05 level, one-tailed test.
[c]Significant at the .01 level, one-tailed test.
[d]Each Wilcoxon test statistic results from comparing model at the top with model on the side.

that both RWD models and RW models statistically outperform the UBJ forecasts at the .01 level, with no statistically significant difference between the RWD and RW forecasts. For the CDAIM rate of return on equity series, the Friedman test statistics indicate no significant difference among the three forecast models. Using the Wilcoxon test, for both error metrics, the evidence indicates that RWD and RW models provide a significant (α = .05) difference among the three forecast models. Using the Wilcoxon test, for both error metrics, the evidence indicates that RWD and RW models provide better predictions than UBJ models. In addition, although RWD models predict better than RW models, the difference is not statistically significant. The forecast accuracy results for the CDAIM net income models are provided in Table 2. The Friedman statistics are highly significant when the three forecast models are tested together. Also, the prediction error rankings show that both RW and RWD models provide predictions superior to UBJ models. Using the MARE matrix, the Wilcoxon test statistics indicate a significant difference in favor of RWD models and RW models (at the .01 significant level) when compared with the UBJ models. The MSRE results are consistent with the MARE findings providing evidence of RWD and RW superiority over the UBJ models at the .05 level of significance. Although the RWD outperforms the RW model, its superiority over the RW model, no matter which measure of prediction error is used, is not statistically significant.

Table 3 presents the predictive accuracy of the forecast models for the three CDAEM income series. For the CDAEM rate of return on assets series, the χ^2 values are significant at the .018 and .034 levels based on MARE and MSRE error metrics, respectively. For both error metric, the pairwise comparisons reveal the statistical superiority of RW models over UBJ and RWD models at the .01 and .05 levels of significance, respectively. For the CDAEM rate of return equity series, the χ^2 value indicates that no significant difference exists in the forecasting ability of the alternative forecasting models when MSRE error metrics are used (p = .147). Moreover, the group difference is significant only at the .10 level when using MARE error measure. As for the pairwise comparisons, predictions generated via RW models, regardless of the error metrics used, are statistically superior to UBJ and RWD models. Table 3 shows that for the CDAEM net income series using MARE error metric, the RW model provides significantly better predictions than the RWD and UBJ models at the .05 level of significance. Comparisons of differences based on MSRE for the three forecasting models produced the same results but only at the .10 level of significance. That is, forecasts of the RW model were significantly (α = .10) better than forecasts of the RWD and UBJ models.

In conclusion, the Friedman tests and pairwise Wilcoxon Signed Ranks tests of the error measures strongly support the superiority of the RW and the RWD model over the UBJ model for all CDAIM deflated and nondeflated earnings. Moreover, comparisons of the RWD with the RW models in predictive contests reveal that, although in five of six cases the general ranking of the prediction errors favored RWD, the differences were not statistically significant. With respect to the CDAEM deflated and nondeflated earnings series, no matter which measure of prediction error is used, the statistical tests provide an overwhelming dominance of the superiority of the RW over the UBJ and RWD models. Moreover, the UBJ model consistently generated the least accurate forecasts. Therefore, the evidence suggests that the RW model provides more accurate forecasts of CDAIM earnings, while the RWD model is a reasonable description of the deflated and nondeflated CDAEM earnings.

CONCLUSIONS

The objective of the present study was twofold: first, to explore the interstructure of both deflated and nondeflated CDA earnings measures and to compare the predictive ability of the parsimonious models with the random walk models, both with and without drift; and second, to assess the possible effects of the inclusion of purchasing power monetary gains or losses on the time-series characteristics of the CDA earnings. In general, the empirical evidence provided in the chapter indicated that the time-series behavior of the CDAEM and CDAIM earnings measures is consistent with the description of the process as random walk and random walk with drift processes, respectively. This observation can be attributed to the effects of the net monetary gains or losses on the time-series behavior of the CDA earnings data. That is, since most industrial companies are in a net monetary liability position, they will have purchasing power monetary gains during inflationary periods. Similarly, as the assets size of a company grows over time, so will its monetary gains. Therefore, the inclusion of monetary gains/losses should introduce an upward drift in the time-series characteristics of such data. The evidence provided in this study was consistent with this connotation. Specifically, while the random walk model showed superiority over other models for the CDAEM series, the inclusion of the monetary gains/losses in the determination of earnings resulted in a random walk with drift process to best predict future CDAIM values. This finding was consistent across the deflated and nondeflated earnings measures. The implication of this finding from the point of view of researchers and other users of earnings expectation models is that given the superiority of RW and RWD models over the univariate B-J models, the use of this sophisticated and costly approach cannot be justified. The empirical evidence provided in this study implies that researchers, financial analysts, and investors do not need to be concerned with the firm-specific time-series models for the CDA series. Instead, the appropriate random walk processes would be sufficient to develop the necessary earnings expectation models for CDA earnings.

REFERENCES

Albrecht, W. S., L. L. Lookabill, and J. C. McKeown. 1977. The time series properties of annual earnings, *Journal of Accounting Research* 15(2):226–244.

Bamber, L. 1986. The information content of annual earnings releases: A trading volume approach, *Journal of Accounting Research* 24(1):40–56.

Barn, A., J. Lakonishok, and A. R. Ofer. 1980. The information content of general price level adjusted earnings: Some empirical evidence. *The Accounting Review* 55(1):22–35.

Beaver, W., and W. Landsman. 1983. *Incremental Information Content of Statement 33 Disclosures,* Stamford, CT: Financial Accounting Standards Board.

Beaver, W., A. Christie, and P. Griffin. 1980. The information content of SEC Accounting Series Release No. 190, *Journal of Accounting and Economics* 2:127–157.

Beaver, W., P. Griffin, and W. Landsman. 1982. The incremental information content of replacement cost earnings, *Journal of Accounting and Economics* 4:15–39.

Box, G. E. P., and G. M. Jenkins. 1970. *Time Series Analysis: Forecasting and Control,* San Francisco: Holden-Day.

Brown, L., and M. Rozeff. 1978. The superiority of analyst forecasts as measures of expectations: Evidence from earnings, *The Journal of Finance,* 1–16.

Bublitz, B., T. Frecka, and J. McKeown. 1985. Market association tests and FASB statement No. 33 disclosures: A re-examination, *Studies on Accounting Earnings and Security Valuation: Current Research Issues* (Supplement to the *Journal of Accounting Research*) 23:1–23.

Financial Accounting Standards Board. 1979. *Statement of Financial Accounting Standards No. 33: Financial Reporting and Changing Prices,* Stamford, CT: FASB.

Foster, G. 1977. Quarterly accounting data: Time-series properties and predictive results, *The Accounting Review* 52(1):1–21.

Foster, G. 1978. *Financial Statement Analysis,* Englewood Cliffs, NJ: Prentice-Hall.

Fries, C. 1985. *Preliminary Evidence Regarding the Transfer Function Relationship of Quarterly Earnings for Closely-Related Industries,* Fayetteville: University of Arkansas.

Givoly, D. 1985. The formation of earnings expectation. *The Accounting Review* 60(3):372–386.

Granger, C. W. I., and P. Newbold. 1977. *Forecasting Economic Time Series,* New York: Academic.

Griffin, P. 1982. *Usefulness to Investors and Creditors of Information Provided by Financial Reporting: A Review of Empirical Accounting Research,* Stamford, CT: FASB.

Hillison, W., W. Hopwood, and K. Lorek. 1983. Quarterly GPPA earnings data: Time-series properties and predictive ability results in the airline industry, *Journal of Forecasting* 2:363–375.

Hopwood, W. S. 1980. On the automation of the Box–Jenkins modeling procedures: An algorithm with an empirical test, *Journal of Accounting Research* 18(2):289–296.

Hopwood, W., and J. McKeown. 1981. An evaluation of univariate time series earnings models and their generalization to a single input transfer function, *Journal of Accounting Research* 19(2):313–322.

Modigliani, F., and M. Miller. 1966. Some estimates of cost of capital to the electric utility industry, 1954–57, *American Economic Review* 56:333–391.

Ronen, J., S. Sadan, and C. Snow. 1977. Income smoothing: A review, *The Accounting Journal* 1:11–26.

Shalchi, H., and C. H. Smith. 1985. Research on accounting for changing prices: Theory, evidence, and implications, *Quarterly Review of Economics and Business* 25(4):5–37.

Siegel, S. 1971. *Nonparametric Statistics*, New York: McGraw-Hill.

Watts, R. L., and R. W. Leftwich. 1977. The time series of annual accounting earnings, *Journal of Accounting Research* 15(2):253–271.

Chapter 17

Survival Analysis of Business Failures

Rafael Solis

Business failures are viewed here as a life and death process. Traditionally, these processes have been extensively studied by actuaries when designing mortality and life tables used by insurance companies throughout the world. The basic tool used in building such tables is called survival analysis (Abramowitz, 1965; Johnson and Elandt-Johnson, 1980; Johnson and Kotz, 1970). This chapter presents a simplified version of this theory and its application to the analysis of business mortality (failure). In particular, we study the following topics:

(1) In most types of businesses the early years are the most difficult and time mortality is highest.
(2) Generally, the longer the business survives, other things being equal, the smaller its probability of failure.
(3) Mortality rates differ among business types.

SURVIVAL ANALYSIS

Traditional survival analysis deals with mortality rates. These data arise from recording times of death of individuals (or laboratory animals) that possess a specific characteristic. The data collection process is carried out over time, starting at a specific time ($t = 0$) at which all individuals in the group (called the cohort) are alive. The recorded times of death of the individuals in the cohort are used to produce life tables, which in turn can be used to fit certain functions that will provide a model of the mortality (failure) behavior of the population that the cohort represents.

In applying the above idea to business failures (bankruptcy, closings, etc.), a cohort may represent a particular type of business (retail, banking/financial, manufacturing, etc.). The data collection process of a business cohort, if applied in the traditional sense (i.e., longitudinally following the cohort until everyone dies (fails)), may become a very difficult task. Instead, a sampling process may be used to produce observed frequency counts of the number of businesses (of a particular type) that failed within a specific time period, say within t years from opening ($t = 1, 2, 3, \ldots$). This frequency histogram constitutes the basic data on which our analysis is based.

Denote by $F(t)$ the observed (cumulative) probability of failure at time t of a business of a particular type. $F(t)$ can be interpreted as the (empirical) probability that a business will fail within t years. A related but more meaningful expression is the survival function $S(t)$, which can be expressed as follows:

$$S(t) = 1 - F(t) \qquad t = 0, 1, 2, \ldots$$

where $F(0) = 0$

This function measures the probability of surviving at least t years. Table 1 shows the $F(t)$ and $S(t)$ values for two types of businesses: retail and manufacturing (Lomax, 1954). The behavior of $F(t)$ and $S(t)$ for the two types of businesses considered here is shown in Figures 1 and 2.

Although we always observe $F(t)$ and $S(t)$ at discrete intervals of time, these two functions are continuous. An estimate of the density function values $f(t)$ (i.e., $f(t) = F'(t)$) also will be needed. The discrete values of this function will be estimated from the values of $F(t)$ given in Table 1. The estimated function points of $f(t)$ will be used to estimate a related function called the instantaneous failure rate at age t (denoted here by $H(t)$). This function is also known as the hazard rate or force of mortality, and measures the probability of failure within the time interval $[t, t + \Delta_t]$ ($\Delta \to 0$), conditional upon nonfailure prior to t. This quantity can be written as follows:

$$H(t) = \frac{f(t)}{S(t)}$$

Table 1
Probabilities of Business Failure in Poughkeepsie

Business age (years)	Retail		Manufacturing	
	$F(t)$	$S(t)$	$F(t)$	$S(t)$
0	0.000	1.000	0.000	1.000
1	0.296	0.704	0.231	0.746
2	0.438	0.562	0.346	0.654
3	0.532	0.468	0.469	0.531
4	0.594	0.406	0.547	0.453
5	0.643	0.357	0.602	0.398
6	0.684	0.316	0.655	0.345
7	0.715	0.285	0.678	0.322
8	0.741	0.259	0.702	0.298
9	0.762	0.238	0.726	0.274
10	0.782	0.218	0.746	0.254

Source. Lomax (1954).

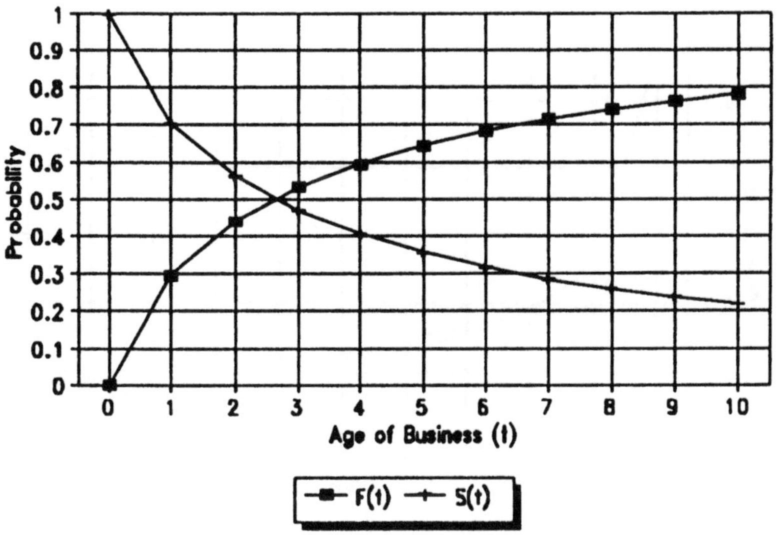

Figure 1 Retail industry: cumulative distribution and survival functions.

The hazard rate $H(t)$ provides information about the probability of failure at a given time t, knowing that a business has survived exactly t years. Figure 3 shows the estimated hazard function for both industry sectors.

Notice that $H(t)$ cannot be computed unless $f(t)$ is known. Two simple procedures can be used to calculate $f(t)$. The first is to estimate the slope of the underlying (continuous) function $F(t)$ for the various values of t for which data were collected. The other (and simpler) is to use the method of finite differ-

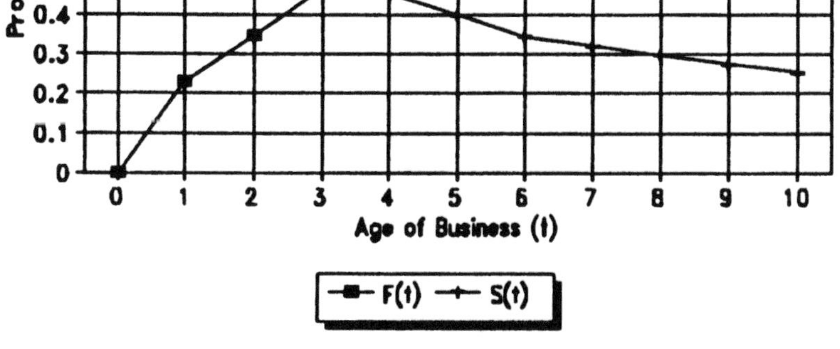

Figure 2 Manufacturing industry: cumulative distribution and survival functions.

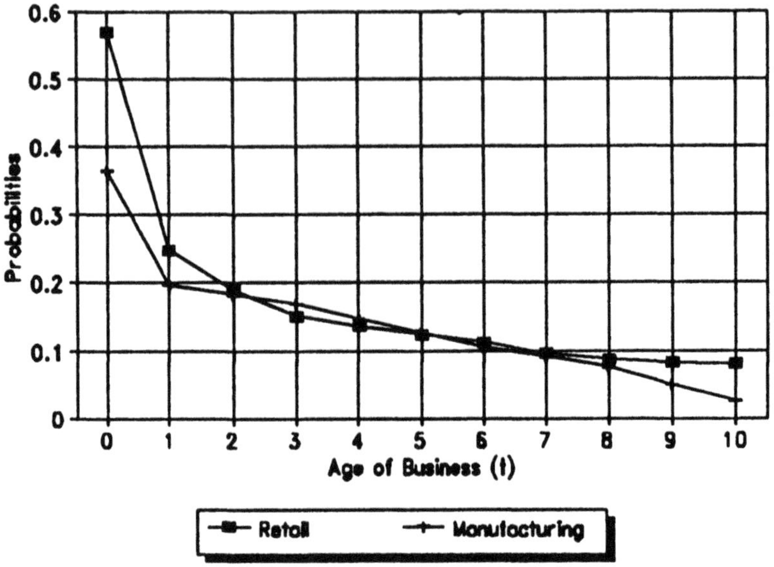

Figure 3 Estimated hazard functions.

ences (see, for instance, Abramowitz and Segun (1965)). The latter method is used here. The estimated values of $f(t)$ and $H(t)$ are shown in Table 2. Of primary importance in this analysis is the fitting of parametric functions to the estimated hazard and/or survival functions ($H(t)$ and $S(t)$). Once the parameters of such functions are estimated, statistical inference about the (unknown) characteristics of the phenomena under consideration (e.g., business failure) are

Table 2
Estimated Values of the Density Function and Hazard Rates for Business Failures in Poughkeepsie

Business age (years)	Retail $f(t)$	Retail $H(t)$	Manufacturing $f(t)$	Manufacturing $H(t)$
0	0.570	0.570	0.365	0.365
1	0.175	0.249	0.152	0.204
2	0.107	0.190	0.119	0.182
3	0.071	0.152	0.090	0.169
4	0.056	0.138	0.067	0.148
5	0.045	0.126	0.051	0.128
6	0.036	0.114	0.037	0.107
7	0.028	0.098	0.030	0.093
8	0.023	0.089	0.023	0.077
9	0.020	0.042	0.014	0.051
10	0.018	0.083	0.007	0.028

possible. In the next section we discuss some approaches used to solve this problem.

ESTIMATION OF SURVIVAL DISTRIBUTIONS

Theoretically, any proper probability function for which $S(0) = 1$ might be used as a survival function. In real situations, however, certain families of distributions are especially useful for fitting survival data (see, for example, Johnson and Elandt-Johnson, 1980; Johnson and Kotz, 1970). Here we discuss only the one that we consider appropriate to fit business failures.

The Gompertz Family

The survival function is

$$S(t) = \exp\left[\frac{b}{a}(e^{-at} - 1)\right] \qquad t > 0, \quad a > 0, \quad b > 0$$

The corresponding hazard rate is

$$H(t) = be^{-at} \qquad t > 0$$

Estimation

Two basic methods of estimation are used to fit survival distributions (Johnson and Johnson-Elandt, 1980; Johnson and Kotz, 1970): maximum likelihood (MLE) and least squares (LS). Both methods can be used for most situations arising in survival analysis. Here we discuss only the simplest of the two: LS. The idea is to linearize the observed hazard function $H(t)$. We exemplify this with the Gompertz distribution and the data from Table 2. We can readily transform the observed $H(t)$ values taking (natural) logarithms to both sides of the proposed hazard rate function (i.e., Gompertz's). The left side of the expression obtained can then be equated to the (natural) logarithm of the observed points of $H(t)$. A linear model like the one below is then used to fit the transformed values of the observed $H(t)$:

$$Y_t = \log[H(t)] = \log(b) - at + \epsilon_t$$

where ϵ_t is a random error. Relabeling $\beta = \log(b)$, $\alpha = -a$, we can now use the ordinary least squares method to fit the model:

$$Y_t = \beta + \alpha t + \epsilon_t$$

The following Gompertz survival distributions and hazard rates were estimated from the data:

Retail data

$$S(t) = \exp[1.9874(e^{-0.158t} - 1)]$$

$$H(t) = 0.3134e^{-0.158t}$$

Manufacturing data

$$S(t) = \exp[1.5596(e^{-0.204t} - 1)]$$

$$H(t) = 0.3181e^{-0.204t}$$

Of interest is the fact that the manufacturing data fits the present distribution better than the retail data (r^2 = .82 for retail, r^2 = .92 for manufacturing). Figures 4 and 5 show the fitted and the observed hazard functions.

DISCUSSION AND CONCLUSIONS

We can now support the belief that retail businesses have a larger chance of failing than, in particular, manufacturing businesses. It can also be confirmed that mortality is higher in the early age of a business (regardless of type) than later on in its life. This behavior makes business mortality analysis different to, say, the mortality analysis of individuals or laboratory animals.

The fitted survival distributions and hazard functions obtained in the previous section can be used to analyze the behavior of the failure data under

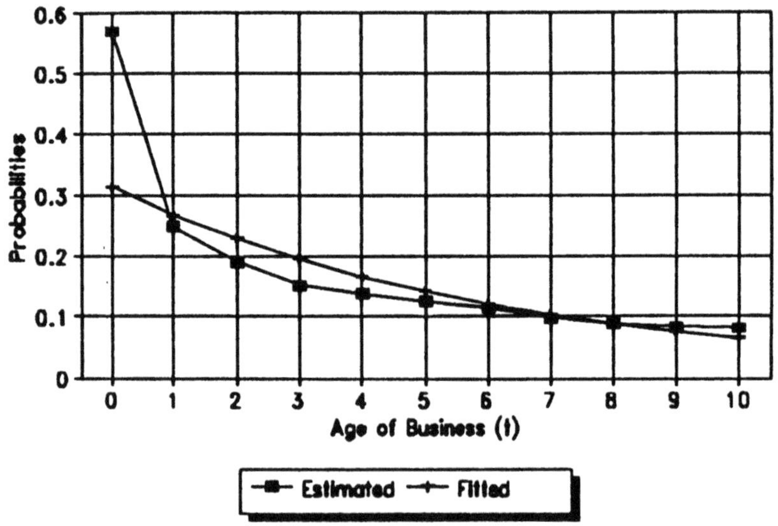

Figure 4 Estimated and fitted hazard functions: retail industry.

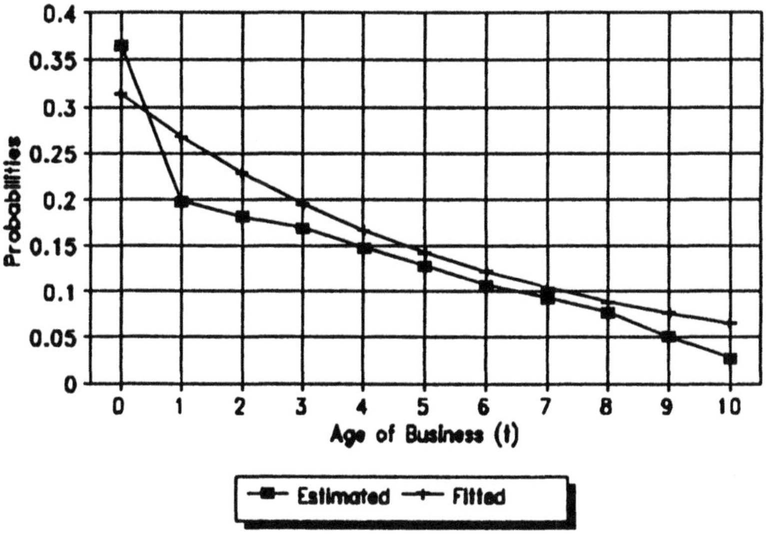

Figure 5 Estimated and fitted hazard functions: manufacturing industry.

consideration. From either $S(t)$ or $H(t)$ we can infer that retail businesses exhibit a larger hazard rate (instantaneous failure rate at a given age t) than manufacturing businesses over all the time periods considered here.

The analysis is by no means complete or exhaustive. For instance, we have fitted only one possible distribution to our data. This detail alone could produce an entirely new study. On the other hand, we hope that the ideas developed here will serve as a starting point for more detailed studies.

REFERENCES

Abramowitz, M., and I. A. Segun. 1965. *Handbook of Mathematical Functions with Formulas, Graphs and Mathematical Tables,* National Bureau of Standards, Applied Mathematics Series 55, Washington, DC: U.S. Government Printing Office.

Johnson, N. L., and R. C. Elandt-Johnson. 1980. *Survival Models and Data Analysis,* New York: Wiley.

Johnson, N. L., and S. Kotz. 1970. *Distributions in Statistics: Continuous Univariate Distributions* Vols. 1, 2, New York: Wiley.

Lomax, K. S. 1954. Business failures: Another example of the analysis of failure data, *Journal of the American Statistical Association* 49(3): 847–852.

Chapter 18

Stakeholder Objectives and Government Incentives in East European Joint Ventures

David C. Bangert

The changes in Eastern Europe are providing scholars a unique opportunity to test their most basic theories. The rapidly changing political and economic environments allow for the study of an economy's evolution from centrally planned to market economy. For example, in Hungary, a country moving quickly through this transition, discussion and debate of economic theory has moved from the halls of the Karl Marx University of Economics to the pages of the popular press. The legislature has moved rapidly, in the best traditions of a democracy, to debate openly and to vote and pass laws and regulations designed to move its country from a centrally planned economy to a market economy.

Central to this legislation are Act VI 1988 on Economic Associations (Company Law), Act XXIV of 1988 on Foreign Investment in Hungary, and Act XIII 1989 on the Transformation of Business Organizations and Companies. These laws provide strong incentives to attract foreign investment and expertise through the formation of international joint ventures. The ventures have at least two parents, one Hungarian and the other foreign. In the legislature and press, there has been speculation of abuse by individuals and institutions who were placed in positions of power by the old and now despised regime. Similar laws are being promulgated and corresponding changes are occurring elsewhere in Eastern Europe.

To examine the dynamics of the transition, the major stakeholders in the joint ventures and their associated objectives are identified and then examined considering the incentives the governments are putting in place. Finally, recommendations are made on which incentives will encourage the formation of joint ventures while maintaining the aspiration levels of all major stakeholders.

EVOLUTION OF AN EASTERN EUROPEAN ECONOMY: HUNGARY

After the Second World War, the state took ownership of most firms in Hungary. To make central administration easier, it amalgamated the nationalized companies, yielding an over-centralized structure. The number of companies per thousand inhabitants is 70–80 in Japan, 60–70 in the United States, 30–40 in Western Europe, and 10 in Hungary (Bakonyi, 1990). Over the past 20 years, the government has moved from a "planned economy" approach to a market approach. Even so, Hungary and other countries of the Council of Economic Assistance (CMEA) face two interrelated economic problems: indebtedness to the Western world and an aging industrial base that is inflexible and lags behind the worldwide development of technology (Rejto, 1983). During the last two years, the CMEA has established the mechanism for private ownership of firms by Hungarians and foreigners. Janos Martonyi, head of the privatization effort by the government, believes that by 1995 over 50% of the state-owned companies will be in the private sector (Anonymous, 1990). The Blue Ribbon Commission, Project Hungary (1990) noted that "the fundamental objective of transforming ownership is the wholesale transfer of most state assets to new owners, who, with the rights of ownership and their interest in dividends and capital gains, will improve the utilization of those assets. . . . The book value of state-owned enterprises is about $30,000 million. The current annual flow of private (domestic) currency savings that could be available for purchasing assets (other than real estate) is not more than $300 million per year. . . . The annual flow of foreign direct investment from 1988 to 1990 has been between $300 to $400 million per year." Therefore, a great increase in the foreign direct investment is mandated if Hungary is going to achieve its privatization goals.

To attract foreign investment, the government has given incentives that put a foreign owner or joint venture with a foreign partner at a competitive advantage over a 100% Hungarian firm, privately or state-owned. The competitive advantage stems from a foreign investment tax holiday, ability to take profits in hard currency, relaxed import–export regulations, and liberal labor laws. Corporate representatives and individual entrepreneurs are flocking to Budapest with their dollars, yen, and deutsche marks to form joint ventures or buy complete companies. Their investment flows are accelerating from under $100 million in 1987 to $300 million in 1990 and $700 million in 1991, giving Hungary more total foreign investment than Czechoslovakia and Poland combined (State Property Agency, 1991).

Though the Western firms are investing in Eastern Europe and governments are encouraging this investment, there exists an asymmetry in interests between the various stakeholders. This arises partially from the unequal economic characteristics of the joining partners that are different in quality, structure, management, and environment; partially from the superior strength of the Western firms; and finally from contradictory economic expectations of the various stakeholders. Even the aims of the newly formed joint venture and the objectives set by the host government's national economy may clash. Often the main interest of the venture is to build a powerful and lasting competitive advantage, but the government is stressing the momentary advantages of increasing its exports for convertible currency (Rejto, 1983). The documentation of this multiobjective problem with conflicting points of view is at the heart of this study.

STAKEHOLDERS

The changes in profit repatriation, the ability to use foreign management, relief from labor laws, and tax holidays have realigned objectives and responsibilities of the major stakeholders in state-owned firms. The stakeholders include the firm's management, the firm's work force, and the host government. New stakeholders are entering the picture with the formation of joint ventures. The new, most prominent stakeholder is the foreign firm. These four stakeholders are discussed below.

The Firm's Management

Previously, in a planned economy, the objectives of the firm's managers coincided with the objectives of their superiors through a strong system of incentives and disincentives. Each level of the state hierarchy closely monitored managers at lower levels. Through the party system, the hierarchy severely disciplined any who strayed from the well-defined objectives. In return for this "forced loyalty," consumption of nonwage benefits was high. Kornai (1990) observed, "I looked upon the successful manager of a state-owned firm as a highly esteemed official, whose prestige was no less than that of an ambassador, a mayor, or a general" (tense changed). Now the managers were on their own. Being loyal to the state was not a guarantee of position or wealth any more than being loyal to a political party in the United States is a guarantee of power or money. The managers' objectives became ones of financial and societal survival, yet these managers were positioned to guide their firms from state ownership to private ownership. There exists a deep distrust of the managers as they guide their firms. Kornai (1990) expresses this distrust well: "The managers of the state-owned firm do not have the right to sell the enterprise. This is the right of the *owner,* whereas the manager is only a paid employee."

As the managers guide their firms into the formation of joint ventures with foreign companies, they aspire to maintain their combined wage and nonwage benefits at a level equal to their position under the former regime. They are in a position to make these gains since they are often the principal negotiator for the government with the foreign entity. Their nonwage benefits were immense compared to their wages. They must negotiate an apparent great increase in the visible wage since the summer homes, mistresses, and foreign travel will be curtailed by the foreign partner's controls.

The Firm's Work Force

Workers in Eastern Europe have suffered through years of a shortage economy. They have seen the riches of Western Europe through television while their economy has not grown from a post-World War II economy. To compensate for the lack of a minimum level of quality of life, the workers have taken second jobs in the gray economy. While on their state job, they earned the right to the state benefits. Their productivity and attendance were poor. They rested on the state job to save energy for their second job. At the gray market job, they tried to earn the funds for "a piece of the good life." The results for the workers were long hours and a quality of life that continued to fall behind their cousins in Western Europe. The results for the state-owned company were poor quality, low production, and a dissatisfied work force.

The worker's objective is to have one job that will provide fair compensation for a day's work. The minimum aspiration level would be one job that provided what the two jobs provided previously.

Host Government

The government is presently the owner of most firms in the Eastern Bloc countries. By Western measures of firm value, the net present value of future cash flow, the firms have negligible value. Because of the lack of market discipline, most of the firms, if rigorously measured, are producing a negative profit. The host government's objective is to infuse the firms with managerial expertise, funding, technology, marketing techniques, and credibility. Thus, the firms would provide better quality jobs for the citizens and tax revenues for the government, whose aspiration level is for each firm to produce a profit.

Besides being the owner of the firm, the government is responsible for the financial well-being of the nation. The Eastern European countries have amassed large national debts and foreign exchange deficits. Therefore, an objective of the host government is for the newly formed venture to increase and promote exports. As the Hungarian economist Jeno Barsony observed, this is contrary to the objectives of the foreign partner. "The exports of capital would be mostly motivated by the extension of the market, but the reality of this is dubious, too, for on behalf of Hungary we can hardly offer any new market, what is more, it is rather we who expect the mixed ventures to increase and promote the Hungarian exports" (Rejto, 1983). The aspiration level for the government would incur no increases in the national debt or the balance of payment deficit, while providing jobs and revenue.

Foreign Firms

In 1983, Andras Inotai asked, "Why should foreign capital come with open arms to Hungary when it can make investments elsewhere under more favorable conditions? . . . Capital even in the Western countries is interested in buying up the well-operating enterprises and it is unlikely that this should be different in the case of Hungary with a much lower economic efficiency" (Rejto, 1983).

Contractor and Lorange (1988) point out that firms forming a joint venture can achieve at least seven overlapping objectives: (1) risk reduction, (2) economies of scale or rationalization, (3) technology exchanges, (4) co-opting or blocking competition, (5) overcoming government-mandated trade or investment barriers, (6) facilitating initial international expansion of inexperienced firms, and (7) vertical quasi-integration advantages of linking the complementary contributions of the partners in a "value chain." For a Western company entering Eastern Europe, risk reduction, blocking competition, overcoming government-mandated barriers, and initial expansion into the planned economies with their unique distribution and marketing channels are the most common objectives. For a country to attract a Western firm, its regulations and incentives must address these potential objectives.

INCENTIVES

The incentives put in place in the planned economies have varied greatly, causing the desirability of investing in the emerging economies to vary from country to country. As William Hough (1990) observed, "establishing a joint venture may often prove more difficult and time-consuming in the Soviet Union than starting a similar enterprise in Poland or Hungary." The incentives used by some countries include convertibility of local currency profits into hard currency, relaxation of limits on percentage of foreign ownership, exemptions from labor laws, tax holidays, lower import and export tariffs, allowing the purchase of real estate, and the construction of an infrastructure in support of the firm. The following subsections examine the use of four incentives in Eastern Europe and the USSR: convertibility of local currency profits, lifting limits on foreign ownership percentage, relief from labor laws, and tax holidays. The data for this section are drawn from Razvigorova and Djarova (unpublished).

CONCLUSIONS

Four principle stakeholders and their objectives have been identified. Four common incentives have been discussed that the Eastern European and Soviet governments are using to attract outside investment and its accompanying managerial and technological expertise. Table 5 summarizes the interaction between the incentives and the stakeholders.

The four main stakeholders view the incentives differently. The workers and the foreign firms view the four incentives as positive, coinciding with their objectives. The firm's management sees two of the incentives as threats to maintaining the positive of control over the plant because it allows the joint venture to bring foreign managers into the country. The local managers' confidence needs to be built to alleviate their fear. The government or foreign partner may offer management training for a market economy. Since there is a shortage of qualified managers in Eastern Europe, those selected for training programs should be well compensated to bind them to the joint venture and allow them to reach their aspiration levels. The management sees the other two incentives as positive improvements. Finally, the host government remains divided. The continuing threat of the internal and external debts facing all the Eastern Bloc must be balanced against the import of capital and expertise. For external debt aspiration level, the incentive needs to encourage the generation of enough foreign exports to offset the exportation of profits. For internal debt aspiration, the additional wages created must generate enough taxes to offset the lost corporate taxes.

Since the workers caused the dramatic changes we are seeing in the planned economies and the countries must compete for the scarce capital and expertise of international firms, employing all four incentives appears logical. The tax holidays and profit repatriation are the most controversial. The long-term effects of extended tax holidays must be carefully evaluated. The profit repatriation incentive is not as important. Most of the economies under discussion are moving toward having a convertible currency. When that occurs, the incentive will be moot.

Convertibility of Local Currency Profits

Table 1
Profit Repatriation

Country	Profit repatriation
Bulgaria	• Foreign partner's profit share on hard currency earned by the joint venture can be repatriated. • Some relief concerning the repatriation of leva earned under contracts with state bodies. The levas are equally transferable into the desired foreign currency.
Czechoslovakia	Foreign partner's profit share in any foreign currency earned by the joint venture.
Hungary	Foreign partner's share in hard currency only out of the joint venture's own currency earnings.
USSR	There is no limitation on profit repatriation. Foreign partners have the right to transfer their foreign exchange profit share (in any currency) abroad without special approval and/or authorization. The foreign partner also has the right to receive and transfer in cash and foreign exchange the residual value of his contribution.

Lifting Limits on Foreign Ownership Percentage

Table 2
Maximum Foreign Ownership

Country	Maximum foreign ownership
Bulgaria	No limitation.
Czechoslovakia	No limitation, but at least one of the parties has to be Czechoslovak.
Hungary	No limitation.
Poland	20–100% of capital stock, to be defined in consultation with the FIA (Foreign Investment Agency).
USSR	No limitation.

Relief from Labor Laws

Table 3
Employee Salaries and Management's Nationality

Country	Employee salaries
Bulgaria	In Bulgarian levas and hard currency to be specified in the labor contract.
Czechoslovakia	In national currency with the right to pay social security insurance of its foreign employees abroad.
Hungary	The salaries are paid in Hungarian forints. Foreign employees can transfer 50% of their salary abroad without permission.
Poland	While cash payments are generally in zloty, a certain percentage of salaries are usually in foreign exchange.
USSR	• Salaries of Soviets have to be paid in roubles. • Regulated in individual contracts for foreign citizens.

Note. For the five countries listed above, there is no limitation of the nationality of the joint venture's management.

Tax holidays

Table 4
Tax Holidays

Country	Tax holidays
Bulgaria	Five years in free trade zones or for companies in priority fields.
Czechoslovakia	Initial two years.
Hungary	Depending on industry, five years tax free and reduced tax.
Poland	Three years for all, may be six years in priority areas.
USSR	Two years for all, three years after initial profit in Far East regions.

Table 5
Stakeholder Evaluation of Incentives

Stakeholder	Profit repatriation	Ability to use foreign management	Relief from labor laws	Tax holidays
Firm's management	Positive: Attracts foreign investment and its capital and know-how.	Negative: Perceived as a threat to job security.	Negative: Perceived as a threat to job security.	Positive: Allows increases in the firm's wealth.
Firm's work force	Positive: Attracts foreign investment and its capital and know-how.	Positive: Attracts foreign investment and its capital and know-how. Negative: Insists on more rigid work rules.	Positive: Attracts foreign investment and its capital and know-how. Negative: Perceived as a threat to job security.	Positive: Allows increases in the firm's wealth.
Host government	Negative: Increases the foreign exchange debt of the country.	Positive: Attracts foreign investment, capital, and technical and managerial know-how.	Positive: Attracts foreign investment and its capital and know-how.	Negative: Increases the country's internal debt.
Foreign firms	Positive: Allows return on investment.	Positive: Allows executives with market economy experience.	Positive: Permits attracting good executives.	Positive: Increases profits.

REFERENCES

Anonymous. 1990. Janos Martonyi addresses Amcham on privatization, *Amcham Today* 1(2).

Bakonyi, E. 1990. Recent changes in the Hungarian economy: Problems of privatization, unpublished manuscript.

Blue Ribbon Commission, Project Hungary. 1990. Action program for 'Hungary in Transmission to Freedom and Prosperity'.

Contractor, F. J., and P. Lorange. 1988. Why should firms cooperate? The strategy and economics basis for cooperative ventures, pp. 3–28 in F. J. Contractor and P. Lorange (Eds.), *Cooperative Strategies in International Business*, Lexington, MA: Lexington Books.

Czako, R. 1990. Hungary: The small birds sing! A review of the (sic) Hungary's efforts to increase foreign investment, unpublished manuscript.

Hough, W. J. H. 1990. New incentives lure Western investment, *Management Review*, 38–41.

Hungarian Chamber of Commerce. 1988. Act VI of 1988 on economic associations (company act), *HungaroPress: Economic Information.*

Hungarian Chamber of Commerce. 1989a. Act XXIV of 1988 on foreign investment in Hungary, *HungaroPress: Economic Information.*

Hungarian Chamber of Commerce. 1989b. Act XIII of 1989 on the transformation of business organizations and companies, *HungaroPress: Economic Information.*

Kornai, J. 1980. *Economics of Shortage*, Amsterdam: North Holland.

Kornai, J. 1990. *The Road to a Free Economy*, New York: Norton.

Razvigorova, E., and J. Djarova, Dymanics of East–West economic relations and the role of joint ventures, in E. Razvigorova and G. Wolf-Laudon, Joint Ventures: New Practice in East-West Relations, unpublished manuscript.

Rejto, G. 1983. Reviews: A debate in Hungary on the possibilities of cooperation with Western firms, *Acta Oeconomics* 31(3/4):327–340.

State Property Agency of Hungary. 1991. *Invest Hungary*.

Zeira, Y., and O. Shenkar. 1990. Interactive and specific parent characteristics: Implications for management and human resources in international joint ventures, *Management International Review* 30(special issue):7–22.

Part Four

International Banking and External Debt

Chapters 19–22 examine risk-reduction and linking external debt to exports, the International Finance Corporation syndications of its less-developed country investments, the relationship between external debt and economic development, and the operation of the multilateral Investment Guarantee Agency.

Chapter 19 by Per Mokkelbost utilizes financial innovations techniques associated with contingent financial claims to model the financing project needs of Central Europe. Chapter 20 by James Baker explores the syndication of a significant portion of its loans to developing countries by the International Finance Corporation to encourage international commercial banks and other financial institutions to participate in the development process of developing countries. In Chapter 21, M. Zaman contends that until indebted nations drastically reform their economic policies, debt-restructuring packages will achieve only debt restructuring and not a meaningful reduction in debt burdens. In Chapter 22, James Baker examines the operation of the Multilateral Investment Guarantee Agency, the new affiliate of the World Bank, in encouraging the flow of foreign direct investment to developing countries by providing investment guarantees to foreigner investors.

Chapter 19

Export Earnings Indexed Debt: Risk-Reduction and Linking External Debt to Exports

Per B. Mokkelbost

The financing needs of Central Europe have led to the charter of the European Bank for Reconstruction and Development, whose mission is to provide financing for public infrastructure and private sector loans to both Central Europe and the USSR. The capital of the bank is Ecu 10 billion, of which 51% would come from the European Community (EC). The bank is headquartered in London.

In the European Community, concerns are being expressed that the preoccupation with Central Europe may derail some of the EC progress one would otherwise expect, particularly with regard to the redirection of Germany's resources to complete the German unification. Based on experiences in the USSR, the United States, and Canada, where distance and location are important parameters in business decisions, these emerging regional disparities are not surprising. Presently there is little evidence of how much, if any, investment has been redirected to Central Europe at the expense of EC's hinterland.

The financing needs of Central Europe and the USSR that will have to be met by external sources are estimated to be Ecu 75 billion over the next four years. These anticipated financing requirements are bidding away savings needed in many EC member countries and other deficit nations such as the United States. The first impact of this was felt in January 1990 when estimates of the West German deficit doubled due to the requirements associated with the unification of the two Germanys. In this instance, the Bundesbank was required to increase interest rates to stem inflationary pressures building from deficit expectations. This interest rate increase was then transferred to other countries, and as the DM bond yields increased, the long-term end of the yield curves in New York and Tokyo was pushed upward. Consequently, the U.S. dollar and Japanese yen softened for a period until the yield differential was re-established at a higher level of interest rates. Fears were expressed in the press that these interest rate increases could trigger difficulties for the economies of Japan and the United States. Who would have thought that the effects of Gorbachev's Perestroika would impact on interest rates in Tokyo and New York?

The economic restructuring of Central Europe requires financing of infrastructure and pollution control equipment as well as of new plants and machinery. The savings rates in these countries and the level of product available for export are not sufficient to generate funds to cover the financing demands of the optimistic economic scenarios. There is no doubt that the countries need the money, but according to *The Financial Times* on 1 March 1990, they cannot afford financing on commercial terms. Furthermore, *The Financial Times* reports that since January 1990 the downside of lending to these countries is growing faster than the upside. Economic growth is negative, waste continues, and quality of output is deteriorating. Consumer necessities are increasingly in short supply, and inflation is increasing as subsidies are removed and wage demands increase. Exports to the West are declining while imports are increasing, resulting in current account deficits and rising indebtedness.

Thus, the ability of Central European countries to service external debt is declining and the cost of borrowing is increasing. LIBOR is up from a year ago and the risk premiums charged the countries have increased, by some estimates, from 1/8 to 1%. In March 1990 the credit rating of the USSR was de facto downgraded and Soviet debt traded at a 3 to 5% discount, which added 1% of the cost of servicing of new Soviet debt. In addition, the chairman of the French Bankers Association warned against lending to Central Europe, citing that the credit risks are beyond what is considered prudent in lending transactions.

Financial inflows to Central Europe are necessary but not possible on commercial terms, because the needs are too great and the risks too large. Hopefully, the proposed development bank will provide some accommodation of these needs, risks, and financial inflows. The upside potential of investing in Central Europe is very good 5 to 10 years into the future. However, the possibility exists that the financing of Central Europe could become an EC 1992 "LDC problem" analogous to the British and North American banking experience in the 1980s. The challenge then for the development bank (or anyone else involved in lending to Central Europe) becomes how to manage the high short-term credit risks against the longer run upside potential. The structure of debt financings that avoids the obvious pitfalls of the Latin American type debt of the early 1980s is indexed debt, known as collar or alley financing in the Euromarket.

INDEXED DEBT

It is in the Euromarket that a substantial part of the less-developed country (LDC) debt of the early 1980s was booked and later restructured. The Euromarket originated as a vehicle to avoid the costs associated with the regulatory burden imposed on national and cross border transactions. Later, it became the place of origin of most products of financial innovation, such as swaps, forward rate agreements, indexed debt, and basket instruments, just to mention a few (A Special Issue . . . , 1988). The Euromarket has been the arena for the fiercest competition between capital market-based and intermediary-based financial transactions, as well as the site of combinations of the two in the form of securitization, repackaging and stripping of financial transactions. The competitive environment in the Euromarket has made it the financial engineer's laboratory, wherein economists have derived most applications of financial engineering that involve financial arbitrage between different markets and against institutions and markets as well as regulatory arbitrage to bypass regulatory costs and constraints.

Indexing debt on the cost of living has been tried in the United Kindgom, Israel, and Brazil to protect against hyperinflation (Brown and Shafer, 1988). Since 1988, debt indexed on commodities, currencies, and securities baskets has been issued in the Euromarket by sovereigns, quasi-sovereigns, and corporate entities (Schwartz, 1982). The need for indexed debt to finance Perestroika is evident in the recent Organization for Economic Control and Development data on the debt export ratios of the USSR and Central Europe, as shown in Table 1.

FINANCIAL IMPLICATIONS: AN ILLUSTRATION

Estimates of external debt requirements of the USSR and Central Europe are about Ecu 75 billion over the next four years. However, as seen in Table 1, Central Europe's ability to service debt is weak and for some the ability to service debt is deteriorating. The ratios in Table 1 represent the number of years required to pay off net external debt with the proceeds of annual export earnings. Poland, for example, would need 4.57 years to pay off its debt if export earnings remain at the 1989 level. Rumania on the other hand was exporting most of the food it produced in order to retire debt and therefore is ranked better (*The Economist,* 1990).

Table 1
Central European External Gross Debt/Export Ratios

Country	1985–1988 average	1989
Bulgaria	1.62	2.84
Czechoslovakia	0.86	0.96
East Germany	1.52	1.67
Hungary	2.70	2.23
Poland	5.22	4.57
Rumania[a]	0.76	0
USSR[a]	0.77	1.13
Yugoslavia	1.78	1.10

Source. Swiss Bank Corporation, *Prospects* (3/1990).
[a]Net external debt.

In the following illustration the reciprocal of the ratio in Table 1 is used, expressing export earnings to debt as an index, the export index, which will determine the amount of ultimate payment at maturity of external borrowings. The export index is an index of a country's capacity to pay down external debt denominated in Ecus. As the export earnings fall relative to indebtedness, the capacity to pay deteriorates; as export earnings increase, the capacity to pay increases (Gibson and Schwartz, 1990).

Let us begin by assuming that since Central Europe is unable to service interest payments at this time, the debt in this example is structured as a zero coupon issue. The debt is thus issued at a discount, with a face value of Ecu 100 billion, payable in the year 2000. To bridge or arbitrage the deep downside in the short term and the upside in the long term, the debt is indexed on I, the export index. If in the year 2000 the ratio I is less than 20%, then the debt is forgiven; if the ratio is 100% in 2000, then the payment is Ecu 100 billion. To allow the lenders to capture the upside potential, if the ratio is between 100 and 150%, the payment is between Ecu 100 billion and Ecu 150 billion.

Would this form of financing raise the Ecu 75 billion needed over the next four years? The boundary value of the loan value is the present value of Ecu 150 billion maturing 10 years into the future, which is Ecu 67.40 billion at an 8% rate of interest. This is approximately the value of Ecu 75 billion spread out over four years. However, when the payment in the year 2000 is dependent on the export index, then the loan value will depend upon the level of the index in 2000.

The possible payment scenarios in the year 2000 if the index is between 20 and 100% are

$$[\text{Max}(I - 20\%, 0) - \text{Max}(I - 100\%, 0)]\text{CF}_1 \tag{1}$$

The conversion factor (CF_1) translates the index to Ecus and is equal to

$$\text{CF}_1 = \frac{\text{Ecu } 100 - \text{Ecu } 0}{100\% - 20\%} \tag{2}$$

The possible payment scenarios when the index is between 100 and 150% are

$$[\text{Max}(I - 100\%, 0) - \text{Max}(I - 150\%, 0)]\text{CF}_2 + \text{Ecu } 100 \text{ billion} \tag{3}$$

This conversion factor (CF_2) is

$$\text{CF}_2 = \frac{\text{Ecu } 150 - \text{Ecu } 100}{150\% - 100\%} \tag{4}$$

The loan value is the present value of the possible future payment scenarios. It is a plausible assumption that the export index follows a diffusion process such that

$$\frac{dI}{I} = \mu dt + \sigma dz \tag{5}$$

where I = export index (export to net debt ratio)
μdt = the mean drift over time
σdz = the volatility of the diffusion process.

When the export index follows the diffusion process described in Eq. 5, the loan value can be calculated using the options pricing algorithm. Thus, the loan value is as follows:

$$\text{PV}\{[\text{Max}(I - 20\%, 0) - \text{Max}(I - 100\%)]\text{CF}_1 + [\text{Max}(I - 100\%) - \text{Max}(I - 150\%)]\text{CF}_2\}$$

The loan value and the various payment scenarios are both plotted in Figure 1, where loan values are the lower curve and payment scenarios are straight line segments. The loan value depends on the level of the export index today, the volatility of the export index, and the Ecu interest rate. If we assume that the risk-free interest rate on Ecu transactions is 8%, the present export index is 50%, and the volatility is 10%, then the loan value is Ecu 47.37 billion. Figure 1 demonstrates that as the export index increases toward 100%, the loan value approaches the maximum value of Ecu 67.40. Table 2 shows the sensitivities of the loan value to interest rates and volatility. The table values demonstrate that the loan value peaks at a given volatility for different interest rates. In general, the higher the volatility and the higher the interest rate, the lower is the loan

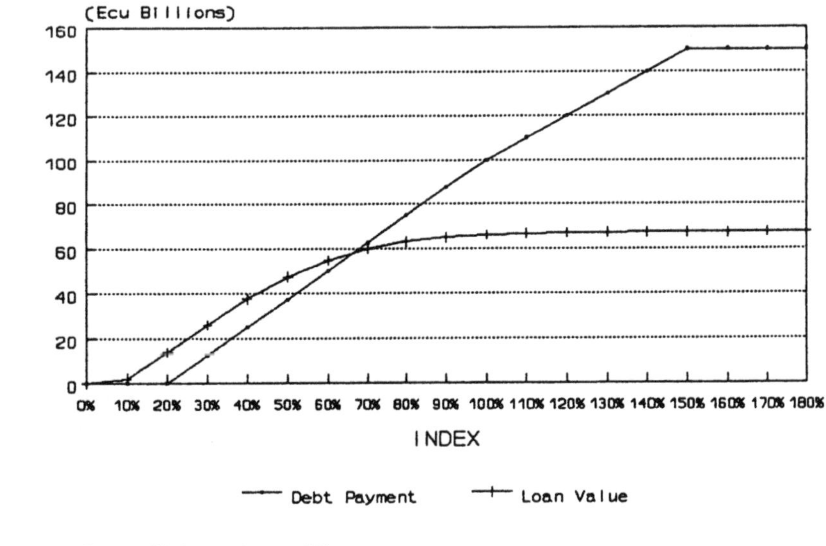

Figure 1 Loan values and payment scenarios.

Table 2
Relationship Between Loan Value and Interest Rates and Export Index Volatility

Rate of interest	Volatility 5%	10%	15%	20%	25%	30%
2%	42.03	41.89	41.10	39.47	37.27	34.76
4%	45.71	45.20	43.62	41.06	38.04	34.90
6%	48.42	47.18	44.63	41.32	37.77	34.27
8%	49.62	47.37	44.00	40.27	36.52	32.92
10%	48.64	45.37	41.74	38.05	34.44	30.99
12%	44.00	41.24	38.14	34.92	31.71	28.60
14%	36.92	35.75	33.67	31.19	28.56	25.91
16%	30.28	29.99	28.89	27.21	25.21	23.08

Note. An export index of 50% is assumed.
Source. Author's computations.

value. Selected loan values for volatility rates of 5, 10, and 15% and interest rates are plotted in Figure 2.

To increase the loan value, the export index (export earnings per Ecu of debt) must increase. The loan value will also increase if the cap on the upside participation is set higher. However, setting the cap too high will make the loan similar to an equity participation and may not be acceptable to Central European countries, where there is documented resistance to foreign ownership. To

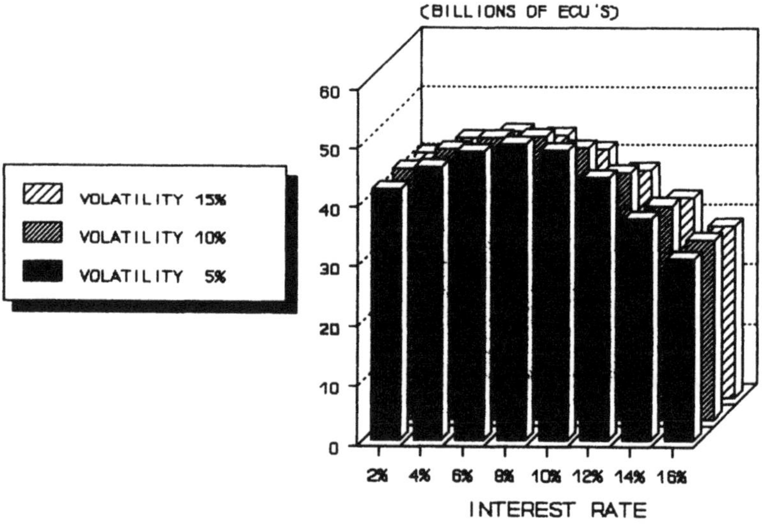

Figure 2 Loan value, volatility, and interest rates. Index is at 50%.

raise Ecu 67.4 billion the cap must be higher than Ecu 150 billion on an export index of 150%.

If the 1989 export indices reported in Table 1 are an indication (an average of approximately 50% when Rumania is excluded), then the caps have to be set much higher. If there is little chance that these export ratios will improve in the future, then it will be difficult to structure debt financing that would raise the needed amount unless most of the upside is signed off to the lenders.

CONCLUSION

The recent debt servicing statistics for Central Europe are not encouraging. Therefore, funds bound for Central Europe will have to be considered outright aid or equity, either of which would constitute a drain on savings in the EC and reduce the prospects of prosperity in Europe after 1992. There are concerns that the needs of Central Europe could slow down the harmonization process targeted for 1992 within the EC. The energy of some members of the community such as France and Germany could be diverted to attempts to help Central Europe at the expense of the EC harmonization process.

There are some signals indicating that the export index could be better than the numbers reported for 1989. Recent news accounts indicate that increases in output and productivity could be achieved, thereby increasing export earnings. For example, large pools of underutilized labor, if retrained and motivated, could increase output substantially. Furthermore, tourism in Central Europe is increasing. With tourists spending hard currency, Central Europe's export of services increases, which eases balance of payment problems (as long as Central Europeans stay at home). With such improvements, the export index, which determines available types of financing, could be improved. And with reasonable export indices, equity financing in joint ventures could be combined with indexed debt to satisfy Central Europe's financing needs.

REFERENCES

Brown, R. H., and S. M. Schafer. 1988. Testing the Cox, Ingersol & Ross model on British government index-linked securities, *London Business School.*

The Economist. 1990. p. 71.

Gibson, R., and E. S. Schwartz. 1990. Stochastic convenience yield and the pricing of oil contingent claims, *Journal of Finance,* 959–976.

Mokkelbost, P. B. 1991. Financing the new Europe with participating debt, *Management International Review* 31:7–18.

Schwartz, E. S. 1982. Pricing commodity-linked bonds, *Journal of Finance,* 523–539.

A special issue on financial engineering. 1988. *Financial Management.*

Chapter 20

The International Finance Corporation and Banks: IFC Syndications of Its LDC Investments

James C. Baker

This chapter contains an examination of the function of syndication, which the International Finance Corporation (IFC) uses to encourage international commercial banks and other financial institutions to participate in the development process in the developing world. A brief overview of the IFC will precede an analysis of the agency's syndication process.

The IFC has completed 35 years of operations (Baker, 1992). At the inception of its operations, planned capital to be subscribed by member nations was $100 million. The IFC officially began operations with 31 member nations and subscribed capital of $78.4 million (Baker, 1968a, p. 31). Its initial capitalization made it a fledgling development finance agency by today's standards. Today, the IFC is the world's largest multilateral organization that provides financial assistance by means of loans and equity investments to private enterprise in less-developed countries (LDCs). It does so only without government guarantee. It is affiliated with the World Bank and utilizes the Bank's public sector infrastructure development programs to support its investments in private sector projects. However, the IFC operates as a separate, legally independent agency with its own staff and funding. Its share capital is provided by 142 member countries and now amounts of $1.1 billion subscribed. The IFC's total capital, including retained earnings, amounts to $2.1 billion. The IFC has invested in projects in LDCs whose capital cost totals more than $70 billion. These projects have involved more than 2000 companies and financial institutions in support of more than 1000 businesses in 96 countries.

At the end of fiscal year (FY) 1991, the IFC's Board of Directors approved a capital increase of $1 billion, bringing authorized capital to $2.3 billion. Member countries will pay this increase in equal annual installments until August 1996. This additional capital will permit the IFC to increase its investment activity greatly. For example, annual approvals will rise from $1.5 billion in FY

1991 to $4 billion by the end of the decade. Total cost of IFC-supported projects will increase during this period from $10.7 billion to $31 billion annually (A Private Affair, 1991).

In addition to these financial resources, as well as principal and interest payments on its investments and sales of some of its investments to private investors, the IFC has recently begun to use international capital markets as a source of funds (IFC, 1991, p. 68). In FY 1990, the IFC borrowed $799 million and in FY 1991, $702 million. These funds have been obtained by issues in the Eurobond market as well as in Japan, Spain, and Portugal. The IFC is also permitted to borrow from the World Bank in amounts not generally more than 20% of total funding.

IFC'S PURPOSE

The general purpose of the IFC is

> to further economic development by encouraging the growth of productive private enterprise in member countries, particularly in the less developed areas, thus supplementing the activities of the International Bank for Reconstruction and Development (World Bank). (IFC, 1956, p. 3)

To implement its purpose, the IFC Articles of Agreement requires the IFC to:

> (1) in association with private investors, assist in financing the establishment, improvement, and expansion of productive private enterprise which would contribute to the development of its member countries by making investments, without guarantee of repayment by the member government concerned, in cases where sufficient private capital is not available on reasonable terms;
> (2) seek to bring together investment opportunities, domestic and foreign private capital, and experienced management; and
> (3) seek to stimulate, and to help create conditions conducive to the flow of private capital, domestic and foreign, into productive investment in member countries. (IFC, 1956, pp. 3–4)

When the IFC began operations, it performed several functions to implement these objectives. In addition to the financing of industrial projects, it has (1) underwritten shares issued by companies; (2) encouraged financial institutions in capital exporting nations to participate in development projects by selling them investments from its own portfolio; (3) financed private development finance companies, a type of development bank that is privately owned and whose capital is invested in local private enterprise; (4) appraised investment proposals submitted to the World Bank by industrial and mining companies; (5) advised the management of companies in which it has invested; and (6) assisted these companies in drafting market surveys (Baker, 1968b, pp. 290–291). Only the IFC, of all the development agencies, clearly states in its mission that economic development sought by it is to be attained by private enterprise. The IFC is unique in that it not only invests in private enterprise projects in LDCs, it does so without government guarantee. In fact, it will not consider any project in which the least hint of government interference may be present.

In recent years, the IFC has added several other services, designed to facilitate the implementation of its general purpose. These include syndications, privatization, development of securities exchanges and country investment funds (closed-end investment companies whose portfolios include the securities of companies in a specific country), project facilities such as the Africa Project Development Facility and the Caribbean Project Development Facility, the Foreign Investment Advisory Service, and Technology Transfer and Project Development.

SYNDICATIONS (IFC N/A)

The IFC has, from its inception, had two major goals: to finance as many profitable private sector projects as possible given the finite amount of funds available and to encourage as many international financial institutions as possible to participate in the development finance process. One of the IFC's most active programs has been instrumental in the achievement of both of these goals: the syndication of participation by banks and financial institutions around the world in IFC loans.

Syndication encourages financial institutions worldwide to furnish funds for IFC-financed projects in the private sector of LDCs. The fact that IFC is a sponsor of these projects is an added inducement for the participating financial institution, especially because the project credit risks are shared with the IFC. In fact, the special status of the IFC has insured that no portion of a loan in participation with the IFC has been included in the rescheduling of the foreign debt of any LDC.

The IFC has placed participations in its loans with more than 200 international financial institutions since it began syndication operations. Most of these participations have been by European banks. Japanese banks do participations only if another Japanese company is involved in the project.

THE SYNDICATION PROCEDURE

Although one agreement is generally made between the IFC and the borrower, the IFC loan is divided into two parts: the IFC's portion of the loan, subject to IFC's own peculiar terms, and a second part funded by the participating financial institution(s), with terms agreed to between the borrower and the participants. Finally, the participation will involve a separate agreement between the IFC and each participating institution. The process, in short, has been one of the IFC's most effective catalytic operations.

To encourage a particular bank to participate in a loan, the IFC outlines the project for the bank and follows this with an appraisal report and the principal conditions of the loan, including pricing, if the bank shows an interest in the participation. The bank is then invited to participate in the loan. The IFC acts as lead manager for the transaction and if a large amount of funds is needed from several banks, either the IFC or the borrower may request one or more banks to assist syndication of the IFC loan.

The IFC administers the loan since it is the lender of record. Thus, it is responsible for collections of principal and interest, distribution of proceeds to the participant, the availability of financial statements and other necessary information to the participant, and insurance of compliance with loan documentation by the borrower.

RESULTS OF SYNDICATIONS

The IFC developed and initiated the syndication process in the early 1960s. Since then, more than $3.1 billion of IFC investments has been placed with more than 250 financial institutions, mostly international commercial banks. At the end of FY 1990, the IFC was administering a portfolio of syndicated loans for participants totaling $1.1 billion. During FY 1990, syndicated loans amounted to $622 million, more than a third of the IFC's total loans approved during the year. A total of 37 financial institutions participated in these syndications, compared with a record 67 financial institution participants in FY 1989. A representative list of institutions that have participated in IFC loans is provided in Table 1.

Syndicated loans were quite representative, geographically speaking, in FY 1990. In Asia, the IFC syndicated loans in six projects in four countries, including $100 million as part of the $529 million Vinythai integrated PVC plant and a $30 million loan to Shin Ho Paper Company for a newsprint paper mill and de-inking pulp plant, both in Thailand. In Latin America, the IFC syndicated loans totaling $157 million for nine projects in six countries, including a $35 million loan to Oleoducto de Colombia, S.A., a joint-venture company constructing a $321 million oil pipeline in Colombia. In Africa, the IFC syndicated $150 million in loans to three projects in three countries, including a $35 million loan, part of a $93 million project to expand the Sansu gold mine complex for Ashanti Goldfields Corporation in Ghana, and a $52 million loan, part of a $92 million IFC loan to finance a number of foreign-exchange earning tourism projects (IFC, 1990, p. 38).

CONCLUSIONS

A significant number of IFC loans to private sector projects in LDCs have been syndicated with more than 200 international financial institutions, most of which have been European banks. These banks have participated in IFC loans

Table 1
Selected Participating Banks in IFC Loans

Al Saudi Banque	Handelsbank NatWest
American Express Bank Ltd.	Industrial Bank of Japan
Amsterdam-Rotterdam Bank N.V.	Irving Trust Company
The Arab Investment Company S.A.A.	Landesbank Rheinland-Pfaiz Girozentrale
Banco di Napoli	Midland Bank plc
Banco Sudameris S.A.	Morgan Guaranty Trust Company of New York
Bank of America N.T. & S.A.	National Westminster Bank plc
Banque Bruxelles Lambert S.A.	NMB Bank
Banque Paribas	The Nippon Credit Bank, Ltd.
Baring Brothers & Co., Ltd.	Norwest Bank Minneapolis N.A.
Burgen Bank S.A.K.	Postipankki
Chemical Bank	The Royal Bank of Scotland plc
Crédit Suisse	The Siam Commercial Bank, Ltd.
DG Bank Deutsche Genossenschaftsbank	Standard Chartered Bank
The First National Bank of Maryland	The Taiyo Kobe Bank, Ltd.
The Gulf Bank K.S.C.	UBAF Bank Ltd.
Hamburgische Landesbank-Girozentrale	Wells Fargo Bank N.A.

Source. IFC, *How IFC Works with Commercial Banks*, Washington, DC: International Finance Corporation (1989).

totaling nearly $3 billion during the IFC's 35 years of operations. The IFC has also sold 283 investments totaling $117 million during the 1956–1987 period.

Syndications represent an important method for the IFC to recycle its investment funds by turning them over into new investments. As the private sector of IFC's member countries becomes more efficient and as a global investment becomes more diversified globally, the IFC should be able to encourage more international banks to participate in syndications of its loans.

REFERENCES

Baker, J. C. 1968a. IFC in the developing countries: A method of indirectly financing foreign trade, *Foreign Trade Review (India)* 3:289–298.

Baker, J. C. 1968b. *The International Finance Corporation: Origin, Operations, and Evaluation*, New York: Praeger.

Baker, J. C. 1992. *Business Expansion Into Less-Developed Countries*, New York: Haworth.

IFC. 1991. *Annual Report 1991*, Washington, DC: International Finance Corporation.

IFC. 1990. *Annual Report 1990*, Washington, DC: International Finance Corporation.

IFC. 1956. *Articles of Agreement*, Washington, DC: International Finance Corporation.

IFC. *How IFC Works with Commercial Banks*, Washington, DC: International Finance Corporation.

1991. A private affair, *Asian Finance* 17:4.

Chapter 21

Some Issues in External Debt, Domestic Policies, and Economic Development

M. Raquibuz Zaman

Developing countries' debt servicing problems began in earnest in the late 1970s, when OPEC-induced oil price increases brought economic recession and large-scale imbalances in their trade accounts. Countries such as Zaire, Sierra Leone, Gabon, Turkey, Sudan, and Togo had to negotiate rescheduling of official debts between 1976 and 1979 (Kuhn and Guzman, 1990, p. 2). Although external factors played a significant role, domestic economic policies and mismanagement were primarily to blame for their external payments' imbalances and consequent debt servicing problems. Autocratic governments with ironclad control over the operation of the economic sectors made it impossible for the market forces to bring the proper adjustments in economic activities of these countries.

The debt servicing problems, however, did not become a major crisis until August 1982, when Mexico, the world's second largest debtor nation after Brazil (not counting the United States), announced its inability to meet debt service payments (Corrigan, 1988; *The Economist,* 1988, pp. 70–71). This happened in a country that experienced a 3.2% annual growth rate in per capita income during 1965–1983 (*World Development Report 1985,* p. 175), a rate that by no means was a meager one. The causes of this debt crisis are now well documented (Reisen and Van Trotsenburg, 1988; Eichengreen and Lindert, 1989, pp. 148–151; Balassa, 1986, pp. 75–78; Krueger, 1987, pp. 159–164; Zaman, 1988, pp. 155–158) and will not be discussed here. What is important is that the Mexican debt crisis of 1982 encouraged the formulation of the debt restructuring program that later came to be known as the Baker Plan. The Baker Plan did not solve the debt crisis of the major debtor nations, including Mexico. Now we are dealing with the Brady Plan (Zaman, 1989, pp. 158–165), and if history is any indication, the debt service burden will continue to overwhelm the economies of the majority of the debtor nations.

DEBT AND ECONOMIC DEVELOPMENT PLANS

Large-scale borrowing from multilateral agencies, such as the International Bank for Reconstruction and Development (popularly known as the World Bank), for inducing economic growth began in earnest in the early 1950s. During the 1950s and 1960s, the emphasis of economic development was placed on the overall growth in the GNP by both the lenders and the borrowers. It was believed that aggregate economic growth was the only way to achieve the "take-off stage" and that the internal economic imbalances would be taken care of by the interplay of market forces. (For a fascinating study on the subject, see the Pearson Commission Report (1969); and for a summary of the changing objectives of economic development, see Morawetz (1977), particularly Chapter 1.) As is now well known, growth in GNP in many of the debtor nations was achieved at a high cost of regional and sectoral economic imbalances and worsening income distribution (Pakistan, Nigeria, and Brazil are some of these debtor nations). The Pearson Commission's deliberations and its final report are ample testimony to the serious nature of the maladjusted economic growth in the developing countries in the 1950s and 1960s. While the developed countries' per capita GNP grew at an annual rate of 3.2% between 1950 and 1975 at constant dollars (1974 dollars), the growth rate for the developing countries (excluding China) was only 3% (see Morawetz, 1977, Table I, p. 13) with a much lower economic base.

A careful country-by-country analysis of development plans and their implementation largely by borrowed funds would show that domestic economic policies (often suggested and at times required by the experts from the aid donor nations, the World Bank, and the International Monetary Fund) were as responsible for failures in achieving economic development as external factors, such as discriminatory trade policies toward exports from these countries imposed upon by the developed world, unfavorable terms of trade induced by market manipulation, and occasional random factors such as armed conflicts, economic recessions, and natural calamities. Moreover, there has been little attempt by the aid-giving agencies and nations to extend aid in proportion to the needs of the borrowing nations. Aid was given according to the political expediencies of the major power brokers of the world. Thus, in 1988, per capita aid received by Israel, a developed country with 1988 GNP per capita of $8650, was $282.07, as against $14.62 by Bangladesh with a per capita GNP of $170 (see Table 1). This continues to this day. Rich Israel continues to receive the highest per capita aid in the world year after year (over a thousand dollars per capita if all types of aid are taken into consideration), whereas the countries that are termed "basket cases" receive less than a fraction of what Israel gets from the donor countries, especially from the United States. Since 1967, Israel received $77 billion from the United States as "aid" (Bradsher, 1991, p. A10). Politics and "strategic significance" of a country seem to be the determinant of amounts of aid received, not the need for its economic betterment. When a country receives too

Table 1
Per Capita Aid Receipts, 1988
(U.S. Dollars)

Country	Aid receipts per capita	GNP per capita
Israel	$282.07	$8650
Jordan	108.95	1500
Egypt	29.91	660
Nepal	22.05	180
Ethiopia	21.05	120
Bangladesh	14.62	170
Pakistan	13.32	350
Indonesia	9.34	440
India	2.58	340
Nigeria	1.09	290

Source. The World Bank, *World Development Report 1990,* Table 8.3, p. 128.

much aid, it is likely to postpone the badly needed reforms that are essential for a sustained economic growth (Collins, 1991, p. 221).

When a country receives too little aid, it is quite likely that the aid money would be spent on projects and programs that are grandiose in nature and which bolster the images of the autocratic rulers who often impose themselves on the people of the poorer countries. Pakistan, a nation that has been ruled by military dictators most of its life, spent billions of dollars in gigantic hydroelectric cum irrigation projects, changing the rural landscape that did little to help the landless laborers or poorer farmers downstream whose lands were ruined by waterlogging and salinity (Dorfman, 1974, Appendix 5). The Egyptian Aswan Dam brought similar miseries to many poor farmers who received none of the benefits of the project but all its ill winds (Caputo, 1985, p. 583; El-Baz, 1985, p. 595).

SHARING BLAME FOR DEBT CRISES

Very often, the analysts from the World Bank, the International Monetary Fund, the Organization for Economic Cooperation and Development, banking and financial sectors, and academia blame the debtor nations for lack of discipline in exercising proper fiscal and monetary policies (for example, see Reisen and Van Trotsenburg, 1988; Eichengreen and Lindert, 1989; Fischer and Hussain, 1990, pp. 24–27; Sachs, 1989; Sachs and Collins, 1989), for their failure to achieve sustainable economic growth through debt. To some extent, this is true. The major debtor nations of Latin America have consistently failed to institute monetary policies that would stem inflationary pressures and fiscal discipline that would raise tax revenues while cutting wasteful government handouts and subsidies. When political and economic situations permitted, they were able to achieve economic growth. Brazil, for example, enjoyed a reasonable rate of economic growth from 1960 to 1980 (*World Development Report 1990,* p. 48), Argentina from 1970 to 1974, and Mexico from 1976 to 1981 (Sachs, 1989, pp. 51 and 148, respectively, for Argentina and Mexico). Turkey, another major debtor nation, enjoyed significant real economic growth from 1972 to 1978 (Sachs, 1989, p. 195), yet had to reschedule some of its external debt in May 1978 (Kuhn and Guzman, 1990, p. 2).

It is not that the developing countries do not have the determination to improve their lot, but at times they are simply unable to control the events that are imposed on them from external sources. The rising interest rates of the late 1970s and early 1980s, along with rising oil prices, escalated the cost of debt services for many of the heavily indebted countries precisely at the time when the world was hit with a major economic recession that virtually shut the doors to developing countries' exports to the developed world. Table 2 data show the impact of external shocks in the 1980s to the various regions of the Third World countries. These figures do not even take into consideration the fact that during that period, all these countries experienced significant growth in their population and, hence, there were substantial declines in their per capita income.

It has been claimed that some of the major debtor nations could have substantially reduced their external debts if they were able to reduce enormous amounts of capital flight out of their countries. According to Morgan Guaranty Trust Company, the 1987 year-end value of the flight capital assets from Mexico stood at $84 billion, Venezuela at $58 billion, Argentina at $46 billion, and Brazil at $31 billion (Pauly, Thomas, and Evans, 1989, p. 46). The 1988 estimated total capital flight from the 15 largest debtor nations amounted to $340

Table 2
Impact of External Shocks to GDPs
of Various Regions During 1985–1989 Compared to 1970–1980
(Percentage decline in GDP)

Region and country	Terms of trade shock	Interest rate shock	Total
Sub-Saharan Africa	−10.1	−4.4	−14.4
East Asia (excluding China)	−3.9	−4.3	−8.1
China	−0.6	−0.6	−1.2
South Asia (excluding India)	−7.9	−2.3	−10.2
India	−4.6	−1.0	−5.6
Latin America and the Caribbean	−6.3	−4.0	−10.3

Source. The World Bank, *The World Development Report 1990,* p. 107.

billion (McNamee and Ryser, 1989, p. 74). One can argue that the insistence of multilateral agencies, commercial bank lenders, and other aid donors that the debtor nations follow strict domestic autarky, trade liberalization policies, and devaluation of currencies to receive further assistance or to get some of their debts rescheduled, might have contributed to the growth of flight capital in the mid 1980s. The debt–equity swap arrangements under the Baker Plan could have resulted in some forms of capital flight (Zaman, 1989, p. 161). It is the economic uncertainties that are often created by the IMF-induced policy changes in monetary and fiscal management that often force private investors to cover their foreign exposures through the flight of capital out of currencies that are soon to be devalued. In a rather candid note, the World Bank elucidated conditions "when aid can be ineffective." Some of the points raised in this section are confirmed by the Bank. In addition, the aid giving agencies at times recommended "incompatible technologies and deliver(ed) conflicting projects and advice" (*World Development Report 1991*, p. 48).

DEBT RESTRUCTURING AND DEBT SERVICING BURDENS

The mechanisms by which debt rescheduling packages have been implemented since 1982 consist of such measures as (1) currency denomination, (2) interest rate options, (3) interest timing, (4) onlending and relending, (5) new trade credit facilities, (6) cofinancing, (7) debt conversion including debt–equity swaps, and (8) secondary market transactions. (For a detailed discussion of these modalities, see Regling (1988, pp. 6–9), and Zaman (1990, pp. 47–53). A critical analysis of these measures will show that these restructuring modalities are meant to safeguard the interest of the lending institutions and countries, rather than to reduce the debt burden of the borrowing nations.

Since 1987, debt restructuring has taken a new approach called the menu approach, which consists of (1) fees, (2) alternative participation instruments (APIs), (3) securitization, (4) prioritization of debt, (5) interest capitalization, and (6) debt buy-backs (Regling, 1988, pp. 8–9; Zaman, 1990, pp. 49–53). Of these six instruments, APIs, also known as exit bonds, and debt buy-backs hold some promise for actually reducing debts. The Brady initiative, consisting of these two modalities, may actually reduce debts of the borrowing nation if the commercial lenders can be persuaded to go along with it. Agreements were reached in recent months along the Brady Plan with Mexico, thc Philippines, Costa Rica, and Venezuela (Fischer and Hussain, 1990, p. 25). According to the World Bank (*World Development Report 1991*, p. 24), these institutions so far have reduced the debts of these countries by $9.5 billion. The economic recession triggered by the Gulf crisis, and the disintegration of Eastern Europe and the Soviet Union have interfered with the future success of the Brady Plan. It may not be long before newer debt crises crop up all over again.

THE FUTURE OUTLOOK

The International Monetary Fund, in its *World Economic Outlook, October 1990,* projected a 9% increase in debt liabilities of developing countries during 1990/91. These projections were made before the full economic consequences of the Gulf crisis and the crisis in Eastern Europe and the Soviet Union could be comprehended and before the U.S. economy entered into a recession. It is difficult to be optimistic about the future prospects of any reduction in debt service burden of the indebted countries. The Gulf War further worsened the already precarious external balances of countries, such as Egypt, Jordan, Pakistan, India, Bangladesh, and the Philippines, as they no longer can count on receiving hefty remittances from their nationals working in that region (*World Economic Outlook, October 1991,* p. 20). The ongoing bank crisis in the United States and the deepening economic recession will make it difficult for the Latin American borrowers to negotiate further reductions in their debts through the Brady Plan initiatives.

The developing debtor nations must learn to manage their economies better if they desire to improve their lot. Many of them with large populations and limited natural resources cannot hope to achieve economic miracles on borrowed funds. What worked for Taiwan, Korea, and Singapore (i.e., export-led economic growth) may not work for India and Bangladesh (see Collins, 1990, pp. 104–107; Krueger, 1990, pp. 108–112; Srinivason, 1990, pp. 113–117; Park, 1990, pp. 118–121). Such countries must find their own miracles with their own efforts and initiatives.

REFERENCES

Aggarwal, V. K. 1989. Interpreting the history of Mexico's external debt crises, pp. 140–148 in B. Eichengreen and P. H. Lindert (Eds.), *The International Debt Crisis in Historical Perspective,* Cambridge, MA: The MIT Press.

Balassa, B. 1986. Policy response to exogenous shocks in developing countries, *The American Economic Review* 76(2):75–78.

Bradsher, K. 1991. U.S. aid to Israel: $77 billion since '67, *The New York Times,* p. A10.

Caputo, R. 1985. Journey up the Nile, *National Geographic* 167(5): 577–633.

Collins, S. M. 1990. Lessons from Korean economic growth, *The American Economic Review* 80(2):104–107.

Collins, S. M. 1991. Policy watch: U.S. economic policy toward the Soviet Union and Eastern Europe, *Journal of Economic Perspectives* 5(4):219–227.

Corrigan, G. E. 1988. A balanced approach to the LDC debt burden, *Federal Reserve Bank of New York Quarterly Review* 13(1):1–6.

Dorfman, R. 1964. *Report on Land and Water Development in the Indus Plain,* U.S. Department of Interior Panel on Water Logging and Salinity in West Pakistan, Washington, DC: The White House, Appendix 5.

The Economist. 1988. School-brief: Lender of last resort, *The Economist,* 70–71.

Eichengreen, B., and P. H. Lindert. 1989. *The International Debt Crisis in Historical Perspective*, Cambridge, MA: The MIT Press.

El-Baz, F. 1985. A dam against famine, *National Geographic* 167(5):595.

Fischer, S., and Hussain, I. 1990. Managing the debt crisis in the 1990's, *Finance & Development*, 24–27.

International Monetary Fund. 1990. *World Economic Outlook, October 1990:* A Survey by the Staff of the International Monetary Fund, Washington, DC: International Monetary Fund.

International Monetary Fund. 1991. *World Economic Outlook, October 1991:* A Survey by the Staff of the International Monetary Fund, Washington, DC: International Monetary Fund.

Krueger, A. O. 1987. Debt, capital flows, and LDC growth, *The American Economic Review* 77(2):159–164.

Krueger, A. O. 1990. Asian trade and growth lessons, *The American Economic Review* 80(2):108–112.

Kuhn, M. G., and J. P. Guzman. 1990. *Multilateral Official Debt Rescheduling: Recent Experience*, World Economic and Financial Surveys, Washington, DC: International Monetary Fund.

McNamee, G., and J. Ryser. 1989. Can this flight be grounded? The exodus of capital from the big debtor nations looks unstoppable, *Business Week*, 74.

Morawetz, D. 1977. *Twenty-five Years of Economic Development: 1950 to 1975*, Washington, DC: The World Bank and The John Hopkins University Press.

Park, Y. C. 1990. Development lessons from Asia: The role of government in South Korea and Taiwan, *The American Economic Review*, 80(2):118–121.

Pauly, D., R. Thomas, and J. Evans. 1989. The dirty little debt secret: Searching for ways to stem Latin capital flight, *Newsweek*, p. 46.

Pearson, L., et al. 1969. *Partners in Development: Report of the Commission on International Development*, New York: Praeger.

Regling, K. P. 1988. New financing approaches in the debt strategy, *Finance & Development*, 6–9.

Reisen, H., and A. Van Trotsenburg. 1988. *Developing Country Debt: The Budgetary and Transfer Problem*, Paris: OECD.

Sachs, J. D. (Ed.). 1989. *Developing Country Debt and the World Economy*, National Bureau of Economic Research, Chicago: The University of Chicago Press.

Sachs, J. D., and S. M. Collins (Eds.), 1989. *Developing Country Debt and Economic Performance*, National Bureau of Economic Research, Chicago: The University of Chicago Press.

Srinivasan, T. N. 1990. External sector in development, China and India, 1950–89, *The American Economic Review* 80(2):113–117.

The World Bank. 1985. *World Development Report 1985*, Washington, DC: The World Bank.

The World Bank. 1991. *World Development Report 1991*, Washington, DC: The World Bank.

Zaman, M. R. 1988. Reducing debt burden through debt swaps: The Latin American experience thus far, pp. 155–158 in R. L. King (Ed.), *Proceedings of the 1988 Conference of the Academy of International Business*, U.S. Southeast Region.

Zaman, M. R. 1989. The Brady Plan and the status of debt swaps by the major Latin American debtors, pp. 158–165 in W. H. Thielbar and J. S. Kaminarides (Eds.),

Proceedings of the 1989 Conference: Selected Papers and Notes, Association for Global Business.

Zaman, M. R. 1990. Debt restructuring and debt burden: Is one really a cure for the other? pp. 45–53 in W. H. Thielbar, W. E. Nelson, and J. S. Kaminarides (Eds.), *Proceedings of the 1990 Conference: Selected Papers and Abstracts*, Association for Global Business.

Chapter 22

MIGA: A New Kid on the Block

James C. Baker

The plight of less-developed counties (LDCs) since 1980 has been quite dismal. Since the rescheduling of sovereign debt by Mexico in 1982, many of these countries have had to reschedule their burgeoning external debt, totaling more than $1.2 trillion at present, or have resorted to temporary moratoriums on their loan or interest payments. Although world energy prices have declined somewhat (except for the price spike caused by the Persian Gulf War) and interest rates have declined since the early 1980s, real prices have remained relatively high and industrialized nations have not significantly increased their imports of LDC goods and services. Thus, the economies of LDCs have remained, with a few exceptions, relatively weak. Foreign direct investment (FDI) could greatly benefit these countries. However, general political and economic conditions in most of these nations discourage increased flows of FDI.

The purpose of this chapter is to discuss and analyze an institution designed to cope with and alleviate some of the problems that discourage FDI. This institution is MIGA, the Multilateral Investment Guarantee Agency, an affiliate of the World Bank created specifically to guarantee FDI in LDCs.

RECENT LDC TRENDS IN PRIVATE INVESTMENT

A study of trends in private investment in 30 LDCs (Pfeffermann and Madarassy, 1989) revealed that total investment, public and private, as a percentage of gross domestic product (GDP), increased steadily during the 1970s, but that this trend was reversed in the 1980s. The private share is higher on average than the public share of total investment, according to this study, and started rising as a percentage of GDP by 1986/87, although such investment fell in four countries surveyed: Bangladesh, Malaysia, the Philippines, and Tunisia.

One important source of private investment is foreign direct investment (FDI). However, the LDCs' share of FDI is only about 30% of the total (Shihata, 1984, p. 6). In some regions of the world, both private investment and FDI are at paltry levels. For example, in Africa, private investment is only 5% of GDP, and FDI is nearly nonexistent, being 0.5% of GDP, one-third of the level of FDI in all LDCs (Ryrie, 1989, p. 1). The global level of FDI in LDCs, 1.5% of GDP, is abysmally low.

Role of FDI

FDI presents several benefits to host LDCs (Marsden, 1989, pp. 1–2), including (1) additional equity capital; (2) transfer of patented technologies; (3) access to scarce managerial skills; (4) creation of new jobs; (5) access to overseas market networks and marketing expertise; (6) reduced flight of domestic capital abroad; (7) more rigorous appraisal of investment proposals; (8) diffusion of improved techniques; (9) long-term commitment to successful FDI projects; (10) catalytic effects leading to associated lending for specific projects.

Several benefits also stem from FDI by home countries. These include overcoming of trade barriers to foreign markets, securing of raw materials supplies, reduction of costs of component supplies and finished goods that require labor-intensive operations, and the reinforcement of global marketing strategies of their principal exporters.

Restrictions on FDI

Despite the benefits that accrue to the host LDC from FDI, these countries present environments that create restrictions on foreign investors, thus causing the extreme paucity of FDI in many regions. Several of these factors have been identified by a study carried out by the U.S. Agency for International Development (Marsden, 1989, pp. 6–7). For example, many LDCs place controls on ownership, limiting foreign investors to some maximum percentage or requiring foreign investors to divest their interest within a certain period of time, as in the Andean Pact countries. Bureaucratic snafus in the project approval process are prevalent in many LDCs. Contract disputes that arise between foreign investors and host states are often difficult to resolve, although the International Centre for Settlement of Investment Disputes (ICSID) was created by the World Bank to facilitate resolution of such disputes (Baker, 1990).

Other host country practices that inhibit FDI include quotas that require employment of a certain proportion of local nations regardless of their qualifications, or the imposition of residency requirements that limit expatriate employment. Some LDCs impose performance requirements, including local content or the offsetting of imports with exports, countertrade, barter, or devotion of some production to exports. LDCs often impose exchange controls, restrictions on repatriation of capital, investment incentives that may distort efficient allocation of resources, and tax policies that discriminate against foreign firms.

In addition, local political conditions may increase the risk of operations significantly. Threats from political turmoil and strife inhibit FDI, as does the instability of the local political regime. Labor unrest may reduce productivity of projects entered into by foreign investors.

Other more specific obstacles to FDI are present in some LDCs (Marsden and Belot, 1987, pp. viii–ix). For example, internal political pressures may lead to price controls. Contractual obligations may not be respected. Local governments may grant preferences to large prestige projects. Excessive legalism is often practiced in LDCs, or precision in legal texts may be inadequate. And decisions by the government may be slow or arbitrary, making it difficult for foreign investors to implement their decisions in a sufficiently prompt manner.

In addition to political obstacles, financial restraints inhibit FDI in many LDCs (Marsden and Belot, 1987, p. ix). Inadequate investment funds and working capital inhibit development of the private sector. Financial restraints include restrictive financial regulations, inadequate financial intermediaries that can efficiently mobilize and allocate project funds, insufficient foreign exchange reserves, public sector crowding out of the private sector for funds, heavy taxation that squeezes corporate profits and reduces private sector incentive, and public sector monopolization of foreign loans and grants.

In light of these restrictions on FDI and the resulting paucity of foreign investment flows into LDCs, the risk is, thus, quite high for such investment. Some mechanism was needed to guarantee FDI flows into LDCs on a global basis. The major objective of such facility is the encouragement of increased private capital flows to LDCs (Shihata, 1984). Through the auspices of the World Bank, such a mechanism was created in the form of the Multilateral Investment Guarantee Agency (MIGA).

Precursors to MIGA that insure foreign investors against losses from commercial and political risk include the Overseas Private Investment Corporation (OPIC) and the Inter-Arab Investment Guarantee Corporation (IAIGC). OPIC is a U.S. Government agency that guarantees foreign investment by U.S. investors against political risk arising from expropriation, war, insurrection, coups, and other confiscatory activities in LDCs. It gained impetus after the expropriation of U.S. investments by Fidel Castro after the Cuban Revolution in the late 1950s. The IAIGC, formed in 1974, is a regional agency offering investment guarantees only to investments flowing among its Arab member countries (Shihata, 1985, p. 14). This agency furnished the pattern for MIGA. Both OPIC and IAIGC have been relatively successful during the past 20 years.

MIGA: ITS FORMATION

The regional success of the IAIGC coupled with the international debt crisis and its subsequent highlighting of the importance of FDI motivated top management of the World Bank to explore the creation of a global investment guarantee agency (Shihata, 1985, p. 14). Such an agency, it was believed, was needed to encourage the flow of FDI into LDCs. Development had been financed in the 1970s by commercial bank lending. Such lending, at first in the form of project financing, turned into nothing more than balance of payments financing by the early 1980s. By year-end 1985, such lending amounted to nearly $1 trillion and many reschedulings and temporary payment moratoria had been necessary. FDI, on the other hand, would bear the risks of project failure, resulting in an easier process of adjustment to economic disturbances. An agency to guarantee FDI should encourage increased flows.

This idea was kept alive with a proposal in 1951 for an international agency. Development of this proposal was continued by the World Bank in 1961, producing several studies over the next 20 years. None resulted in a new agency. At the Bank's Annual Meeting in 1981, A. W. Clausen, President of the World Bank, announced plans to establish an agency that eventually would become MIGA. After consultations between the Bank and member governments, other international organizations, and professional and business associations, a Convention Establishing the Multilateral Investment Guarantee Agency (*Convention,* 1985) was drafted and presented to member governments. Several discussions were held on the draft Convention and, on 11 Oct 1985, the Bank's governors adopted a resolution that opened the MIGA Convention for signature by Bank member governments and Switzerland (Shihata, 1986, p. 328).

The MIGA Convention entered into force when five capital-exporting countries and 15 capital-importing countries ratified it and total subscriptions of these countries amounted to one-third of MIGA's authorized capital. This occurred in April 1988 and MIGA then was constituted as an affiliate of the World Bank.

The new agency withstood some temporary problems during the ratification process (Viehe, 1987). Because of the trade deficit problems of the United States, U.S. Congressional approval of the authorized capital to be contributed was delayed for a short time because of debate over proposed protectionist trade legislation. Since the United States holds more than 20% of MIGA's authorized capital, this delay raised some concerns. However, the United States did approve the appropriation and MIGA's establishment then advanced without further delay.

MIGA'S OBJECTIVE

The objective and purpose of MIGA are contained in Article 2 of the Convention (*Convention,* 1985, p. 2). The objective is as follows:

> To encourage the flow of investments for productive purposes among member countries, and in particular to developing member countries, thus supplementing the activities of the World Bank, the International Finance Corporation and other international development finance institutions.

To implement this objective, MIGA shall (1) issue guarantees, including coinsurance and reinsurance, against noncommercial risks in respect of investments in a member country which flow from other member countries; (2) carry out appropriate complementary activities to promote the flow of investments to and among developing member countries; and (3) exercise such other incidental powers as shall be necessary or desirable in the furtherance of its objective. The supplementary activities include the conduct of research and provision of technical assistance and information on investment opportunities. MIGA is not intended to displace national and private investment insurance programs that operate in industrialized and developed countries.

MIGA was established on the basis of 10 principles (Voss, 1987, p. 9):

(1) Flexibility in the design of its coverage
(2) Underwriting on the basis of project specifics rather than on host country assessments
(3) Combination of guarantee operations with technical activities to improve investment conditions
(4) Special attention to the promotion of investment among LDCs
(5) Host governments' control over MIGA's involvement in investments in their territories
(6) Legal and financial independence from the World Bank and International Finance Corporation but cooperation with these institutions
(7) Complementarity with existing investment guarantee and insurance programs
(8) Financial self-sufficiency
(9) Joint political oversight and financial responsibility of both developed and developing member countries
(10) Voluntary membership.

ADMINISTRATION AND OPERATIONS OF MIGA

The capital base established for MIGA is one billion SDRs initial share capital, with 10% to be paid in cash, 10% in promissory notes, and the remainder subject to call. Eligible members include World Bank member countries and Switzerland. As of 17 Jan 1991, the Convention had been signed by 98 countries, 17 of which are industrialized, and of these, 71 have ratified the Convention while 64 have completed membership requirements. Nearly 73% of MIGA's authorized capital has been subscribed (MIGA, 1991).

Some countries have been slow to join MIGA, particularly Latin American nations, which often adopt the so-called Calvo Doctrine in their foreign investment contracts. The Calvo Doctrine essentially holds that, in case of contract disputes, foreign investors must exhaust local remedies for dispute resolution before they can utilize their own national remedies or those of international organizations (Baker and Yoder, 1990).

Although MIGA is an affiliate of the World Bank, it is an autonomous organization that includes a council of governors, board of directors, and president and staff. The council delegates responsibility to the board, but has a vote on admission, changes in capitalization, and amendments. The President, actually the President of the World Bank, delegates responsibility for ordinary business operations to the Executive Vice President.

MIGA's Guarantees

MIGA will reinsure some of its portfolio with private insurers and will develop cooperative agreements with these insurers to leverage underwriting capacity and diversify risks (The Multilateral Investment Guarantee Agency, 1985). The emphasis of MIGA's guarantees will be concentrated on investments not eligible for national or private coverage and will not fully cover losses. MIGA will cover 70–95% of the investment. Thus, the deductible feature is meant to discourage irresponsible behavior by investors. Initial MIGA guarantees will not exceed 1.5 times capital plus reserves and a portion of MIGA's reinsurance coverage. This ratio may be increased, if experience warrants, to 5:1.

Risk Coverage

The risks covered by MIGA guarantees are (1) risk of government restrictions on currency conversion and transfer; (2) risk of loss resulting from legislative or administrative actions that deprive foreign investors of control or benefits of their investments; (3) risk of repudiation of government contracts where investors have no access to due process; (4) risk of armed conflict or civil unrest; (5) other noncommercial risks, to be decided on a case-by-case basis.

Eligibility for Guarantees

Eligible investments are new investments, as well as reinvested earnings, of a medium- to long-term nature that are judged sound and in accordance with the host country's declared development objectives. These will not include export credits already guaranteed by a government agency. Commercial loans directly related to FDI are eligible.

Eligible investors include nationals of MIGA member countries or corporations located in member countries. Nationals of LDCs who invest in their own country are eligible if the assets are obtained abroad.

Eligible host countries include only LDC members of MIGA. Priority will be given to the lower income countries. However, MIGA is able to guarantee investments that are sponsored by member countries as trustees for these countries. Revenues from such operations accumulate in a separate fund from which claims and expenses are paid.

Payment of Claims

Investors that have claims must first attempt administrative remedies in the host country. After such relief is denied, MIGA will assess claims and provide for prompt reimbursement. If disputes arise, the parties may resort to arbitration. ICSID, a World Bank affiliate, is specifically qualified to handle such disputes, provided the MIGA member in the dispute is also a signatory of ICSID.

MIGA Operating Procedures

MIGA charges premiums and fees for its services with its board setting their level. Eligible investors must make a preliminary application for guarantee to insure that the investment will be eligible for MIGA guarantees. The premium rates and the method by which they are calculated are published by MIGA and are subject to change (*Premium Rates,* n/a). Premium rates can range from 0.3 to 1.5% of the amount of guarantee per annum. The guarantee is issued for a maximum term of 15 years, but may be extended to 20 years. The investor may terminate the guarantee after it has been in effect for three years (*Investment Guarantee Guide,* n/a).

After the preliminary application is filed by the investor, other steps must be taken to finalize the guarantee. The investor then completes the Definitive Application for guarantee submitted with other documentation about the investment. The Definitive Application determines investor, investment, and project eligibility, details of investment to be insured and types of guarantees desired, economic and development effects of the project on the host country, and the basis for confirming the economic viability of the project enterprise. Finally, the approval of the host country must be obtained.

A Unique MIGA Function

One MIGA function that distinguishes it from other proposed FDI guarantors concerns its promotional activities (Berger, 1988, p. 38). MIGA provides research including technical advice and assistance. It serves as consultative forum for its members and offers a data bank for investment opportunities, the ability to organize investors, and arrangement of sectoral workshops dealing with foreign investment. It also serves as an intermediary for the purpose of bringing together joint venture partners.

MIGA'S OPERATIONS TO DATE

MIGA's first guarantees were announced in late 1989 (Lawrence, 1989). The first of these was issued 1 Jan 1990 and covered 10% of a $500 million expansion project by Freeport McMoran Copper Company of Indonesia. The guarantee is for a period of 14 years and the project is for expansion of a copper, gold, and silver mining project (Recent developments in MIGA, 1990, p. 7).

Three other guarantees were issued during 1990. First, MIGA issued a reinsurance contract with the Export Development Corporation of Canada (EDC) that extended coverage to Placer Dome, Inc. a Canadian company that invested $335 million to develop a gold and silver mining project in Chile. EDC had made a $250 million loan guarantee against political risks for seven years. MIGA is reinsuring $49.8 million of this (Recent developments in MIGA, 1990, p. 7).

Second, MIGA has reinsured $30 million of a $150 million guarantee issued by OPIC to cover an investment by General Electric Company to acquire an interest in the Tungsram Company, Ltd. of Hungary, a large lighting products manufacturer. The guarantee covers risk of currency transfer and expropriation (Recent developments in MIGA, 1990, p. 7).

Finally, MIGA issued a $2.5 million guarantee to provide security for Mariculture Partners, a U.S. partnership that will establish a new scallop breeding facility in coastal waters of northern Chile (Recent developments in MIGA, 1990, p. 7).

By mid 1990, MIGA had received 115 applications for insurance in 35 LDCs whose project investment totaled $17 billion (Lawrence, 1990a). During its second fiscal year of operations, ending 30 June 1991, MIGA was expected to insure 10 new investments, five of these having combined project costs of $1.5 billion (Lawrence, 1990b).

MIGA'S NONGUARANTEE OPERATIONS

MIGA also sponsors conferences with member countries designed to promote FDI. One such conference was held in February 1990 in Ghana and was a macro level meeting to increase international awareness and confidence in the business community of the favorable investment climate in Ghana. A similar conference was held in Budapest, Hungary, in September 1990 (Recent developments in MIGA, 1990, p. 7). In fiscal year 1991, 25 such meetings were planned (Lawrence, 1990b).

Some of these countries are coordinated with the Foreign Investment Advisory Service (FIAS), a department within the International Finance Corporation (IFC), a global development finance institution that invests in private sector projects. FIAS's major role is the encouragement of foreign investment in LDCs (Baker, 1992). FIAS is a joint venture of the IFC and MIGA (*FIAS: Foreign Investment Advisory Service*, 1990).

MIGA has also executed "bilateral legal protection agreements" in accordance with Article 23(b)(ii) of the Convention. These have been initiated with Bangladesh, Ghana, Hungary, and Poland. Similar agreements are being negotiated with Angola, Congo, Pakistan, Sri Lanka, and Zaire. Such agreements strengthen the investment protection environment for prospective investments to be guaranteed by MIGA and they insure that MIGA will be treated appropriately by the host country if MIGA subrogates to the rights of an indemnified guarantee holder (Recent developments in MIGA, 1990, p. 7).

CONCLUSIONS

To develop adequately, LDCs need more investment. To develop efficiently, they need private investment. Host country financial markets are not sufficiently developed to furnish the necessary private investment. Thus, FDI is needed to fill the gap. Regardless of the stated benefits from FDI, the investment climate in most LDCs does not encourage a free flow of FDI. Therefore, the development of institutions designed to encourage FDI is a necessary ingredient of economic development.

MIGA represents the most recent multilateral agency whose objective is to encourage FDI by insuring a certain type of investment for a certain type of investor in a certain type host country. MIGA has just entered its second year of operations and, after issuing guarantees on investments whose total cost was $1 billion, had 10 additional guarantees in the planning stage, half of whose total investment costs amounted to $1.5 billion. The agency also had more than 100 additional applications for investment guarantees. MIGA has held or planned 25 or more conferences to promote FDI. The cooperative nature of the agency is unique in that it is an autonomous agency controlled by industrial countries and LDCs alike. It offers comprehensive coverage of investment risks. It also furnishes other services, including research and provision of information, policy advice to member governments, and technical assistance. All of this suggests that MIGA will successfully perform its role as one more development institution designed to encourage foreign investment in LDCs.

REFERENCES

Baker, J. C. 1990. Setting foreign investment disputes via ICSID, *Business* 40:43–44.

Baker, J. C. 1992. *International Business Expansion Into Less-Developed Countries*, New York: Haworth.

Baker, J. C., and L. J. Yoder. 1990. ICSID and the Calvo clause, *Ohio State Journal of Dispute Resolution* 5:75–95.

Berger, K. P. 1988. The New Multilateral Investment Guarantee Agency globalizing the investment insurance approach towards development, *Syracuse Journal of International Law & Commerce* 15:13–58.

1985. *Convention Establishing the Multilateral Investment Guarantee Agency*, Washington, DC: International Bank for Reconstruction and Development.

1990. *FIAS: Foreign Investment Advisory Service*, Washington, DC: Foreign Investment Advisory Service.

Investment Guarantee Guide, Washington, DC: Multilateral Investment Guarantee Agency (n/a).

Lawrence, R. 1989. Investors in Third World get boost, *Journal of Commerce* 382:1A, 10A.

Lawrence, R. 1990a. Insurance arm of World Bank expects pickup, *Journal of Commerce* 384:10A.

Lawrence, R. 1990b. Investment insurance agency to expand coverage, members, *Journal of Commerce* 385:1.

Marsden, K. 1989. The role of foreign direct investment, extract from FIAs Background Paper on the Private Investment Climate in Sub-Saharan Africa, Washington, DC.

Marsden, K., and T. Belot. 1987. *Private Enterprise in Africa: Creating a Better Environment*, Washington, DC: World Bank.

1985. The Multilateral Investment Guarantee Agency: An update, *Finance & Development* 21:54.

Multilateral Investment Guarantee Agency. 1991. *List of Signatures and Ratifications of the Convention Establishing the Multilateral Investment Guarantee Agency*, Washington, DC: Multilateral Investment Guarantee Agency.

Pfeffermann, G. P., and A. Madarassy. 1989. *Trends in Private Investment in Thirty Developing Countries*, Washington, DC: International Finance Corporation.

Premium Rates, Washington, DC: Multilateral Investment Guarantee Agency (n/a).

1990. Recent developments in MIGA, *News from ICSID* 7:7.

Ryrie, W. S. 1989. Keynote address, FIAS Conference on Promotion of Foreign Investment in Sub-Saharan Africa, Washington, DC.

Shihata, I. F. I. 1984. Increasing private capital flows to LDCs, *Finance & Development* 20:6–9.

Shihata, I. F. I. 1985. Bringing MIGA to birth, *Euromoney*, 14–15.

Shihata, I. F. I. 1986. MIGA and the standards applicable to foreign investments, *ICSID REVIEW Foreign Investment Law Journal* 1:327–339.

Viehe, K. W. 1987. The Multilateral Investment Guarantee Agency, *International Financial Law Review* 6:37–38.

Voss, J. 1987. The Multilateral Investment Guarantee Agency: Status, mandate, concept, features, implications, *Journal of World Trade Law* 21:5–23.

Index

www.ingramcontent.com/pod-product-compliance
Ingram Content Group UK Ltd.
Pitfield, Milton Keynes, MK11 3LW, UK
UKHW022027061126
477531UK00002B/73
9780415538800